KC WOLF: FAITH, FAMILY & FUR

WOLVES CAN'T FLY

DAN MEERS

D1004647

Contents

CROSSTRAINING
PUBLISHING

For additional books and resources available
through Cross Training Publishing contact us at:

Cross Training Publishing
15418 Weir Street #177
Omaha, NE 68137
(308) 293-3891
www.crosstrainingpublishing.com

For more information on Dan Meers, Rod Handley and
Character that Counts contact us at:

Character That Counts
512 N.E. Victoria Drive
Lee's Summit, MO 64086
www.characterthatcounts.org

Preface

For many years people told me I should write a book about my experiences as a professional mascot. I would smile politely and say, "That is a great idea; maybe one day I'll do that," while what I was actually thinking was, "Are you crazy? Who wants to read a book about a man who wears feathers and fur to work and arrives home each night smelling like a junior high locker room?" It sounded like a fun and challenging project, but I wasn't convinced my life was interesting enough to be captured in the pages of a book.

It seemed to me that most books are written about important people, the kind who get dressed up for work in a suit and tie, not a suit and tail. I also noticed that many books are written about great athletes. I definitely didn't see myself fitting into that category. In high school I was a three sport benchwarmer, sitting the bench in baseball, basketball and football. I didn't think there would be a high demand for a book about a mediocre athlete who watched the games from the sidelines.

I did, however, begin thinking about writing a KC Wolf children's book. Then it dawned on me that might not be a good idea either because in every kid's book that has a wolf, the wolf is always the bad guy (The Three Little Pigs, Little Red Riding Hood, The Boy that Cried Wolf, etc.). I put the idea of becoming an author on the shelf. I decided that if I did write a book I would do it when I got older and wiser, a time still many, many years away.

As the years went by I wasn't sure if I was getting any wiser, but there were several things hinting that I must be getting older. In 2011, I spoke at a Chiefs cheerleader chapel service. As I was sharing my story, it occurred to me that I had been the Chiefs mascot longer than several of those young women had even been alive. That thought made me feel old. Then in 2012 I was buying breakfast cereal in a local grocery store. Instead of looking to see if there was a prize in the bottom of the cereal box, I caught myself checking to see how many grams of fiber I would get per serving. Once again I was reminded that I was getting older. In 2013 I finally had to break down and get reading glasses. I realized that I either needed to buy glasses or begin to carry a LARGE PRINT BIBLE to church with

me every Sunday. I knew only old people read LARGE PRINT
BIBLES.

Later that year, at the Chief's Christmas party, I was visiting
with my friend Jack Steadman. Jack is the former president and general manager of the Chiefs, but more importantly, he is a wonderful
Christian man for whom I have a great deal of respect. As we were
visiting, Jack said, "Dan, remember this; life is like a roll of toilet
paper, the closer you get to the end the quicker it goes." He encouraged me to make a bucket list and start working to check things off
of it.

A few weeks later, on January 7, 2014, I celebrated my 47th
birthday. That afternoon I came across a website that allowed you
to type in your birth date and the current date, and it would tell you
exactly how many days you had been alive. After typing in the nec-
essary information, I learned I had been alive for 17,167 days. The
other important piece of information I learned was that the average
lifespan for an American male was approximately 28,251 days. I
quickly broke out my calculator and figured out that, if I'm average,
I only had 11,084 days left on Planet Earth.

I thought back to what Jack Steadman had told me at the
Christmas party. For the first time in my life, I realized I probably
have more sidewalk behind me than in front of me. If I'm an average American male, then the numbers tell me that on my 47th birthday I've already used up almost 61% of my life expectancy.

For many people that news might be depressing. For me, it
served as a reminder that I still have many things I'd like to accomplish with the remaining 39% of my life before my toilet paper roll
runs out.

Several months later I decided that if I was going to write a
book, I'd better get started. In the Bible, James 4:14 says, "What is
your life? You are a mist that appears for a little while and then van-
ishes."

Life is short and since you are investing part of your life reading
this book, my goal is to give you a return on your investment. My
hope is that as you read about the experiences and the lessons I have
learned during my time as a mascot, you will also be encouraged and
challenged to live life to the fullest.

I once read, "If you ask a man his occupation you will find out how he pays his bills. If you ask a man his preoccupation you will find out the passion of his life." My occupation is a professional mascot. For many years I have paid my bills by acting like a nut dressed in a costume. My preoccupation, what I am most passionate about in life, is what I hope to share with you in the pages of this book.

My career in feathers and fur has been a long and exciting journey, filled with both successes and failures. For more than 25 years I have worn a mask and covered up my true identity. I've run around in costumes at sporting events and appearances pretending to be something I'm not. I confess I'm a fake when I'm wearing a costume and trying to create the "mascot magic." A good mascot tries to bring to life a certain magical personality for his character. Unfortunately, being fake does not give people the true picture of who I am as a person.

I meet thousands of people every year, and I am always much more attracted to those who are genuine and authentic rather than superficial and showy. In the pages of this book I want you to meet the "real" man inside the costume. I've made a living out of being a fake; I've made a life out of being authentic. I promise to be authentic as I share with you my life and my stories. Thank you for taking the time to read my book. I hope you have as much fun reading it as I've had writing it.

Foreword by Tony Dungy

In 1989, my family and I experienced a major life change. We moved from Pittsburgh, Pennsylvania to Kansas City, Missouri as I started a new job. I had worked the previous eight years as an assistant coach for the Pittsburgh Steelers and had just gotten hired by the Kansas City Chiefs. Having spent my whole married life in Pittsburgh, going to Kansas City was venturing into the unknown. However, we soon found out it was a great place to live and raise a family, and we would come to make some lifelong friends. I met one of those friends in a most unusual way. He was a man known in Kansas City as KC Wolf.

I first met Dan Meers in 1990 when he was hired to work as the team's new mascot. The Chiefs had not enjoyed many winning seasons in the mid 1980's, and attendance had dropped dramatically from their earlier championship days. They had a beautiful place to play, Arrowhead Stadium, which seated over 70,000 fans, but it was half-empty on many game days then. Our job as coaches was to put a winning team on the field. Dan's job, as mascot, was to bring some life to the sidelines and connect with the fans. Even though we worked in different departments we shared a common goal—to get the fans coming back out to watch Chiefs football.

As I got to know Dan, I learned that he not only brought excitement and energy to his job, but he also had a passion for life. I also saw that he and I shared three common loves: a love for the Lord, a love for our families, and a love for football. With as much time as we both spent at the stadium, it was our love for the Lord and our love for our families that caused us to really bond.

While my coaching career took me to Minnesota, Tampa Bay and Indianapolis, Dan remained in Kansas City. Each time I returned to Arrowhead Stadium to coach against the Chiefs, I could always count on Dan to be there to greet me. After the game, win or lose, he would always come by the visiting locker room to say goodbye with that infectious smile that unfortunately is covered up when he is in costume.

In 2004, Dan and I finally got to work together again. We were asked to speak at a military prayer breakfast at the Pro Bowl in Hawaii. It was an honor to speak to our military and talk about our Christian faith. It was then I realized that the real bond between us was our commitment to Jesus Christ. Inside that crazy costume is a man of deep faith, and although we wore different NFL logos on our shirts, in the end he and I would always be on the same team.

Dan and I each spent over 25 years in the NFL. My time was spent as a player and a coach, while Dan spent his entire career entertaining fans as KC Wolf. Although we had very different roles on game day, we both agreed that our most important roles in life are being a husband, a father and a follower of Christ. Dan is truly an example of a man who strives to live his life with purpose and passion.

For those who have watched Dan perform as KC Wolf, it's easy to see that he is quite a character. For those of us who know the man inside the costume, it is obvious he is also a man of character. Dan is a great combination of fun and faith, and that is what makes him an inspiration to so many people. I'm glad to call him a friend and glad that you are going to learn more about him through this book. Hearing his incredible story will not only give you an appreciation for Dan Meers the mascot but, more importantly, for Dan Meers, the man behind the mask. – *Tony Dungy, former NFL head coach*

Foreword by Clark Hunt

In the summer of 1972, my father Lamar became the first representative from the American Football League to be enshrined in the Pro Football Hall of Fame. Standing on the steps there in Canton, Ohio, just a few weeks before his 40th birthday, it was clear that the toil and turmoil of the previous decade had subsided. His upstart AFL had successfully expanded the footprint of professional sports, merged with its old-guard rivals in the National Football League and forged a path that would make football America's game.

My father accepted pro football's highest individual honor the same way he accepted every achievement throughout his career—with character, his trademark humility, and a focus on others.

"Basically, I just consider myself a fan," he said. "Pro football belongs to the fans, and I want to acknowledge this honor in the name of the pro football fans of America." He also took time to salute the great fans of the Chiefs' Kingdom and specifically, "the Wolfpack"—a special group of wild, loud and loyal supporters who were the heart and soul of the Chiefs in the early years.

Today, the spirit and tradition of the Wolfpack is carried on by the "Chiefs' #1 Fan," KC Wolf. For more than two decades, KC Wolf has entertained generations of Chiefs' fans at Arrowhead Stadium and throughout the Chiefs' Kingdom. KC Wolf's wacky antics and innovative game-day stunts have made him a fan favorite and a hall-of-famer in his own right.

But while KC Wolf is quite a character, it is the character of Dan Meers, the man inside the suit, that brings true meaning to this book. Like my father, Dan has had a profound impact on the Chiefs' Kingdom because of his character, humility and focus on others. With endless energy, an infectious positive spirit and a gift for entertaining and inspiring young people, Dan's message of character and encouragement has made KC Wolf much more than a mascot.

The principles Dan shares in this book about his faith, his family and his football team are more than just good suggestions—they are essential to a life of passion and purpose. Those of us blessed to work with Dan know that these are the values that drive him, and I hope that after reading Dan's story they will inspire you as well.

- *Clark Hunt, Kansas City Chiefs Owner*

Introduction

The stunt went terribly wrong. It was a cold Saturday afternoon in November, and I was at Arrowhead Stadium to practice a bungee jump and zip line stunt that I would perform the next day at the Chiefs game. KC Wolf was well known for his crazy antics, and this was going to be the most exciting pregame entrance ever. I've always been a bit of a thrill seeker, and I was very excited about my first bungee jump.

Now, however, I found myself hanging over 200 feet above the football field, shaking uncontrollably in excruciating pain. As I struggled to breathe, it was obvious something had gone horribly wrong. Just seconds before I had jumped out of the lights at the top of Arrowhead anticipating the thrill of a lifetime. Instead I experienced the spill of a lifetime. My body was in shock, and I felt dazed as I struggled to understand what had just happened.

I looked down at the tarp covering the field and noticed a trail of blood stretching from the sideline all the way to midfield. Directly beneath me was a pool of blood. Fear slowly began to overcome me as I realized it was MY blood pooled below.

What had gone wrong? Where was I bleeding? Why couldn't I breathe? So many questions were racing through my mind as I felt fear welling up inside. I whispered a prayer, "Lord, I'm scared. Please help me."

For years I had been telling others my faith was the most important part of my life. That faith was about to be tested like never before. The days, weeks and months ahead would prove to be the most challenging time of my entire life.

Merriam-Webster's dictionary defines 'miracle' as "an extraordinary event manifesting divine intervention in human affairs." As I think back on the events of November 23, 2013, I truly believe God intervened and miraculously saved me. I came within inches of losing my life, and the fact I am still here to tell my story is truly a miracle.

1

The Early Years - Family, Friends and Faith

"You don't choose your family.
They are God's gift to you, as you are to them."
Desmond Tutu

The first Super Bowl took place on January 15, 1967, at Memorial Coliseum in Los Angeles. The Green Bay Packers of the National Football League defeated the American Football League's Kansas City Chiefs 35-10. I don't remember much about that first Chiefs' Super Bowl appearance because my mom tells me I slept through it. You see I was born just eight days before the big game. At the time I wasn't a big Chiefs' fan—but that would change.

On January 11, 1970, just four days after my third birthday, the Kansas City Chiefs beat the Minnesota Vikings 23-7 to win their first and only Super Bowl. I don't remember much about that Chiefs' Super Bowl victory either because my mom tells me I was way too busy at age three to sit still and watch a football game. At that time I still wasn't a big Chiefs' fan—but that would change.

Twenty years after the Chiefs celebrated their Super Bowl victory, I finally became a huge Kansas City Chiefs fan. If you're wondering how that conversion took place, I can tell you it happened the day the Chiefs offered to pay me a salary to be their #1 fan, KC Wolf. It doesn't take long to become a fan when someone hands you a check every few weeks. Growing up, my favorite football team had been my hometown St. Louis Cardinals, but they moved to Arizona in 1988 and beginning in 1990 the Kansas City Chiefs became my new #1.

In 1990, fresh out of college, my plans were to have fun being a professional mascot for the Chiefs for a few years. Then I would do what everyone else does, grow up and get a "real job." God had other plans for my life. As I look back now, more than 25 years later, I realize I never quite got around to getting a "real job." Instead I have been extremely blessed to do something I love and make a career out of doing it. If you had told me in 1990 I would have a 25 year NFL career running around in a Wolf suit, I would have said, "You're nuts." Never in my wildest dreams did I think I would be a professional mascot for that long.

Time has a way of passing quickly, and before I knew it I was an NFL veteran. As the years passed I began to notice that the hair on my head slowly started to match the gray fur on my costume. I also noticed that my body needed more ibuprofen after Chiefs games to relieve my aches and pains. Looking back I can honestly say that all of the aches, pains and cramps have been worth it because being a mascot is the most fun filled, rewarding job on the planet. When my friends give me a hard time about being one of the oldest mascots in professional sports, I just smile and remind them that "Old mascots never die; they just smell like it."

When people find out what I do for a living I get a lot of questions. Being a mascot is an unusual and strange occupation, and people are naturally curious about it. The most frequently asked question is, "How does someone become a professional sports mascot?" I've sat on many airplanes next to complete strangers who wanted to know where I am from originally, and how I ended up in Kansas City cheering for the Chiefs. This is my story.

My journey began in St. Charles, Missouri, which is located about 25 miles west of St. Louis. I was born and raised in this great town for the first 18 years of my life, the second of three boys. My oldest brother Anthony is ten years older than me, and my younger brother Dave is exactly one year and nine months younger than me. Our family lived in a brown brick ranch style home on a half-acre near my grandfather's farm. When my dad, Ken Meers, married my mom, Rene Cannon, they built this house on this half-acre of land given to them by my grandfather. Our house sat by itself in the middle of a big cornfield. My closest neighbors were relatives whose houses sat on the edge of the cornfield in both directions.

I loved living near the farm because there was plenty of room to roam and explore. I had a lot of energy as a kid, energy that came in handy later in life when I became a mascot. Mom liked my brothers and me to burn off our energy outside.

During the first 18 years of my life I spent most of my time with my brother Dave. The two of us were inseparable. We would laugh, cry, fight, play and do chores together. Of course it seemed to me I always worked harder than he did. I found it very suspicious that whenever my parents asked us to do the dishes, Dave would rush to the bathroom. I accused him of having "Dishwater Diarrhea" because every time he heard the dishwater running, he felt a sudden bowel movement coming on.

As kids, Dave and I shared a bedroom until my oldest brother Anthony went into the army. and then we each got a room to ourselves. Although my oldest brother's real name is Anthony, Dave and I have always called him "Honey." Trust me, he doesn't look like a Honey and definitely doesn't act like a Honey, but we call him that name because as little kids we couldn't pronounce Anthony. Now that we are adults it's fun to watch people's faces at the grocery store when we call our bearded and tattooed older brother Honey.

Even though Dave was almost two years younger than me, he was close to my size because he was big for his age. We tried our best to get along, but like most brothers occasionally a fight would break out. We tried to fight quietly because if mom caught us fighting, she would make us come inside and sit on the couch together. We always sat at opposite ends of the couch making angry faces at each other. We knew we couldn't talk because if mom heard us she would add 15 minutes to our punishment. After we sat there for what felt like an eternity, mom would come in and say, "Now if you boys think you can get along, you can stand up, hug each other and then go back outside and play." We always pretended we were very sorry for fighting, faked a hug and then ran back out the door before she changed her mind. On our way out the door she would say, "If I hear you boys fighting again I'm going to let your dad deal with you when he gets home." Mom was a smart lady who knew dad meant business. Dave and I were also well aware that dad could spank harder than mom. My dad was old school and knew the best way to straighten up a wayward child was to bend him over. I'm grateful I was raised this way because I learned at a very early age that bad choices always come with bad consequences, and bad consequences can be painful.

Most of my fights with Dave were arguments that resulted from playing sports around our house. Dave and I were both very competitive; neither of us liked to lose. Many of our driveway basketball games ended with one of us getting mad and kicking the basketball out into the cornfield. Then we fought about who had to go get the ball.

Although we had our fair share of fights, I'm convinced having my little brother around made us both better athletes because we always had each other to compete against. Dave ended up becoming the best athlete in the long run. He had a very good high school football, basketball, and baseball career and went on to play college basketball and baseball at Maryville University in St. Louis. I was a decent athlete who was good enough to make every team I tried out for, but I ended up sitting on the bench in football, baseball and basketball. Even though Dave had a much better athletic career, I'm the three sport benchwarmer who ended up with a 25 year NFL career.

My first love was baseball, and at age eight my parents signed me up to play in the St. Charles Little League Baseball Association. Our team sponsor was McDonalds, and we wore blue shirts with the golden arches on the front of our uniforms. Dave managed to talk his way into being our team bat boy. My guess is that he just wanted to get free ice cream and pop after the game like the rest of us.

As one of the starting pitchers, I relied solely on the one pitch I knew how to throw, a fastball which wasn't very fast. My fastball got even slower as the game progressed and my arm got tired. Although I wasn't the fastest pitcher at age eight, I was fairly accurate and could hit the strike zone. Since most boys at that age couldn't hit very well, I looked like Cy Young on the mound. All those hours I spent playing catch with my brother in the backyard apparently paid off because our team won the championship.

The following year I was picked to play for a new team, sponsored by the local Optimist Club, but my second year of organized baseball didn't go nearly as well as my first. I was still a pitcher, but midway through the season our team was still winless. Our team looked like the Bad News Bears, and I think even the Optimists were pessimistic about our chances of winning. Even though we didn't win many games that year, I still had fun. My favorite thing about little league baseball was that after every game, win or lose, we raced to the concession stand for a snack. I learned at an early age that winning was nice, but even losing wasn't bad as long as you had fun and got to walk away with an ice cream cone at the end of the day.

I had great little league coaches who not only taught me how to play the game but also stressed good sportsmanship. Whether I hit a home run or struck out, I was expected to conduct myself with class. They taught me that being a good sport is just as important as winning. I've met a few fans over the years who need to be reminded of this lesson. I'm thankful I had coaches who used sports not only to develop my skills as a player, but more importantly, to develop my character.

One of the stories my mom likes to tell about me as a child is the story of my green frog. Every night I used to sleep with a green corduroy frog filled with beans. My mom bought it for me at our church craft show and gave it to me as an Easter gift. Unfortunately, as a child I had a bed wetting problem. My brother still tries to say I wet the bed until I went to high school, but I don't remember the problem lasting quite that long. I always enjoyed getting to sleep on the top bunk because it made my brother on the bottom bunk a nervous wreck.

One day when my mother was cleaning house she discovered our bedroom smelled exceptionally bad. A bad smell coming from our bedroom wasn't uncommon, but this smell took the term "offensive odor" to a new level. As my mom began to investigate, she discovered the odor was actually coming from my green frog. Apparently I kept the frog so well watered at night that the beans had begun to sprout. Mom did emergency surgery that day, cutting open my frog, removing the beans, and throwing it in the washing machine with extra laundry detergent. After a trip to the dryer, mom finished up the surgery. She filled it with pillow stuffing and sewed the frog back together. I still have that frog today, but I no longer sleep with it. My green frog is now a reminder to me that no matter what people look like on the outside, if they don't keep their insides clean, their lives will eventually start to stink. This lesson taught me how important it is to guard the things I allow into my life, because those things will eventually affect my insides (my heart). I first read this poster as a kid:

Guard your thoughts because they become your words
Guard your words because they become your actions
Guard your actions because they become your habits
Guard your habits because they become your character
Guard your character because it becomes your destiny

The poster still reminds me that it all starts with my mind. What I allow myself to think about will eventually affect my words, actions, habits, character and ultimately my destiny.

There is a story told about an old Cherokee Indian who was talking to his grandson about a battle that goes on inside people. He said, "My son, the battle is between two wolves inside us all. One is Evil….It is anger, envy, jealousy, sorrow, regret, greed, arrogance, self-pity, superiority and ego. The other is Good….It is joy, peace, love, hope, serenity, humility, kindness, benevolence, empathy, generosity, truth, compassion and faith. The grandson thought about the story for a minute and then asked his grandfather, "Which wolf wins?" The old Cherokee simply replied, "The one you feed." This simple story reminds me I can choose what my mind feeds on.

I learned at an early age to be very selective about what I allow into my mind and ultimately into my heart. Attending Sunday school as a child influenced me greatly. I still remember a Bible verse I learned that taught me the importance of keeping my thought life positive.

"Fill your minds with those things that are good and that deserve praise: things that are true, noble, right, pure, lovely and honorable" (Philippians 4:8, GNB).

The Sunday school teachers I had were a wonderful group of people with a tremendous amount of patience. Many days I'm sure they left church feeling more like babysitters than teachers. I'm very thankful for the lessons I learned from them and for the investment they made in the lives of a bunch of rowdy boys.

I attended grade school at Immanuel Lutheran School in St. Charles. I made good grades in school, but I was your typical boy with loads of energy. At Immanuel Lutheran spanking was an acceptable form of discipline. I received several swats on my rear end with a paddle. As a matter of fact, I led my class in swats during most of my sixth grade year until my friend Jeff Fischer finally took the lead late in the school year. Although I was very competitive, I was more than happy to let him win that contest. I never enjoyed getting those swats, but as I look back, I'm thankful I went to a school where my teachers reinforced what my parents were teaching me at home—poor choices come with painful consequences. I owe a great deal to the Sunday school teachers and the elementary school teachers who invested in my life. I was a high energy child who learned from them the importance of showing love and respect for others.

My favorite times during the school day were recess, PE and lunch time. As long as I was either eating or running around, I was having fun. Sitting behind a desk wasn't my idea of a good time. Even as an adult the idea of sitting behind a desk doesn't sound like fun to me. This is probably why I chose to become a mascot instead of getting a white collar desk job.

My mom was the biggest encourager in our home. As a kid I still remember her telling me how cute I was. When I look back on my elementary school pictures, I realize mom was either a liar or she needed glasses. I've seen the pictures for myself, and I'll admit that I wasn't nearly as cute as she made me out to be. Whenever I smiled, I had a large space between my two front teeth with an over bite to accompany it. In school the mean kids called me "Bucky Beaver." The name calling didn't bother me much because I knew they were just being hateful, and I also knew I could shoot water between my front teeth farther than anyone else in class.

In seventh grade I got braces, not the clear Invisalign brand of today where your classmates can hardly see them. No, these were the bright silver train track variety that announced to the world tinsel teeth had arrived. Overnight I went from being called "Bucky Beaver" to "Brace Face." The worst part about braces wasn't getting called names, it was trying to play sports with them. During our basketball or kickball games at recess I would occasionally get hit in the mouth with the ball. When this happened I had to spend the next 20 minutes in the school nurses' office trying to dig my lip back out of my braces. Anyone who has ever worn them knows exactly what I'm talking about.

Thankfully my braces came off right before I entered high school. When I started at St. Charles West, I only had to wear a retainer. The worst thing about my retainer was that I had to take it out and sit it on my tray while I ate lunch. As a freshman I learned it was really hard to impress the girls in the lunch room when you have your retainer sitting on the tray next to your milk carton. I also learned it's hard to impress the girls while you are digging around in the trash can because you accidentally threw your retainer away.

I was thankful when my orthodontist told me at the end of my freshman year that I no longer had to wear my retainer. My new nickname at school became "Smiley" because I always walked around with a grin on my face. I knew a smile was the best way to improve my looks, and I also learned it was the easiest way to make friends. I decided that since my parents had spent a lot of money on my teeth, I should start showing them off. The nickname Smiley stuck with me throughout high school.

I was very active in high school. I was involved with Fellowship of Christian Athletes (FCA), Key Club, National Honor Society, and I served as a class officer. People often think since I'm a mascot that I must have taken theatre classes in school. Actually, the only theatre class I ever took was one semester of drama because it was a requirement to graduate. I took it the first semester of my senior year, and we had to perform a class play for about 100 other students. Since it was December our class decided to perform "*A Christmas Carol.*" I was selected for the lead role as Scrooge. My classmates thought it was funny that Smiley Dan Meers got the role of crabby, old Mr. Scrooge. I must admit trying to look grumpy and mean on stage was very difficult. I enjoyed performing for others, but at the time I didn't realize I would one day make a career out of performing. Drama class was fun, but I enjoyed playing sports a lot more.

My senior year of basketball was very memorable. My friend Tom Booker and I spent most of our time sitting on the bench together during our four years of high school basketball. On Senior Night we decided to do something special since it was our last home game. During the fourth quarter we arranged for the pizza delivery man, who was a friend of ours, to walk down the stairs and deliver a pizza to the end of the bench. Tom and I enjoyed eating pizza while we watched our final home game together. Everyone in the crowd thought our little stunt was hilarious except for one guy, our head coach. Unfortunately for us we still had practice the next day because we had several more away games on our schedule. Needless to say, Tom and I ran a large number of wind sprints at the end of practice. I don't know how many calories were in the pizza, but I guarantee we worked off all of them.

My first job in high school was working at a fast food restaurant called Lion's Choice. I became really good at washing dishes, learning to run a cash register and making roast beef sandwiches. I enjoyed it because my boss was a really nice guy, and several of my friends also worked there. With the help of a loan from my parents, and the money I saved from working at Lion's Choice, I bought my first vehicle. I purchased a used 1979 Jeep CJ5 special Silver Anniversary Edition. It had a soft top, but anytime I had an opportunity I drove around town "topless." My parents told me that as long as I stayed on the honor roll, they would pay for the insurance which was good enough incentive for me to keep my grades up. Since I was making just over minimum wage, it took me about two years to pay off the loan. On my final payment I went to the bank and got 150 one dollar bills, stacked the bills in a brief case and laid it on my parent's bed. I was relieved to be debt free and no longer have a car payment due each month.

On my 18th birthday I received the perfect gift from my parents, a cow horn for my jeep. The horn mounted underneath the hood and had a cable that ran through the fire wall and to the floor board on the side of the driver's seat. All I had to do was reach down and pull the lever attached to the cable and the horn would make a "Mooooo" sound. No one else at my school had a cow horn, and my friends and I had fun driving around town "Mooing" at joggers along the road. The jeep was a perfect vehicle—except in the winter when I could see my breath all the way to school.

I ran around with a good group of friends during high school, guys who liked to have fun but stayed out of trouble. My parents were right when they told me, "People are judged by the company they keep and the company they keep away from." During high school I learned a very important lesson that I have been able to share with thousands of students over the past 25 years. It is possible to go through school and have a great time without using drugs and alcohol. I was blessed with friends who got high on life, not on drugs.

Near the end of my senior year six of my friends and I decided to play a senior prank. We wanted to do something memorable but not something destructive that would get us into trouble. After coming up with several ideas, we finally decided that throwing car tires over the flag pole in front of our high school was our best option. My friend Brad owned a pickup truck, and we found a large pile of used tires in a ditch near my house. A month before graduation, Brad and I loaded the tires in the back of his pickup and parked his truck at my house. At midnight we all met at my house, drove to the school and pulled off the prank under the dark of night. The prank worked perfectly. We brought a long extension ladder that we leaned up against the flagpole. We carried the tires up to the top of the ladder one-by-one. When a tire reached the top of the ladder, we put it over the flagpole and carefully pushed the ladder away from the flagpole allowing the tire to drop to the ground. We completed the prank around 2:30 a.m.

When students arrived at school the next morning, there were 36 tires stacked up around the flagpole and around the school totem pole. The school custodians spent an hour trying to lift the tires back over the flagpole. They finally gave up and used a chainsaw and a giant wire cutters to cut the tires off.

Assistant principal Mike Johnson was quoted in the school newspaper saying, "Any prank is wrong, but if there is going to be one, I would say this is an appropriate one." We stayed up late pulling off the prank, but the result was well worth losing a few hours of sleep.

We pranksters revealed our identities by taking out a small ad in the school year book. We posed in a picture together under the flagpole holding tires. The caption read: "The 1985 Seniors of St. Charles West High School officially reTIRE. GOOD LUCK SENIORS!" - From the Tire Bandits.

I have many fond memories of high school, but my favorite occurred in the spring of my senior year. I signed up to attend a Fellowship of Christian Athletes (FCA) weekend conference at

Camp Wyman in Eureka, Missouri. I was excited about the trip because I was going to be hanging out with friends for the entire weekend, listening to motivational speakers and competing in sports against hundreds of other high school boys from around the St. Louis area. I normally wouldn't have been excited about the motivational speakers, but I had heard through the grapevine that many of the speakers were current and former members of the St. Louis Cardinals baseball and football teams. The thought of meeting professional athletes and competing in sports all weekend with my buddies was all I needed to know. I couldn't wait to sign up and get the weekend started.

When I arrived on Friday evening, I learned my friends and I would all be staying in different cabins. We were each assigned to different small groups called huddles and placed with guys we had never met before. I'm an extrovert by nature so being separated from my friends didn't really bother me. I just saw it as an opportunity to make some new friends.

The weekend ended up being a life changing experience. Making new friends with the other high school guys and competing in sports together helped create a special bond within our huddle. I was amazed at how a group of total strangers became close friends in such a short period of time. However, what had the greatest impact on my life were the speakers.

Throughout the weekend I listened as several professional athletes stood up and shared their testimonies of faith. They spoke about how their successes on the field were not what gave their lives meaning and purpose. They each gave credit for their success to their Lord and Savior Jesus Christ. These humble athletes were men who shared that the talents they had were given to them by the Lord, and they in turn used those talents to honor Christ. By the end of the weekend what really impressed me about these men was not the fact that they were professional athletes, but that they were men of God. I was inspired with their personal devotion to the Lord. I had always considered myself religious, but it seemed like these athletes had something I was missing in my own life.

I had grown up going to church, but to me God always seemed like a distant deity way off in the sky. I thought He was busy watching everything I did, and I assumed He was keeping score. In my mind God was up in heaven with two chalkboards. When I went to church or said my prayers or did something kind, I thought God gave me good marks on my good chalkboard. However, when I said something I shouldn't say, or did something that was hurtful to others, I thought He placed bad marks on my bad chalkboard. I thought that one day when I died and stood before God in heaven, as long as I had more good marks than bad marks I would be fine. I assumed if I had done more good things during my lifetime than bad things, God would allow me into heaven. Like most people, I grew up believing good people go to heaven, and bad people go to a much warmer location. According to my way of thinking I was in control, and my eternal destiny was entirely based on my performance. I just needed to work hard at being good, and I could earn my way into heaven.

On Saturday evening of the FCA weekend conference one of the athletes shared a Bible verse that completely changed my way of thinking.

Ephesians 2:8-9 (GNB) says, "For it is by God's grace that you have been saved through faith. It is not the result of your own efforts, but God's gift, so that no one can boast about it."

The speaker shared how a person could never be good enough to earn God's favor and approval. This statement troubled me because all my life I'd been trying hard to be a nice person so I could get into heaven. Obviously I was still confused about what I needed to do to get into heaven, but I definitely wanted the assurance that if I died I would spend eternity with God. Growing up in the church, I had heard of a place called heaven that was with God and I'd heard of another place called hell that was separated from Him. I wasn't the brightest kid in the world, but even I knew which of those two places I wanted to go, given a choice. I knew I wanted to end up in heaven. The biggest question in the back of my mind was how do I get into heaven if I can't get there by being good?

The speaker shared Romans 3:23, "For all have sinned and fall short of the glory of God."

He explained to us that one thing everyone in the world has in common is we are all sinners and our sin separates us from God. No amount of effort can close the gap between us and God. He then read what he called the Bad News/Good News verse in the Bible.

Romans 6:23 (GW) says, "The payment for sin is death, but the gift that God freely gives is everlasting life found in Christ Jesus our Lord."

The Bad News was that because of the sin in my life I deserved death and eternal separation from God. However, the Good News was that God loved me so much that He was offering me the free gift of everlasting life with Him, and it was found in His Son, Jesus Christ.

Romans 5:8 says, "But God demonstrates His own love for us in this: While we were still sinners, Christ died for us."

First Peter 3:18 (NLT) says, "Christ suffered for our sins once for all time. He never sinned, but He died for sinners to bring you safely home to God.

After hearing these verses I realized Jesus had already done the work to restore my relationship with God. Although there was nothing I could do to get myself into heaven, Jesus made a way for me by paying the price for my sins when He died on the cross. I couldn't pay that sin debt on my own, but Jesus paid it for me. Why would Jesus pay such a high price for me? I realized He died in my place for one simple reason, because He loves me. It wasn't because I was great and wonderful but simply because of His great love for me. The speaker closed his talk with a Bible verse I had heard many times before but now it took on a whole new meaning.

In John 14:6, Jesus says, "I am the way and the truth and the life. No one comes to the Father except through me."

The speaker explained that, just like you need a ticket to go to a professional baseball game, you also need a ticket to go to heaven. John 14:6 tells us the only path to God, the one and only ticket to heaven is found in Jesus. When he asked who would like a ticket to heaven, I knew I was ready for mine. I was tired of my boring religion; I was ready to start an exciting relationship with Jesus. I prayed a simple prayer of faith that night asking God to forgive my sins and inviting Jesus Christ to come into my life. The commitment I made to Christ that evening has been the greatest decision of my life. Jesus Christ gives my life direction, meaning and purpose.

I left the FCA weekend conference knowing I was a changed young man. I knew I was a long way from being perfect, but I was

committed to living my days here on this earth in obedience to my
Lord and Savior Jesus Christ. I was excited about my new found
faith, but I had no idea the incredible journey God had prepared for
me as I graduated from high school and headed off to college.

2

Truman Tiger - Kickoff to a Crazy Career

"The best education is caught—not taught."

Many of my classmates knew exactly what they wanted to do with their lives when they graduated from high school. Some who wanted to become engineers enrolled at the best engineering schools. Others wanted to study nursing or education, and some even chose to join the armed forces. Personally, I wasn't sure where I wanted to go or what I wanted to study.

At the end of my senior year the St. Charles West High School newspaper, *"The Smoke Signal,"* conducted a poll. They asked each senior to write down his prediction on which of their classmates was most likely to fit into several categories over the next 20 years. The categories included:

- Most likely to become President of the United States—I wasn't picked for this one.
- Most likely to succeed—I wasn't chosen for this category either.
- Most likely to be a rocket scientist—Not smart enough.
- Most likely to be a model—Not a chance. Not cute or muscular enough.

Out of all the categories listed, Dan Meers was chosen by his fellow 1985 St. Charles West classmates as the person most likely to become a Game Show Host. I wasn't sure if that meant my friends liked me or not, but I figured at least I wasn't chosen as the classmate most likely to end up in jail. Even though being a Game Show Host sounded interesting, I assumed I would have to move to the West Coast to pursue that career. I was ready to get out of St. Charles, but California seemed a little too far. Instead I enrolled in college closer to home at the University of Missouri—Columbia (aka Mizzou).

Mizzou was less than two hours away from St. Charles, which felt like the perfect distance from home. Several of my classmates were going to college there, and one of them was my best friend, Brad Baum. Brad and I decided it would be fun rooming together. We were not only high school classmates and friends, but we also attended the same church. I was excited about rooming with Brad, not only because he was fun to be with but also because I knew he could help hold me accountable in college. The commitment I made to live for the Lord in high school at the FCA conference was real, but I also knew that commitment would be tested when I left home.

My freshman year was definitely a learning experience. After my first load of college laundry, half of my underwear was pink because I completely forgot about separating lights and darks. I guess I was trying to be frugal and save 50 cents by washing both colors together. Brad and I lived on the first floor of Hatch Hall. Many people complained about life in the dorms, but I loved living there. The best part for me was the cafeteria. I've never been a picky eater, thanks to my parents. When I was growing up, our family had the same two choices for dinner every night, take it or leave it. Since I didn't like to go hungry, I learned to eat whatever was placed in front of me. The reason I loved the dorm cafeteria was that I got to eat three buffet meals every day of the week, and I didn't have to do the dishes afterwards.

When I enrolled in college, I had to declare a major. Since there wasn't a specific major for a potential Game Show Host, I put down agriculture, a major I chose because the Ag building was the closest to my dormitory. It didn't take long before I realized I was obviously in the wrong area. Most of the guys in the agriculture school wore blue jeans with large belt buckles and cowboy boots. Since I preferred going to class in shorts and flip flops, I decided I was probably in the wrong area of study. I dropped out of agriculture and switched my major to broadcast journalism.

One of the best choices I made in college was getting involved with a campus ministry called The Navigators. My pastor encouraged me to get plugged in with a group of believers because, as he put it, "The banana that gets separated from the bunch is the first to get eaten." This was his way of saying stay connected with a church. The Navigators ministry made a huge impact on me and taught me how to live out my faith.

One of my favorite memories from my freshman year was the 1985 World Series. The St. Louis Cardinals were playing the Kansas City Royals, and since Columbia is located between those two cities, it made for an exciting week. Half of the students in Hatch Hall were Cardinals fans and the other half cheered for the Royals. Since I had grown up near St. Louis, of course I was cheering for the Redbirds. During the games every time someone hit a home run or made a good play the fans from that team could be heard yelling and screaming up and down the hallways. It was a very exciting series that went the full seven games, but to my dismay in the end the Boys in Blue hoisted the World Series trophy.

In the spring of my freshman year I was reading our college newspaper, and I saw an article about the Missouri athletic department holding tryouts for the school mascot Truman Tiger. Even though I had never been a mascot, the idea sounded interesting, and I thought I would at least attend the informational meeting. I didn't realize it then, but this was a moment in time that would alter the course of my entire life.

At the meeting I learned that originally MU had two tiger mascots, a male and a female, but neither had a specific identity. The university held a contest in 1984 to name the mascot and the winning student submitted the name Truman after the Missouri-born President Harry S Truman. They also explained how Truman Tiger represented Mizzou at appearances and athletic events throughout the year. Being a mascot sounded fascinating and with a little encouragement from my roommate Brad, I decided to try out. There were 25 students competing for four Truman Tiger positions. The athletic department explained that each of the four Tigers had different responsibilities:

- The #1 Tiger would perform at men's sporting events.
- The #2 Tiger performed for the women's sports.
- The #3 Tiger was a backup for #1 (in case he was sick or had a class to attend).

- The #4 Tiger was a backup for #2.
- All of the Tigers would work together to help cover other university appearances.

Although I had never performed as a mascot before, I figured I had just as good of a shot as the others who were trying out. The weekend before tryouts I drove home and called my friend Beth McGuire, who was on the dance team at my old high school. She helped me come up with a skit and a dance routine. As we practiced my dancing, it became obvious that even though I didn't have much rhythm, my routine was filled with high energy.

During the tryout each contestant had to perform a short two minute skit and then dance to the school fight song. Once the performance was finished, each contestant had to interview with the judges from the athletic department. My skit consisted of Truman Tiger dressed in a Hawaiian outfit, hanging out on the beach. I used a beach towel, sunglasses and a beach ball for props and worked in some Surfing Safari music to add to the beach theme. Overall I felt good about my tryout, but I had to wait 24 hours to find out the results.

The next day I walked over to the Hearnes Center where the names of the four students who had won the mascot tryouts were posted. I looked on the sheet, taped to the athletic department door, and noticed my name was not on the list. I was disappointed because I had put a lot of effort into my tryout, but I figured being a mascot just wasn't meant to be.

I finished my freshman year and went home to work for the summer. For my sophomore year I arrived on campus about a week before most of the other students because I had received a position as a Resident Assistant (RA) on fifth floor of Hatch Hall. My floor was known as the "Cockrell House Roaches." Judging by the number of bugs in the bathroom it was easy to see where the floor got its name.

The best part of the RA job was receiving my room and board for free, as well as having a room all to myself. The most challenging part of the job was feeling like a glorified babysitter for 60 college students. Most weekends I felt like a 19-year-old father of a very,

very large, disobedient family. The job was a challenge, but I was very thankful because it was a huge financial blessing in my life. Life was going well, and was about to get better.

A week after classes started, I received a phone call from the Missouri Athletic Department asking if I was still interested in being Truman Tiger. Apparently, I had finished fifth in the mascot tryouts, but one of the four winning students had failed to show up for classes in the fall. The athletic department wanted me to serve as the #4 Truman Tiger. I was very excited and told them I would love to take the position. I never learned who the student was that had dropped out, but I would like to thank him because his decision set my entire career in motion. After my first few appearances as Truman Tiger, I realized I needed to get myself in better physical shape. I started jogging on a regular basis which really increased my stamina. I intentionally tried to jog during the hottest times of the day to help simulate the heat in the costume.

My first performance at an athletic event was at a women's volleyball game held at the Hearnes Center. Although the seating capacity was 12,000, there were only about 30 people in the crowd. Two of those 30 were my mom and dad. My parents had driven almost two hours to watch my first big performance. I'm sure I wasn't overly entertaining but my mom and dad made me feel like I was the best mascot to ever wear a costume. Every kid needs cheerleaders in his life, and my parents were two of the best. They encouraged and supported me in everything I ever did no matter how crazy it might be.

I quickly learned that being a mascot was like snow skiing. The more you do it, the better you get. The more appearances I did in the costume the more comfortable I became. When basketball season arrived, I was finally starting to feel confident. My big break came when I was asked to fill in at one of the Missouri women's basketball games. The women's games were typically played right before the men's games so the crowds were much larger than for volleyball matches. I'm still not sure what I did to impress the athletic department that night, but after the game I was promoted from the #4 Truman Tiger to the #1 Truman Tiger. I went from being the backup for women's sports to the Truman who got to perform at men's sports. The best thing about being the #1 Tiger was the crowds I performed for were much larger, and I occasionally got to travel to away games. That spring I had my first opportunity to travel to an out of town game. I felt like I had finally reached the big time because I was traveling for free, and I even got per diem money to spend on food. I was really excited about the food money because I was just a poor college student often giving blood plasma to make a few extra bucks. For this first away game I hopped on a Greyhound bus along with the pep band and the cheerleaders, and we rode to the Hoosier Dome in Indianapolis for the 1987 NCAA Men's basketball tournament. Unfortunately, we didn't stay very long because Missouri lost to Xavier in the first round, so we drove back to Columbia.

At the end of basketball season the athletic department once again held mascot tryouts. Even though I was already a Truman Tiger, they made me try out again. I was excited when I learned that I was selected as the #1 Tiger again for the 1987-88 school year. I made up my mind that if I was going to be the #1 Truman Tiger, I would spend that summer getting in the best shape of my life.

During the summer I attended a week long college mascot camp. The Universal Cheerleaders Association hosted the camp at East Tennessee State University in Johnson City, Tennessee. The camp was the first official mascot training I had ever received, and I enjoyed meeting other college mascots from around the country. The camp was very informative, and I walked away with many new ideas.

When football season rolled around in the fall, I was ready to go. I will never forget the feeling I had the first time I rode around the track at Faurot Field standing on the back of a fire truck, swinging my Tiger tail. I loved the atmosphere, and performing for large crowds was addictive. My favorite part of the football games was when the student section grabbed Truman Tiger, lifted him over their heads and passed him up the student section. This was known as "crowd surfing," and it was a lot of fun as long as the students did not drop me. Surfing over the fraternity section was never a problem. The sorority girls, however, had a hard time lifting the mascot. My crowd surfing usually ended right in the middle of a group of college girls which was fine since I was a single college guy. The campus police never liked my crowd surfing antics because they were afraid I would get hurt. Mizzou's football team finished that season with a record of 5-6 under head coach Woody Widenhofer. Even though we didn't win much, I really enjoyed performing at the games. What I didn't know at the time was that in two short years I would begin an NFL mascot career which would last for over a quarter of a century.

During the fall of 1987 I put together a highlight video of my Truman Tiger antics. At the mascot camp I had attended during the summer, I learned about the National Mascot Championships that were held annually. In order to enter the competition each mascot had to put together a three minute highlight video and mail it to the Universal Cheerleaders Association judging committee. After watching all of the videos, the committee picked the top four mascots and flew them to Orlando, Florida for the finals.

I really didn't think I would win, but I thought putting together a highlight video would be fun anyway. Since I was studying broadcast journalism, I had access to all of the editing equipment I needed. I mailed off my video in late December and headed home to celebrate Christmas break. By the time I returned to college several weeks later, I had pretty much forgotten about the competition.

On February 4, 1988, I received a letter in the mail from the Universal Cheerleaders Association that read:

> Dear "Truman,"
> Congratulations on being selected as one of the "Final Four" in
> the National Collegiate Mascot Championship. Over one
> hundred mascots entered this year's championship. I'm sure
> that your administration and fans are very proud of you.

I was thrilled because along with the letter was a free airline ticket to Orlando, Florida. The National Championship was being held at Sea World, and each finalist also received a free ticket to Disney World for the day before the competition. I had never been to Disney World, and even though I was 21 years old, I was so excited I felt like a little kid. The championships were held February 26-28, and I would be competing against three other college mascots:

• Buzz, the yellow jacket from Georgia Tech University.
• Aubie, the tiger from Auburn University.
• Big Blue, the lion from Old Dominion University.

On my way to Orlando I had a connecting flight through Memphis. As I walked to the gate to board my flight, I was surprised to see my parents, my brother Dave and my cousin John sitting there waiting. They were flying down with me to watch the competition. I could always count on my family to be there for encouragement and support. We had a great time in Florida together, and I ended up taking second place in the competition. I was beaten by Buzz, but I had fun and decided I would compete again the next year.

Shortly after returning home from the Mascot Championship, I traveled to Kansas City for the Men's Big Eight Basketball Tournament. March was always an exciting month for me because I got to travel to several away basketball games. After the Big Eight Tournament in Kansas City, we hopped on a bus and headed out to Chapel Hill, North Carolina, for a first round game in the NCAA tournament. Even though Missouri was favored, the Tigers ended up losing to Rhode Island. Once again it was a sudden end to a good season, followed by a very long bus ride back to Columbia.

After finishing second in the National Collegiate Mascot Championship, I felt really good about my chances of getting the #1 Truman Tiger position when the athletic department held tryouts again. Sure enough, I got the top job for the 1988-89 school year, a year that turned out to be the most enjoyable one of my college mascot career. Even though the football team only finished 3-7-1, we took some very memorable trips. My favorite game was when we played the University of Miami, in the Orange Bowl stadium in Miami, Florida. Even though the Hurricanes thumped the Tigers (55-0), performing in such an historic venue was still very exciting.

Basketball season also had several highlights. The first was a trip over Thanksgiving to New York City to play in the Big Apple NIT Basketball Championship. The games were played in Madison Square Garden, another historic venue that I had heard of many times. This was my first time in New York, and between games I spent my time visiting the Empire State Building, the Statue of Liberty and all the other New York tourist attractions. While in New

York, I also had the chance to watch the Macy's Thanksgiving Day Parade in person. I never would have guessed that many years later, I would have the opportunity to be back in New York on Thanksgiving to participate in the parade. Instead of being a spectator, I dressed as KC Wolf and rode on the NFL float alongside football Hall of Famer Joe Namath.

The Missouri men's basketball team did very well during the 1988-89 season. Missouri finished second in the Big Eight conference regular season behind Oklahoma. However, when we traveled to Kansas City again for the Big Eight tournament, the Tigers upset the Sooners in the championship game. As a result Missouri received a #3 seed in the NCAA Men's Basketball tournament, and once again the athletic department loaded us on a bus. This time our destination was Reunion Arena in Dallas, Texas. After discouraging upsets the previous two years against Xavier and Rhode Island, everyone was hoping to advance further in the tournament. Missouri earned its way into the Sweet 16 by defeating Creighton and Texas on the first weekend of play. I still remember the excitement on the bus as the pep band, cheerleaders and I traveled back to Columbia. Those bus rides back home always felt shorter after a big win.

A few days after arriving back in Columbia, our group loaded onto another bus and headed north to the Metrodome in Minneapolis. Unfortunately, our season came to an end there when we lost to Syracuse. After the game as I walked back to the locker room to take off my tiger costume, I could see the Syracuse Orange mascot excitedly jumping up and down on the court. I laughed because he looked like a pumpkin with legs.

Even though I was disappointed about our loss in Minneapolis, I was excited about another upcoming trip to San Antonio, Texas. It was time for the annual mascot championships, and for the second year in a row I had received a letter congratulating me on making it to the Final Four. This year the event was being held at the Sea World in San Antonio, and I was excited to be competing for the top spot. Once again my parents, my two nieces, Toni and Trisha, and three of my cousins all made the trip to Texas to support me. The three other finalists included:

• Zippy, the kangaroo from Akron University.
• Aubie, the tiger from Auburn University.
• Baby Pouncer, the tiger from Memphis State University.

On Saturday, April 8, 1989, Truman Tiger was crowned the National Collegiate Mascot Champion. When I watched the video of the judges announcing the winner and handing me the championship trophy, I could hear the fans clapping, my family cheering, and my mom screaming. Meanwhile, dad was smiling, and I was sweating. I had managed to beat out 136 other mascots in the competition. On this very exciting day, I had an incredible feeling of accomplishment as I headed back to college. I flew back to Columbia feeling like a celebrity. Several newspapers contacted me wanting to do stories about Truman being named the top college mascot in the nation. A local television station wanted to do an interview. I enjoyed this fun and exciting time as I basked in my brief moment of fame.

I had been featured in the newspaper several other times during college, but a couple of those articles weren't nearly so positive. One was an article written in the *Kansas City Star* titled, "Mascots Antics Can Go Too Far." I had received a stuffed referee doll for Christmas that was about three feet tall. The arms and legs on the doll were attached with Velcro strips. During a timeout I ran out to half court and ripped the arms and legs off the doll. Of course the crowd loved it, but the referees didn't seem to be nearly so amused. Needless to say, my Christmas gift didn't get any more use after that performance.

The other negative press I received in college was actually an editorial written in the *Columbia Tribune* titled, "Truman's Latest Bit Should Go." I had made a stuffed cheerleader that I affectionately named Suzie who was dressed up to look like the other Missouri cheerleaders. The cheerleading squad was coed, and occasionally they performed stunts together during timeouts. When the male cheerleaders tossed their female partners into the air, Truman Tiger also tossed Suzie into the air. The only difference was that occasionally I purposely dropped Suzie. After Suzie hit the floor, I immediately got down and performed CPR on her. Once again the majority of the crowd enjoyed the skit, but apparently one lady thought my actions were brutal and showed hatred toward women. I never dreamed a guy dressed in a Tiger costume could create such an emotional uproar.

Two days later a second editorial came out in the paper. It said, "Criticism of Truman Goes Too Far." The writer of this editorial thought the lady was blowing things out of proportion. This editorial read, "Truman's job is to entertain (which he does very well) and using this doll happens to be one of the ways in which he gets laughs. If one calls Truman a male chauvinist for dropping a doll, what will be next? Is the animal humane society going to put him behind bars for carrying a rubber Jayhawk?" I decided to give Suzie a rest for the remainder of the season and let the controversy fade away peacefully.

Since I had just won the National Collegiate Mascot Championship, the athletic department decided I should continue the job as the #1 Truman for the 1989-90 school year. I wanted to make my final year in college my best. Because I had decided to double major, I was now on the five year college plan, earning degrees in broadcast journalism and in speech communication. I learned a great deal about public speaking in my communication classes, and being a mascot also taught me how to communicate nonverbally.

The summer before my final year of college I worked as a counselor at Kanakuk Kamps in Branson, Missouri. Kanakuk is a Christian athletic camp that has been making a difference in the lives of young people for many years. My time at Kanakuk had a profound impact on my life. I spent that summer investing my time into the lives of the young people who attended camp.

When I returned to school in the fall, I knew it was no accident that I was a mascot. I also knew that God desired me to use my platform to make an impact in the lives of kids. One of the biggest lessons I learned during my summer at Kanakuk was that God did not put people on earth to make a living. He put us here to make an impact. I began to be intentional about looking for opportunities to be a positive role model in the lives of young people.

In September, when the college football season kicked off there was plenty of excitement because the Tigers had hired Bob Stull as their new head coach. Our season got off to a great start when we beat Texas Christian University in the home opener. TCU brought their mascot to the game, and we had a great time performing together. The character's name was SuperFrog the horned frog, and he looked like something you would see in an alien movie. It was definitely one of the most unusual looking mascots I had ever seen. Unfortunately, our win against TCU was the highlight of our football season. The Tigers struggled the rest of the year and ended up winning only one more game. I had been Truman Tiger for three full seasons and during that time the football team had an overall record of 10-22-1. Even though the team only won two games my final year I had a great time on the road trips. During that final football season I performed at Indiana, Kansas State, Oklahoma, Arizona State and Colorado. The trip to Boulder, Colorado, was especially exciting because on our way home the Missouri Marching band performed at halftime of a Denver Broncos game. This was the first time I ever performed as a mascot at an NFL football game, but it certainly would not be my last. I still find it humorous that, for my first NFL game I was dressed in a Tiger suit, cheering for the Denver Broncos. Little did I know that it was the first and the last time I would be cheering for one of the Kansas City Chiefs' biggest rivals.

Basketball season also started out very well in 1989. The Tigers were scheduled to play in the Maui Classic in Lahaina, Hawaii. I was excited for two reasons:

    #1 - I was going to Hawaii.

    #2 - I didn't have to ride in the back of a Greyhound bus to
        get there.

Of all the trips I took with Mizzou, this one was by far the best. I did everything there was to do in Hawaii except sleep. I knew I could sleep at home so when I was on this trip, I tried to make the most of every moment. One morning a few of my buddies and I woke up at 3:00 a.m. and drove a rental car to Haleakala National Park. This scenic National Park is home to Maui's highest peak. We made the trip early in the morning to watch the sun come up. Since we were in Hawaii, we all dressed in our shorts and tank tops. Our plan after watching the sunrise was to grab breakfast, go rent surf boards and head for the beach. When we reached the top of the mountain, we quickly realized that even in Hawaii the weather is very cold and windy at an elevation of 9,740 feet, especially when the sun isn't up. Five members of the Mini-Mizzou pep band and I sat huddled together trying to stay warm, wrapped in three beach towels. I never dreamed I could get that cold in Hawaii, but freezing was worth the effort when the sun started peeking over the horizon. As I sat there watching the sun come up that morning, I reflected on a Bible verse I had memorized earlier in the year.

"Because of the Lord's great love we are not consumed, for His compassions never fail. They are new every morning; great is Your Faithfulness" (Lamentations 3:22-23).

Once again I was reminded of God's faithfulness and the fact that I was a very blessed young man.

The Maui Classic basketball games were played in a small gymnasium that didn't have air conditioning. There was only one fan circulating air in the corner of the gym so that is where the opposing mascot and I spent most of our time. Not only was the trip to Hawaii exciting, but the team also played very well. The Missouri Tigers beat the North Carolina Tar Heels in the championship game, and I flew back home happy and sun burned.

Shortly after arriving home from Hawaii, I was asked to speak at Paris Junior High School in Paris, Missouri. I had been praying for a chance to use the platform God had given me to make a positive impact in the lives of young people, and this invitation seemed like a great opportunity. I titled my message: Being a Winner in Life. I shared with the students that being a winner is more about who you are as a person than about what you successfully achieve in life. It has more to do with who you are on the inside than about what you look like on the outside. I tried to encourage the students to work hard and never to give up. The message I shared that day was very simple, but apparently it was a hit with both the students and the staff. The following week the University of Missouri athletic department received a letter from the school principal thanking them for allowing me to come and visit the school. The principal mentioned in the letter that the assembly had made a positive impression on the students.

This letter encouraged me, and I made up my mind to work on improving my school presentation. Selfishly, I prayed I would have other opportunities to share because in my four years as Truman

Tiger, speaking to those junior high students was one of the most rewarding experiences of my college career.

Over Christmas break my brother Dave wanted Truman Tiger to help him get engaged to his girlfriend, Stacey. I was able to buy a group of tickets for a Missouri Tigers men's basketball game on December 28 because most of the student body was out of town for the holidays. We purchased 20 tickets so many of our family and friends could be there for the big surprise. During halftime I came up to their seats dressed as Truman Tiger. My brother helped me unroll a huge banner which read:

"Stacey, Truman wants a Sister-in-Law, Will You Marry Me?" Dave

The fans were clapping, our family was cheering, and my mom was screaming. Dave and Stacey were hugging and smiling, and yet again I was inside a costume sweating. Getting to be a part of my little brother's marriage proposal was fun.

Once again the Missouri basketball team had a great season, but it ended in an upset. The Tigers were a #3 seed in the NCAA tournament but we lost our opening game to a #14 seed, Northern Iowa. I had been Truman Tiger for four full basketball seasons, and our final overall record for those years was 98-35. That was much better than our football record, but unfortunately the NCAA basketball tournament was not good to the Tigers in my four years. Three out of my four years the Tigers lost in the first round of the tournament to a lower seeded team.

On a positive note, for the third year in a row, I qualified for the Final Four in the National Collegiate Mascot Championship. The competition was back in San Antonio, and once again my parents were there to support me. My good friend Brad Baum and several other friends and family also came along to cheer me on. This time Marco the Buffalo from Marshall University in West Virginia was crowned the champion, and I ended up in second place. As I held my second place trophy, I was smiling because I realized that even though I hadn't won, I was still blessed to be surrounded by my family and friends. Before I got out of my Truman Tiger suit, I had my picture taken one last time with Shamu the Whale. It had been another great trip, and I knew this was my last collegiate competition.

My final appearance in the Hearnes Center where I had spent countless hours performing as Truman Tiger was on May 12, 1990. Instead of wearing a tiger striped suit with a tail, I was dressed in a black robe and a graduation cap. I had spent five of the best years of my life at Mizzou, and now I was graduating with my collegiate degrees and a mascot resume.

Apparently my mascot resume looked pretty good, because I was offered a professional mascot job that was actually going to pay me. After performing for four years in college for free, the idea of getting paid to mascot was a dream come true. The time had come for me to trade in my fur for feathers.

3

Fredbird -
From Fur to Feathers

*"Find a job you love and you will never have
to work a day in your life."*
Jim Fox

God had all the right people in the right places at the right time for me to become a professional mascot. In 1989 the assistant athletic director at Mizzou was Joe Castiglione. Joe, who knew the 1989-90 school year was going to be my last at Mizzou, encouraged me to get in touch with a friend of his who worked for the St. Louis Cardinals baseball team. Joe told me I should look into the position of 'Fredbird' the mascot of the St. Louis Cardinals. Since I had grown up in St. Charles, about 25 miles from Busch Stadium, I was a huge Cardinals fan. I still remember working hard in elementary school to make the honor roll because the Cardinals rewarded students who made A's on their report card with free tickets to a game.

The idea of possibly working for my favorite baseball team was a dream come true. Joe gave me the address of John Kendall, who was in charge of overseeing Fredbird. I mailed John a letter explaining who I was and expressing my interest in the Fredbird position. I included my resume and a copy of my mascot experience. I also listed the awards I had won. Joe Castiglione and Diane Saale, the Missouri cheerleading coach, agreed to be two of my references. Apparently my letter and resume worked because Mr. Kendall called and set up a meeting with me when I was in St. Louis over Christmas break.

During the meeting I learned the Cardinals already had a full time Fredbird who had worked for the team for several years, but they were looking for a backup bird. John explained that the backup mainly worked community appearances and promotions around the St. Louis area while the #1 Fredbird spent most of his time working the baseball games. John told me that if I was interested I could have the backup job starting in April when the baseball season began. I was thrilled and told him that I would love to wear bird feathers.

The spring of 1990 was a busy and exciting time in my life. I was finishing up college days at Mizzou, working as a Residential Assistant in my dormitory, still performing as Truman Tiger for the Missouri men's basketball team, and now I was also doing occasional appearances as Fredbird back in St. Louis. Life was extremely busy, but I was loving every minute.

In the midst of my crazy schedule I received two surprising phone calls. The first one was from Derrill Martin, one of the St. Louis area directors for the Fellowship of Christian Athletes. He wanted to know if I would be interested in a job with FCA working with junior and senior high schools in the St. Louis area. He said I could continue working part-time as the backup Fredbird and work with FCA as well. This was an exciting opportunity for me since FCA was a ministry that had impacted me greatly during my senior year of high school. I told Derrill I was interested, but I would need some time to think it through and pray about it.

The other phone call I received was from Phil Thomas, who was the Director of Promotions with the Kansas City Chiefs. Phil had received my phone number from his friend Joe Castiglione. I was quickly finding out that Joe was well connected and a great guy to have in my corner. Phil was calling to see if I might be interested in interviewing for the position of KC Wolf, the new mascot of the Chiefs. He explained that the Chiefs had created the KC Wolf character in 1989, when Carl Peterson began as the Chiefs new General Manager. KC Wolf was named after the team's "Wolfpack," a group of rabid fans who used to sit in temporary bleachers at Municipal Stadium. The Chiefs had a performer out of New York City fly in and work the home games in 1989, but they were looking to hire a new full time KC Wolf to move to the Kansas City area and begin working during the 1990 season. I took down Phil's contact information and asked if I could think about it and get back in touch with him. I hung up the phone feeling both excited and overwhelmed with the opportunities God was placing before me.

I knew I had some big decisions to make. I was nervous because all of my options seemed like great opportunities. I called my parents and told them about the two new job possibilities in St. Louis and in Kansas City. My parents were always very loving and supportive, but I knew this was a decision that only I could make. I knew deep down they were hoping I would take the St. Louis job so I would be closer to home, but my dad encouraged me to at least interview in Kansas City. I could always decide later not to take the job.

I set up an interview with the Chiefs on Wednesday, April 4, 1990, at Arrowhead Stadium. I arrived dressed in a suit and tie and brought along my Truman Tiger highlight videos that I had used for the National Collegiate Mascot Championships. Knowing I already had a job offer in St. Louis relieved a lot of the stress during my Chiefs interview. During the interview I told Phil that if I took the job as KC Wolf, I wanted permission to do more than just appearances and games. I was very clear that I wanted to be able to use the KC Wolf platform to go out and speak at schools, churches and other youth events. After speaking at schools as Truman Tiger, I knew God was calling me to use my platform as a mascot to have a positive influence in the lives of young people. Whether I was in St. Louis or Kansas City, I wanted to make sure I was following God's path for my life.

I once read that if a man goes through his life and only makes money, he is not a success. I made up my mind that I wouldn't choose my job based upon who paid the most money. I wanted to work where I felt I could have the greatest impact. There was a part of me that wanted Phil to tell me I was not the man for the job. If that had been his response, my decision would have been much easier. However, Phil was very enthusiastic about the idea of reaching out to kids and said the Chiefs would be very supportive. He told me that I came very highly recommended for the mascot position, and he wanted to offer me the job as KC Wolf. As I left Arrowhead Stadium, I told Phil I needed time to think my options over and pray about them. I promised I would call him in a week with my decision.

The following week was incredibly emotional and difficult for me. I have never enjoyed making big decisions, and at this point in my life this was the biggest decision I had ever had to make. I thought the easiest way to make the decision would be to flip a coin with heads for St. Louis (Fredbird & FCA) and tails for Kansas City (KC Wolf). I realized using a coin flip to decide my fate wasn't a very good idea so instead I took the advice of my Bible study teacher. He suggested I get alone with God and seek His direction for my life. He told me to reflect on Proverbs 3:5-6 which says, "Trust in the Lord with all your heart and lean not on your own understanding; in all your ways acknowledge Him, and He will make your paths straight."

I prayed that God would make it clear to me where He wanted me to work and place me where I could have the greatest impact in the lives of others. As I sought God's direction for my life, He was faithful to answer my prayers. God never showed Himself to me in a vision, and He didn't speak to me in an audible voice, but I know for a fact that He clearly gave me direction.

I only knew a few people who lived in Kansas City and it was about 225 miles from home, but as I prayed, God gave me a peace that Kansas City was the place for me. God was calling me out of my comfort zone, and I knew that my faith was about to be stretched. I was also confident that wherever God leads He also provides. If God wanted me in Kansas City wearing a Wolf costume, then Kansas City is where I would go.

After making my decision I knew I had several phone calls to make. The first call I made was to my parents. When I told them about my decision to move to Kansas City, they were once again very encouraging and supportive. My second phone call was to Phil Thomas to let him know I would love to take the job as KC Wolf. He wished me good luck with my finals and encouraged me to take a few weeks off after graduation. I agreed to begin working for the Chiefs the first week of June. My third phone call was to Derrill Martin telling him I was going to be taking the job in Kansas City, but that I appreciated his offer to work for FCA. My final call was the one I dreaded the most. I had only been working with the St. Louis Cardinals for a few months, and now I was calling to let them know that I had taken a new job with the Chiefs. John Kendall was very understanding when I explained to him about the job opportunity in Kansas City that I couldn't pass up. I told him I would be moving to Kansas City in June, but I would be willing to help out until they could find a new backup Fredbird.

The following day John called to ask if I would be willing to work three upcoming Cardinal baseball games. During the May 4-6 weekend series the full-time Fredbird was going to be out of town, and the team needed me to work the games. He wanted to know if I could help him out one last time. This opportunity was a dream come true. Although I had been dressing up like Fredbird, this was my first chance to perform at an actual Cardinal game in Busch Stadium. This was the stadium where I had grown up watching my favorite baseball team play. Now I was going to get to walk on the field as Fredbird. I called my parents, who immediately bought tickets for all three games. My parents told the youth pastor at our church, who organized a youth group trip to the Cardinal game to come out and see Dan dressed as Fredbird.

On Friday, May 4, 1990, I arrived at Busch Stadium early to make sure I was ready for my professional baseball mascot debut. As I tried on the Fredbird outfit in the dressing room, I realized I was several inches taller than the regular full-time Fredbird. The costume consisted of bird feet, yellow tights, red bird feathers and a head. It was quite obvious that I was a taller bird because when I put on the costume the feathers didn't cover up nearly as much of my yellow tights. Fredbird's game day assistant was a nice gentleman named Don, who quickly encouraged me to squat down when I hugged kids instead of bending over to hug them. I later learned he wanted me to squat instead of bending over because when I bent over to hug a kid, anyone standing behind Fredbird would see a bright yellow "Moon" peeking out from under the feathers. When I squatted I could keep the "Moon" hidden.

The St. Louis Cardinals were going to be playing the Cincinnati Reds. As I stepped onto the baseball field for the pregame festivities, I felt like a little kid on Christmas morning. I couldn't believe I was standing with a group of fans having my picture taken with Ozzie Smith, the Cardinals All-Star shortstop. This game ranked right up there as one of the most exciting experiences of my life.

In the sixth inning Fredbird was scheduled to make an appearance at a designated area out near center field. This appearance gave fans and little kids an opportunity to meet Fredbird and have a picture taken with him. The little kids had a hard time getting to see Fredbird that first night because most of my time was spent taking pictures with family members, friends and my church youth group. By the end of the game I was exhausted, but my tiredness was worth it because this day had been one of the best of my life.

Webster's dictionary defines mascot as "A person, animal or object believed to bring good luck." If that definition is true, then I failed miserably as the Cardinals' mascot during my three games. Friday night the Cardinals lost 8-3, Saturday they lost 4-2, and Sunday they lost again 5-1. I was hoping that when I started my job in Kansas City I would bring better luck to the Chiefs.

Even though my time with the Cardinals was very brief, the experience was truly wonderful. The St. Louis Cardinals are a great organization. When this hometown boy got to dress up as Fredbird, I felt extremely blessed. I was born a Cardinals fan and will be a Cardinals fan until the day I die.

After I finished working the Sunday baseball game, I drove to Columbia for my final week of college, a week filled with tests, tears and goodbyes. It was hard to believe my time at Mizzou was coming to an end. As I drove back home to St. Charles after graduation, I thought back on my time at Mizzou and about all of the places I had visited and all the people I had met. I felt extremely thankful for the many experiences I enjoyed in college. Excited to be moving on to a new chapter in my life, I was also a little anxious. I knew I would soon be leaving my family and my comfort zone in St. Charles and moving across the state to Kansas City.

Confident God was leading me to Kansas City, I had no idea what to expect when I got there. As I pulled into my parent's driveway and turned off my car ignition, I sat for a moment and reflected on a quote that I kept in my Bible. "There are a lot of things about tomorrow that I do not understand but I know who holds tomorrow and I know who holds my hand." I was still uncertain about what my future would look like in Kansas City, but I was certain God was by my side. Life was still an adventure, and I couldn't wait to see what the next leg of the journey held. I enjoyed almost three weeks of summer vacation at home in St. Charles, having fun, relaxing, spending time with family and catching up with old friends before packing my bags and leaving again.

On Friday, June 1, our family loaded up my dad's pickup truck with all of my belongings and drove west to Kansas City. My brother Dave also drove his car so we didn't have to squeeze the whole family into the cab of the truck. In the bed of the pickup, strapped to the top of the load, was a papason chair I had bought in college. As we drove down the interstate, I had to laugh because dad looked like he had a satellite dish mounted on the top of his truck.

Our trip went well until we got to Boonville, Missouri, where my dad's pickup overheated and we had to stop. While dad worked on the truck, the rest of the family went to a local restaurant and ate lunch. We grabbed a sandwich for my dad, and he ate while we continued on our journey west. As we drove into Kansas City, I saw a sign which read:

Welcome to Kansas City, Missouri
Population 435,000

I turned to my mom and said, "That is a lot of people I need to meet." I was joking at the time, but by the end of my first year in Kansas City I had easily performed for twice that many people.

A short time later we finally arrived at the place I would call my home for the next three-and-a-half years. Apartment #11 at the Stadium View apartment complex wasn't the nicest apartment in town, but I loved the location because I could see Arrowhead Stadium from my deck. We spent the weekend getting my apartment organized, and on Sunday afternoon I said goodbye to my family as they headed back home to St. Charles.

On Monday, June 4, 1990, I officially began working for the Kansas City Chiefs. I showed up for work on my first day wearing slacks, a dress shirt and a tie. I look back now and laugh because it was probably the only day I've ever worn a tie to work. I was trying hard to make a good first impression. Over the next 25 years I went to work in shorts and a t-shirt 99% of the time. If the weather was really cold I wore sweatpants and a sweatshirt. One of the perks of being a mascot was I didn't exactly have to show up at work dressed for success. I also didn't spend much time fixing my hair in the mornings, knowing that once I wore the KC Wolf costume, I would come out having a bad hair day anyway. I was one of the few Chiefs employees who was allowed to wear a baseball cap to work. I also carried a duffle bag with an extra pair of clothes and a supply of deodorant and cologne. Even though I didn't always look the best after my appearances, I did attempt to at least smell appropriately.

My first "office" at Arrowhead was a desk and a phone located in the same room with the copy machine. There wasn't a lot of peace and quiet in my first office, but this location was a great place to get to know all of the other Chiefs employees when they stopped in to make copies.

My first official work trip for the Chiefs was a 24 hour trip to New York City. I flew to New York to meet with Wayde Harrison and Bonnie Erickson for a costume fitting and training session. Harrison/Erickson was the company the Chiefs had hired to design and build the KC Wolf costume in 1989. The main purpose for my trip was to get the KC Wolf costume properly fitted for my body. Since I was 6-foot-3 and the costume was originally designed for someone 6-foot, we needed to add extra fur onto the arms and legs.

The husband and wife team ran their mascot design and mer-chandising company out of their Brooklyn Heights apartment. When I arrived, I noticed the apartment was filled with puppets and toys from around the world. Bonnie, who was extremely talented, had helped design characters for the Muppet television shows, including Miss Piggy and Statler and Waldorf, the heckling old men of the *"Muppet Show"* peanut gallery. Bonnie also worked as a con-sultant to Children's Television Workshop which produces *"Sesame Street."* Besides work in television, Bonnie had also helped design sev-eral professional sports mascots, including the Phillie Phanatic of the Philadelphia Phillies, Stuff of the Orlando Magic, Hugo of the Charlotte Hornets, and Youpie of the Montreal Expos. When I real-ized that the same lady who had designed Miss Piggy had also designed KC Wolf, I felt a sudden sibling-like connection to the famous pig.

I arrived back in Kansas City the following day with my newly altered KC Wolf costume. I was eager to get home because the next day, July 1, 1990, was going to be my first official KC Wolf appearance at the Cole Younger Days festival in Lee's Summit, Missouri. Although July is typically not the best time of year to be running around in a hot, furry outfit, I was very excited to get started. After working for the Chiefs for almost a month, I was finally getting a chance to perform as KC Wolf.

Although my trip to New York City was interesting, it didn't compare to the excitement of my second official work trip with the Chiefs. The Chiefs were selected to play the Los Angeles Rams in an American Bowl preseason football game in Olympic Stadium in Berlin, Germany. Other than a trip to the Bahamas when I was in high school, I had never been out of the United States. The Chiefs allowed us to bring one guest along on the trip, so I brought my dad. We flew to Germany a week before the game was played and had a great time sightseeing. The Chiefs were treated like royalty, and Dad and I went on several very interesting tours. We visited the Berlin Zoo and the Pergamon Museum and enjoyed a river cruise down the Spree River, which runs thru Berlin. However, the most interesting part of our trip was seeing what had occurred nine months before our arrival.

The Berlin Wall was both the physical division between West and East Berlin from 1961-1989 and a symbolic boundary between democracy and communism during the Cold War. It had been erected to keep East Germans from fleeing to the West. On November 9, 1989, the Berlin Wall was destroyed. I was in college at the time and remember watching the Germans celebrate its destruction. On one of our tours we visited both East and West Berlin. It was amazing to see the stark contrast between the two cities. My favorite photo from our trip was a picture of my dad and me standing in front of the collapsed Berlin Wall. I still have a piece of the Berlin Wall that sits on my shelf at home and reminds me of how blessed I am to live in a free democracy.

I will always remember my first game as KC Wolf because it was played on August 11, 1990, at Olympic Stadium in Berlin, Germany. Even though the Chiefs lost to the Rams 19-3, my first game working in the NFL was an unbelievable experience and a great way to start my NFL career.

We returned to Kansas City, and one week later I mascoted my first home game at Arrowhead Stadium. The Chiefs played the New York Jets and once again lost, 20-0. I was surprised because no one in the Chiefs' offices seemed to be overly concerned that we had lost our first two games. I eventually learned that in the NFL, a team's preseason record doesn't mean much. Wins and losses become much more important when the regular season arrives. My first Chiefs' victory came in our fourth preseason game against the Green Bay Packers.

The serious football started on September 9 in our regular season home opener against the Minnesota Vikings. On this very hot afternoon, I quickly learned why the players complained about the AstroTurf at Arrowhead Stadium. AstroTurf was a short-pile synthetic turf the Chiefs played on from 1972-1993. The artificial turf retains heat from the sun and tends to be much hotter than natural grass. As a mascot I hated artificial turf. Walking around on the field, I could feel the heat radiating through my costume. I often felt like I was walking around in a furry suit with someone blowing a hair dryer in my face. The biggest lesson I learned from working on AstroTurf for four years was that I had better get myself in incredible shape if I wanted to stay KC Wolf for very long.

My first regular season Chiefs' game as KC Wolf ended in a 24-21 victory over the Vikings played in front of over 68,000 fans. It was one of the largest crowds I had ever performed for, and I could tell being an NFL mascot was going to be a whole lot of fun.

Later in the season, when the Chiefs played the Los Angeles Raiders, I experienced "Raider Hater" week for the first time. The Chiefs and Raiders have had a bitter rivalry for years. Raider Hater week was always exciting because our players and fans would get very passionate.

My boss, Phil Thomas, and I decided KC Wolf should do a special pregame skit for the Raiders game to get the crowd fired up. For the first few games of the season, KC Wolf had ridden out on a four-wheeler, done a little dance, waved at the crowd and driven off. Phil and I thought the Raiders game would be a great time to make KC Wolf skits more memorable and dramatic. We decided the perfect skit would involve a Bo Jackson look alike. Bo Jackson was the 1985 college football Heisman Trophy Winner, as well as the 1989 Major

League Baseball All Star Game MVP. He was very well known, not only for being a two sport superstar, but also for his popular "Bo Knows" Nike commercials. In Kansas City everyone knew Bo because he had spent four years as an outfielder for the Kansas City Royals, but Bo was now a running back for the hated Raiders.

On game day I dressed my old college roommate, Brad Baum, up to look like Jackson. Brad wore a Raiders' helmet, football pants and the familiar #34 Bo Jackson Raiders jersey. Since Brad is white, we also had him wear a long sleeve undershirt and a pair of receiver gloves to cover up his skin color. Brad looked just like Bo, except he was much skinnier and not nearly as muscular.

When time came for the skit, Brad (Bo) rode out on a four-wheeler carrying a baseball bat. The crowd wasn't sure what to think at first, but they eventually began to boo as Brad jumped off the four-wheeler and started pumping his fist dressed as a Raider. When Brad turned to taunt the crowd on the west end of the stadium, I ran out of the east end zone tunnel to tackle him from behind. I sprinted 40 yards down the field and gave Brad a flying cross body block, much to the delight of Chiefs' fans. As Brad continued to lay on the football field pretending to be dazed, I grabbed the baseball bat and snapped it over my knee. That was Bo Jackson's signature move when he was upset because of a strike out in baseball. I threw the broken bat on the field and drove off like a superhero on the four-wheeler. The skit worked perfectly, and the Chiefs' fans loved watching KC Wolf beat up Bo Jackson at midfield. Listening to the crowd's reaction, I knew that KC Wolf skits would never be the same again.

KC Wolf was no longer just a cute and cuddly mascot for kids. He was now popular with the adult Chiefs' fans as well. The crowd thought I was a tough guy snapping a baseball bat over my knee, but they didn't know my secret; I had sawed the bat in half before the game and the two sides were taped together.

My first year in the league as KC Wolf was a blast, and the best part was the Chiefs made it to the playoffs with an 11-5 record. I wanted to take the credit for our success, but most of it deservedly went to coach Marty Schottenheimer and our players. That was fine with me because I was just happy to be along for the ride. Unfortunately, our playoff run ended quickly with a first round loss to the Miami Dolphins.

I did 75 appearances in my first seven months as KC Wolf. What was really encouraging to me was 40 of those appearances were programs in which I spoke to kids. I had asked God to give me opportunities to make an impact on the lives of young people, and clearly He had answered my prayer. My goal was to reach out to even more schools and churches the following year.

On December 21, 1990, I received a very encouraging letter in the mail from a man that I would grow to respect, appreciate and admire over my many years with the Kansas City Chiefs. It read:

Dear Dan:

With the conclusion of the regular season home schedule, I wanted to drop you a note to say "well done" for the extra color and entertainment which you have added to the Chiefs' games this year. We hear a lot of positive comments about "KC Wolf," especially from the fans out in the "hinterlands" who see you on TV.

I was also very pleased to learn you are doing a variety of school programs, some of which feature an anti-drug message. Congratulations on doing this as it is a continually meaningful (and important) message for us to get across. All the best for the New Year.

Sincerely,
Lamar Hunt

I figured if the Chiefs owner Lamar Hunt was sending me a letter, I must have a little job security. My career was off to a great start in Kansas City, but life was about to get even better.

4

KC Wolf Answers
Call of the Aisle

"A good wife is God's smile from heaven."

When I moved to Kansas City there was only one person I knew who lived in the area. His name was Brad Snow, and we had met during college. Brad was a very talented trumpet player in the marching band, and he was also a member of Mini-Mizzou, the pep band that traveled and played at Missouri basketball games. Since the pep band, cheerleaders and mascot all traveled together to away games, Brad and I spent a lot of time together. Brad seemed to have good personal hygiene habits so I tried to sit next to him during those long bus rides. It's amazing how well you get to know someone when you're crammed into a bus seat next to them for hours on end.

Brad was a nice guy; he and I spent many hours playing Uno and other card games with the other band members in the back of a bus. I also got to know Brad's parents because Brad and I stopped in for a home cooked meal whenever we traveled to Kansas City for the Big Eight Men's Basketball tournament.

While I was in Kansas City for the Big Eight tournament in 1989, Brad introduced me to Tom Hufty. Tom was Brad's high school youth pastor, and he asked if I would be willing to do an interview at their youth group meeting while I was in town. Brad attended Pleasant Valley Baptist Church, and Tom thought the students would enjoy asking me questions about being a college mascot and the importance my faith played in my life. I agreed to the interview, and the evening ended up being a lot of fun. I enjoyed meeting the students, and I really enjoyed getting to know Tom. I didn't realize it at the time, but Tom and Pleasant Valley Baptist

Church would play a key role in helping me discover the person with whom I would spend the rest of my life.

After moving to Kansas City, I started looking for a church to attend. Pleasant Valley was only 15 minutes from my apartment and since it was the only church where I knew someone, I decided to visit there. Pleasant Valley was a large church which can sometimes be intimidating for a first time visitor, but the church members quickly made me feel welcome. Brad introduced me to several of his friends, and I also got reacquainted with Pastor Tom. After that very first Sunday I knew Pleasant Valley Baptist was the church for me.

Soon Tom asked me to help out with the youth group at the church, which I was glad to do. During the summer of my freshman year of college I had served as the youth director at Carterville Baptist Church in southern Illinois. It turned out to be one of the best summer jobs I ever had. I've always enjoyed the energy and enthusiasm of junior high and high school students. I once read that if you want to stay young, associate with young people. To get old in a hurry, try keeping up with them. Even though I considered myself to be a pretty energetic guy, I have to admit that by the end of our youth group meetings, I was ready to collapse and the youth still had plenty of energy.

One thing I loved about the Pleasant Valley youth group was that the students were always willing to help me out with community service events I was involved with as KC Wolf. Every year I organized an event called Food Characters Day to help raise money for the Kansas City FCA chapter.

Local companies and food suppliers generously donated money to have their mascot character involved for the weekend. The youth group students participated by dressing up as various costumed characters for the weekend activities. On Saturday morning a bus load of mascots went to Children's Mercy hospital in Kansas City to visit the sick children. The visit was fun and very rewarding for us as we watched the kids' faces light up with excitement. Upon arrival at the hospital, the bus driver would stop in the circle driveway and open the bus door. Out jumped KC Wolf, Mr. Peanut, Twinkie the Kid, Mr. Kool-Aid, Pillsbury Doughboy, Energizer Bunny and many other characters. The children loved our visit, and hopefully seeing a bus load of mascots helped to brighten their day. Visiting Children's Mercy hospital was also a great way for our youth group to learn the importance of doing something nice for others who were going through difficult times.

The day after our hospital visit, all of the mascots made an appearance at the Chiefs' game. The youth group students thought it was pretty cool to dress in a costume and do a dance routine with the Chiefs cheerleaders in front of a huge crowd. They also enjoyed stepping on the field at Arrowhead on game day and seeing the Chiefs players up close. By the end of Food Characters weekend we had excited kids, smelly costumes, and best of all a large sum of money to donate to a great organization. I loved helping support FCA because I knew they were making an impact in the lives of youth in the Kansas City area.

I must confess there was something else I liked about Pleasant Valley Baptist Church besides the youth group, and that was a dark haired girl who attended the 9:30 a.m. service on Sunday mornings. After attending Pleasant Valley for several months, I realized this dark haired girl must be a regular because she sat in the same location every Sunday. You can always tell the regular attenders because they get in a routine and sit in the same seats week after week. After several weeks of Sunday morning scouting, I finally figured out her routine. She showed up about five minutes before the service began and sat about 15 rows back on the left side of the sanctuary. Knowing her routine and her favorite seat location made it easier for me to slowly make my move.

I had done a little investigating on the dark haired mystery woman, and even though I didn't know her name, which was kind of an important detail, I found out she had recently graduated from William Jewell College in Liberty, Missouri. Since my uncle Roger Meers had played football for the William Jewell Cardinals back in the 70's, I just knew she would want to go out with me, or at least that's what I was hoping.

I also learned from my investigation that she drove a red LeBaron and parked in the south parking lot at church. This was helpful information because I definitely didn't want to park anywhere close to her. The Chiefs had given me a company vehicle to drive, and since I needed extra space to carry the KC Wolf suit, they gave me a minivan. I didn't think she would be impressed knowing I was a 24-year-old single guy who drove a minivan. Just by looking at this dark haired mystery woman I could tell she was probably out of my league, but I was willing to take a chance. If she showed no interest in me, it wouldn't be the first time. During my high school dating life I felt like a door-to-door salesman. I learned to deal with a lot of rejection.

One Sunday morning, as I was cruising in my minivan to church, I made up my mind this was going to be the day. I was finally going to get up the nerve to say hello and possibly ask her name. I arrived a little early so I could get in the church pew directly behind her seat. At church there was always a point early in the service where the pastor told everyone to stand up and greet the people around them. This would be my big chance to meet the mystery woman without looking like a stalker. As I sat waiting for the service to begin, I saw my dark haired dream girl walking down the aisle. She slid into her normal spot in the pew directly in front of me. I was getting excited because my plan was working to perfection. I couldn't wait for the pastor to get started so we could get to the "greet your neighbor" part of the service. Just before the pastor stood up to welcome everyone though, a short, dark haired, muscular guy showed up and sat down right next to my dream girl. I wasn't sure who this guy was, but my dream girl sure seemed to be excited to see him. I was hoping it was her brother, but when he kissed her on the cheek and put his arm around her I could tell they weren't siblings.

I couldn't believe what was happening right in front of me. This was definitely not part of my plan. I did manage to shake her hand and found out her name was Cameron. I also politely shook the short guy's hand. I wanted to tell him to try out the other Baptist church across town, but I didn't think that would be a very Christian thing to say. I assumed this was God's way of letting me know Cameron was not the girl for me. I was disappointed, but I remembered the advice of my mother when she used to tell her sons, "There is more than one fish in the sea." I'm convinced my mom said that to encourage me because she was afraid I'd stay single my whole life and someday want to come back and live with her and dad. I figured if Cameron got away, or got caught by another short fisherman, that just meant it was time for me to start fishing again. The next Sunday I went back to sitting in my normal spot in the church balcony, and after about a month I had completely forgotten about her.

Several months later, I was asked to speak at the FCA Weekend of Champions at William Jewell College. This was a weekend filled with inspiration and perspiration. I was excited for the opportunity to once again hang out with high school students all weekend. I had attended several Weekend of Champions events in the past, and I always came away from them challenged and inspired to live out my faith in Jesus Christ.

After I signed in at the registration table, I was standing in the gymnasium waiting for the conference to begin. While I was waiting, I heard a woman's voice say, "Don't you go to Pleasant Valley Baptist Church?" When I looked up I saw Cameron. I said, "Yes, I do attend there." I wanted to say, "Isn't your name Cameron, the girl who always sits in row 15 on the left side of the sanctuary and drives a red LeBaron and has a short, dark haired, muscular, goofy looking boyfriend," but I didn't. Instead I smiled and said, "My name is Dan. Tell me your name again." She said, "My name is Cam, short for Cameron." We talked for a while, and I found out she was going to be a counselor for the high school girls at the conference. I still found her extremely attractive, but I didn't want to get my hopes up because I knew about her short boyfriend. Of course, in the back of my mind, I was thinking, "Why would a beautiful girl like her want to date Mr. Short, Dark, and Muscular when she could date, me Mr. Tall, Blonde and Skinny?"

Out of all the Weekend of Champions events I have ever attended, this FCA conference ended up being my favorite. Once again, the weekend challenged and inspired me to live out my faith, but I also left encouraged because Cam told me she had broken up with her boyfriend. As we were leaving the conference, I asked Cam if she would like to go to a singles Bible study with me later in the week and she said yes. It wasn't an official date, but I knew it would be a great way to get know her better.

After attending Bible study together for several weeks, I finally got up the nerve to ask Cam out on an official date. Amazingly, once again she said yes. In football terms, I would say I had outkicked my coverage because Cam was definitely out of my league. She was smart, beautiful, and she loved the Lord. Those were exactly the qualities I was looking for in a girl. The crazy thing was this dark haired beauty really seemed to like me too. At first I thought she was dating me just to get to my Chiefs' tickets. As KC Wolf I got four tickets for every home game. I figured she would just date me during football season and then dump me once the Chiefs got knocked out of the playoffs. As we continued to date, I noticed many times when I asked her if she wanted tickets to the Chiefs' game, she would say no. So I figured the Chiefs' tickets weren't all that important to her. Cam grew up in a family of three girls who enjoyed singing and music. She told me her family didn't play sports growing up, and she didn't even really like football. I had grown up in a family of three boys and we loved football. If it's true that opposites attract, I knew we were meant for each other.

Cam and I began to get more serious, and after about a year, I decided I had better not let this fish get away. It was time to set the hook because she was definitely a keeper. On November 10, 1992, I decided to pop the question. On a Tuesday evening, I enlisted three of my friends to help me pull off the big surprise. Two of those friends worked with me for the Chiefs, and the other was my roommate at the time. My friend Sheldon Mickey was the man who operated the huge video screen at Arrowhead. I promised to take him out for a steak dinner if he helped me with the proposal.

The plan was for me to tell Cam we were going out to eat, but before we went to dinner I needed to stop in at Arrowhead and get something from one of the suites. This suite just happened to be located directly across from the huge video screen. As soon as Sheldon saw me turn on the lights in the suite, that was his cue to flash the "Will You Marry Me?" message on the video board. A few minutes later my roommate was going to show up dressed as KC Wolf and deliver a dozen roses to Cam, along with a bottle of sparkling cider. Other than the fact that the weather was cold and misting rain, my plan worked perfectly. When we arrived at the suite and I turned on the lights, Sheldon was right on cue. First he showed a picture of Cam and me on the video board. Then he slowly began to type the message:

Will You...
Marry Me?...
PLEASE!!!

Sheldon didn't tell me ahead of time, but he had decided to go ahead and add the 'PLEASE' himself. KC Wolf showed up with the roses and sparkling cider, and the whole surprise went just as planned. The best part of the night was that Cam said yes, and on that cold, rainy evening in November, I was the happiest man alive.

Seven months later, on June 12, 1993, the dark haired mystery girl became my wife. The "Beauty" married the "Beast" at Pleasant Valley Baptist Church with Pastor Tom Hufty performing our ceremony. We were blessed to be surrounded by many of our family and friends. The weather even cooperated this time, because it was a beautiful sunny day with temperatures much warmer than the night we got engaged. Our wedding day was truly one of the happiest days of my life.

The week after our wedding the *Kansas City Star* ran an article in the newspaper with this headline:

KC Wolf Answers Call of the Aisle
Chiefs Mascot Sheds Furry Costume to Wed Girl of His Dreams

The article said: "Cross one more name off of the list of Kansas City's most eligible party animals: KC Wolf, the Chiefs' mascot. 'I'm marrying a fox,' says Dan Meers the man inside the wolf costume."

I have been featured in the newspaper hundreds of times over the years, but that article will always be my favorite. I smile each time I read it because I love the headline, and I still refer to Cam as my fox.

I am proud of the fact that I was a virgin on my wedding night. In high school I made a commitment to God and to my future spouse that I would save myself for marriage. It was not an easy commitment to live out, but I'm very thankful I did because I had no regrets on my wedding day! I still share with high school students that abstinence until marriage may not be the popular way, but it is God's way and God's way is always the best way. I learned from an early age that what is popular isn't always right, and what is right isn't always popular.

Proverbs 18:22 (NLT) says, "The man who finds a wife finds a treasure, and he receives favor from the Lord." The greatest earthly blessing I have received from the Lord has been my wife. She truly is a treasure, one I couldn't and wouldn't want to live without. Cam and I have now been married for over 20 years, and she is still my dream girl. She is my best friend, and I love the life we have created together. As in every marriage we've had our good days, and we've had our bad days, but what really matters is that at the end of every day we know we are committed to each other. When we said our wedding vows, we promised to stay together until death do us part. My wife laughs when she says that divorcing me has never crossed her mind—murder yes, but divorce no.

While marriage is not always easy, working to have a good marriage is well worth the effort. I once read that "a good marriage is like a casserole—only those responsible for it really know what goes into it." Cam and I would tell you that our marriage has taken a lot of work. Sometimes in a marriage people do things or say things they regret. It reminds me of a joke I heard about a man and his wife who got into an argument. As the fighting continued things began to escalate. Finally the husband got so angry he shouted, "How can someone so beautiful be so stupid!" As soon as the words were out of his mouth, he knew he had made a mistake because his wife burst into tears. As she continued to cry, she grabbed a tissue and said, "God made me beautiful so you would marry me and God made me stupid so I would marry you." That joke makes me laugh, but it also reminds me that on more than one occasion I have said and done things that I would like to take back. Thankfully, I am blessed to have a wife who is willing to forgive me, and she and I are committed to starting each and every day with a clean slate.

"Be kind to each other, tenderhearted, forgiving one another, just as God through Christ has forgiven you" (Ephesians 4:32, NLT). This Bible verse gives great advice for those who are looking to have a successful marriage. Cam and I have learned that forgiveness is an essential ingredient in marriage because neither of us is perfect. After 20+ years of marriage Cam and I have also learned love really is a choice, not a feeling. Feelings come and feelings go, but our choice to always stay committed to one another is what has kept us together during both the good times and the bad.

There are many definitions for love in our world today, but once again the best is found in God's Word. 1 Corinthians 13:4-8 says, "Love is patient, love is kind. It does not envy, it does not boast, it is not proud. It does not dishonor others, it is not self-seeking, it is not easily angered, it keeps no record of wrongs. Love does not delight in evil but rejoices with the truth. It always protects, always trusts, always hopes, always perseveres. LOVE NEVER FAILS." What I love most about my wife is she has another man in her life she loves even more than me. That other man is Jesus, and I couldn't be happier to share her with Him. Cam's love for the Lord and her commitment to me has challenged and encouraged me to be a better husband. Cam has been a great wife to me, and she has also been a great mother to our three little pigs.

5

My Three Little Pigs

"A father is a man who carries pictures where his money use to be."

Through the years I have had many people come up to me and say, "You've got the greatest job in the world" and I agree. I do have the greatest job in the world, but it's not being a mascot. I would be the first guy to tell you that being a professional mascot is a great job. I've met some interesting people, traveled to fun places and had a lot of unbelievable experiences. However, I don't consider being a mascot the greatest job in the world. The greatest job in the world is my other job—being a daddy! Psalms 127:3 (GNTB) says, "Children are a gift from the Lord; they are a real blessing." Three of the greatest blessings in my life have been my children Mycah, Aaron and Mallory.

I knew my entire world was about to change when I read a note I received in the mail on July 21, 1995. Cam and I had been married for a little over two years and were living in our first home in Lee's Summit, Missouri. When I was a kid I used to love getting mail, but now that I was an adult the trip to the mailbox wasn't nearly as much fun. Every day it seemed like 50% of the mail was junk mail and the other 50% was bills. On this particular afternoon I was surprised to see a small card addressed to Mr. Dan Meers. The card appeared to be written by a child because the handwriting was rather sloppy. I assumed it must be a card from a student at one of the elementary schools I had visited. When I opened the card it read:

Hi-
You don't know me, but I can't wait to meet you. I'm going to look up to you more than anyone else in the whole world, Daddy.
Love,
Baby Meers

My heart started to pound, and tears filled my eyes as I read the card a second time to make sure I had read it correctly. When I finally looked up at Cam, she had a big smile on her face. I sat the card on the counter, gave my beautiful wife a kiss and began to cry like a baby because I was so excited. What a great way to find out that I was about to become a daddy for the first time.

Earlier in the day Cam had learned she was pregnant and wanted to surprise me. She had written the note card and addressed it to me in her worst handwriting so I wouldn't suspect it was from her. She also placed a stamp on the card and took it up to the post office where a nice postal worker stamped the date on the card to make it look official. Cam then brought it home and stuck it in the mailbox to make sure I received the news the same day.

I've attended a lot of thrilling Chiefs games through the years but nothing compared to the excitement I felt when I learned I was going to be a dad. Cam and I were so elated about becoming parents we immediately bought a copy of the book, *"What to Expect When You're Expecting."* I never dreamed I could get so excited reading a book and knowing that my wife was about to gain weight. I felt like a little kid waiting for Christmas to arrive. As Cam's stomach grew so did my anticipation.

Cam and I wanted to think of a fun way to tell my in-laws, Jim and Nancy Cochran, that their first grandchild would be arriving soon. We decided to break the news to them at a Chiefs game so I got tickets for Cam and her parents. I took a small KC Wolf stuffed animal and placed a disposable diaper around its bottom. I then placed it in a shoebox with a note that said, "Grandbaby #1 is on the way." I wrapped up the box and delivered it to their seats during the game. After unwrapping the box, my mother-in-law got more excited than I had ever seen her at a football game. I can't remember if the Chiefs won that day, but it didn't really matter because some things are more important than football.

When Cam entered the final month of her pregnancy, she and I were anxious, excited and a little nervous about the big day. I promised not to schedule any out of town KC Wolf appearances during the final month of her pregnancy. The last thing I wanted was to get caught out of town when Cam went into labor and miss the birth of our first child. I was even a little hesitant to schedule appearances in town.

One of the appearances I did agree to do was the Kansas City Auto Show at Bartle Hall Convention Center. This event was always a fun appearance because thousands of people showed up, and I ran around as KC Wolf messing with them. As a mascot I loved big crowds. The larger the crowd, the better the appearance. This was also an important event because one of the Chiefs' sponsors had invited me to attend. In the world of professional sports, you always want to keep your sponsors happy.

Cam's due date was still about two weeks away, and she was feeling well. Since she knew this was an important appearance, I headed for the Auto Show, and she went to dinner with friends. I told her that if she needed to get in touch with me to call my cell phone. When I arrived at Bartle Hall, I jumped into my costume and began my appearance. I was having a great time mingling with the crowd and looking at all the new sports cars, which I couldn't afford. I was not in the market for sports cars anyway. With a child on the way, I knew I would be one of those cool dads driving a minivan for several more years. I was having so much fun that I completely forgot about the fact that my wife was pregnant, and I was supposed to be checking my cell phone occasionally. I got so wrapped up in what I was doing that it slipped my mind that my wife could give birth to my first child at any time.

I had left my cell phone in the dressing room, and my plan was to check it every half hour. I didn't carry the phone with me in costume because I was afraid I would sweat on it, and the phone was not water-proof. Even if I did hear it ring, it would be impossible for me to answer it, trapped in a furry costume.

When I finished my two hour appearance, I went back to the dressing room to change. I grabbed my cell phone from my duffle bag and discovered I had several messages waiting. My heart began to race as I listened to the first message from one of our friends, who sounded very excited. She said Cam was going into labor so they were leaving the restaurant to take her to the hospital. A second message followed, "Dan, where are you? Why aren't you answering your phone? We're going to the hospital." The third message, "Dan, answer your phone. You need to come to the hospital!" Followed by a fourth one, "Dan, where are you? Pick up your phone!" And finally, "Hey you idiot get up to the hospital; you're about to miss the birth of your first child." That's not actually what the message said, but that is what I was thinking to myself.

After appearances I usually try to find my contact person to say thanks for inviting me, but not this time. I raced to the parking garage, got into my car, and then exceeded the speed limit to Independence Regional Hospital. Driving to the hospital I had two conversations going on in my head. One conversation was with God, and the other was with myself:

To God: "Oh, Lord please, please, please help that baby take it's time getting here."

To Self: "What were you thinking? You're about to miss the birth of your first child."

God: "I know I shouldn't be speeding Lord. Please forgive me. I promise I'll never speed again in my life if you'll let me get to the hospital in time for the birth of my child."

Self: "Cam is going to kill you!"

God: "Lord, please forgive me for just running that stoplight. I promise I'll never speed or run another stoplight in my life if you'll get me to the hospital on time."

Self: "You're going to hear about this for the rest of your life."

God: "I could really use a little help here Big Guy."

When I arrived at the hospital, I raced through the doors fully expecting to hear the cry of a newborn baby. Instead I saw my wife walking down the hallway dressed in one of those cute hospital gowns that have a slit right up the backside. When she turned around, I was relieved to see her big belly still sticking out. What Cam had originally thought was labor ended up being false labor pains.

About a week later I made the mistake of telling Cam she was welcome to wear my KC Wolf pants with the 85" inch hips if she needed to. I thought my suggestion was funny, but my wife didn't find my comment nearly so humorous. Once again I found myself asking for forgiveness for being insensitive. I was new to this pregnancy business, and I was learning the hard way there were certain things I shouldn't joke about with a woman who was nine months pregnant.

On Saturday, March 30, 1996, Cam woke me up at 3:30 a.m. and said it was time to get to the hospital. Now it usually takes me a while to wake up in the morning, especially at that early hour, but this time was different. I jumped out of bed, threw our packed bags in the trunk, and helped my very pregnant wife to the car.

As we drove to the hospital, I tried to remember everything the nurses had taught me at our Lamaze childbirth classes. The only thing I could remember was a breathing exercise that I called the "HEE..HEE..WHO." Now I was wishing I had paid closer attention during class.

Cam was breathing heavily so I knew I needed to hurry to get to the hospital. Thankfully at this early hour there wasn't much traffic. As I sped toward the hospital, once again exceeding the recommended speed limit, I said a little prayer. I prayed, "O Lord, I know I promised you two weeks ago that I would never speed again and I'm sorry, but please remember that this is Cam's fault not mine. If she had wakened me earlier, we wouldn't have to drive so fast right now to get to the hospital. Please forgive her."

Even though I told myself to remain calm, cool, and collected, I was a nervous wreck thinking I was about to deliver my first child in the backseat of our car. Luckily we arrived at the hospital in the nick of time because our beautiful baby girl was born at 4:55 p.m. That's right P.M. We arrived at the hospital at about 3:55 a.m. and waited 13 hours before our daughter, Mycah Lynne Meers, finally decided to show up. I joked with Cam that next time she should wait until a little closer to the actual delivery time before waking me up. Once again I learned that my wife, who had just given birth, didn't appreciate my sense of humor. Fortunately, I had a dozen roses for her, a gift which helped keep me out of trouble.

I was 20 years old dressed in a Tiger suit the first time I appeared on television at a Mizzou basketball game. My daughter Mycah made her television debut on her second day in this world. When three of the local news stations found out KC Wolf and his wife had welcomed their first child, they sent news teams to the hospital to cover the story. I don't think Cam was excited about being on television the day after giving birth, but I was. I was a proud father getting to show off his beautiful baby girl to everyone in Kansas City. I put on my KC Wolf costume, and the cameramen shot video footage of me sitting in the hospital bed with Cam, holding our new daughter.

After we brought Mycah home from the hospital I quickly understood the saying, "Anyone who sleeps like a baby doesn't have a baby." The next several months were a real adjustment for a guy who enjoys his sleep. Not only did I learn to operate on a very limited amount of sleep, I became an expert at changing diapers. Little did I realize I would be changing diapers for the next eight-and-a-half years.

When Mycah was a toddler, we discovered she didn't like mascots. That is a problem when your dad is KC Wolf and keeps the costume in the garage at your house. "Masklophobia" is the term used to describe a fear of masks or mascots. Some people love seeing mascots from a distance, but if they come too close, they freak out. That is how my adorable little girl responded. Mycah liked KC Wolf from a distance, but if I came too close she would start to scream. Cam and I tried to help her understand that Daddy was inside the costume. When she watched me put the head on, she started to cry; when I took it off she smiled. I put it back on and once again she cried. I took it off again and she was all smiles. Finally, we gave up and just tried to keep her out of the garage. Thankfully, masklophobia is a fear that most children outgrow with age, and that was the case with Mycah. Many people are surprised to learn that KC Wolf's first child had a fear of mascots.

In June 1997, I came home from work one day and found Mycah, now a toddler, wearing a t-shirt that said, "I'm the Big Sister." Once again, my wife was standing in the kitchen with a big grin on her face. Once again, I started to cry with excitement. Meers Baby #2 was due to arrive in early February 1998.

In December I received a letter inviting me to the NFL Pro Bowl in Honolulu, Hawaii. This was going to be my first ever Pro Bowl, and I was excited about going to Hawaii. The day after I received my Pro Bowl invitation, I realized the Pro Bowl was on February 1, 1998. Now I've never been the sharpest tool in the shed, but even I was smart enough to know it probably wouldn't be a good idea for me to be lying on a beach in Hawaii while my wife was lying in a hospital bed giving birth in Kansas City. The next day I made a call to let the organizers know I wouldn't be able to attend, but I would really appreciate it if they would keep me in mind for future Pro Bowls. As much as I hated missing out on a free trip to Hawaii, having to call and decline was a good reminder that life changes when you sign up to be a daddy. My world was no longer just about me; I now had a wife and kids to think about.

On February 9, 1998, God blessed Cam and me with our son, Aaron James Meers. When Cam was pregnant with Aaron, she prayed God would send her a son that was just like his father. Cam should have talked to my mom before praying that prayer because God granted her request. As a little boy Aaron was exactly like his daddy—VERY HIGH ENERGY and HARD HEADED. Cam and I tell people that when it came to discipline, Aaron was like a canoe because he worked better if you paddled him from behind.

Thanks to Aaron, I got to know our local windshield repair man by name. At age three he got into my golf clubs in the garage and managed to put my nine iron through Cam's car window. A few years later he started to play baseball and managed to throw a curveball through my back windshield. Even though Aaron cost me a lot of money in repairs and copays at the hospital emergency room, he also kept us laughing.

One of the smartest decisions I made as a dad was to keep a journal for each of my kids as they were growing up. In their journals I recorded important milestones, such as when they learned to ride their bike or when they lost their first tooth. I also wrote down funny things they said or did. My kids like to look back and read what I wrote in their journals. Many of those journal entries still bring a smile to my face. One of my favorite entries from Aaron's journal was recorded on August 10, 2002. "Today Aaron told me that I wipe his bottom better than anybody in the whole wide world." How encouraging. I never realized I was such a good bottom wiper. By that point in my parenting career I had been wiping bottoms for almost six-and-a-half years, so I had plenty of practice.

In December 2000, Cam and I learned that God was sending a third blessing our way, Meers Baby #3. Cam's due date was August of the following year. Once again I cried when I found out the news. I felt like the most blessed man in the world. Mallory Grace Meers arrived in this world on August 6, 2001. Honestly, I was getting a little nervous because the Chiefs' first preseason game was scheduled for August 12. When Mallory arrived six days prior to kickoff, I breathed a sigh of relief. God had blessed us with three happy, healthy kids, each of whom was born during the off season.

One of the lessons I quickly learned as a father was that I needed to be careful what I said around my kids because they repeated what they heard. Mallory reminded me of this on November 16, 2004. My all-time favorite entry in her journal reads:

> This evening we were playing down in the basement and Mallory started to cry. When I asked what the matter was, Mallory said, "Aaron kicked me in the nuts."
> I said, "What?"
> Again she said, "Aaron kicked me in the nuts."
> Aaron quickly responded, "Mallory, you don't even have nuts."

All I could do was stand there and laugh. Aaron probably did kick her, but I was sure it wasn't in the nuts.

I also noticed something changed as we began to have more kids. With our first child Mycah, we were your typical, overly protective parents. When Aaron came along I realized no matter how protective I was, he would still figure out a way to hurt himself or others. By the time Mallory joined the family, I had mellowed significantly.

I read an article in a parenting magazine several years ago that made me laugh because it reminded me of our family. It described how attitudes slowly change with each successive baby.

DIAPERING

1st Baby: You change your baby's diaper every hour, whether they need it or not.

2nd Baby: You change their diaper every two or three hours, if needed.

3rd Baby: You try to change their diaper before others start to complain about the smell or you see it sagging to their knees.

PACIFIER

1st Baby: If the pacifier falls on the floor, you put it away until you can go home and wash and boil it.

2nd Baby: When the pacifier falls on the floor, you squirt it off with some juice from the bottle.

3rd Baby: You wipe it on your shirt and pop it back in.

SWALLOWING COINS

1st Child: When your first child swallows a coin, you rush the child to the emergency room and demand x-rays.

2nd Child: When your second child swallows a coin, you watch to see if the coin passes.

3rd Child: When your third child swallows a coin, you deduct it from their allowance.

Each time we added a child to our family wolf pack, our lives got busier. After a long day of changing diapers and chasing toddlers, Cam and I would often collapse into bed, exhausted. My next door neighbor, the father of four grown children, often warned us, "The days may drag, but the years will fly." Now that my kids are older, I understand what he meant. It seems like they grew up overnight. Since I love being a dad, I try to enjoy each stage of their lives. My goal is to be intentional about making many fun memories with them.

One of those fond memories was Halloween 2002 when I went trick or treating with the kids. I dressed as KC Wolf (the Big Bad Wolf) and my kids dressed as the Three Little Pigs. We turned a lot of heads walking through the neighborhood that night. Apparently the neighbors liked our costumes because we came home with loads of candy. The following year I decided not to dress up and instead just walked around with my kids sampling their candy. Something I discovered about Halloween was that some of the excitement wore off after I became a professional mascot. When I began wearing a costume to work every day, trick or treating was never quite the same. Getting paid to wear a costume was much more fun than just getting a handful of Tootsie Rolls.

On October 24, 2004, I decided to celebrate my very own "Take Your Kid to Work Day," which ended up turning into "Take Your

Family to Work Day." The Chiefs' were playing the Atlanta Falcons, and I needed to come up with a unique pregame skit. I thought it would be cute to have KC Wolf enter the field with four kids dressed in little wolf costumes. Of course I knew three very cute kids who all happened to be related to me. What a great opportunity for me to not only show off my kids to Chiefs fans, but for my kids to get a taste of what Daddy did at work. All I needed was another cute kid and a bad guy to dress up in an Atlanta Falcons jersey. Every good skit needs a bad guy dressed in the opposing team's jersey who we could pretend to beat up. My kids were a little apprehensive because they had always been taught to show respect for others and live out the Golden Rule. However, they were also excited because this was their chance to beat up a bad guy in front of 78,000 people, and they even had dad's permission. I wanted to find a bad guy my kids were familiar with so they would feel comfortable during the skit. It dawned on me that I had the perfect guy, someone I had beat up many times as a kid. My younger brother Dave would make a great victim.

My kids were looking forward to the idea of beating up uncle Dave. He and his wife Stacey also have three kids, Blake, Abbey and Bo. I was sure I could talk one of them into being my other little wolf. I called Dave and promised him that if he would let us beat him up, I would get his whole family tickets for the game. He was excited about the idea, and they came to Kansas City for a fun weekend.

The skit we performed that day will go down as one of my alltime favorites. Not only did I get to perform with my kids at Arrowhead Stadium, I also got to beat up my little brother without getting yelled at by my mom.

I have been a dad since 1996, and I can honestly say it truly is the greatest job in the world. Each of my kids has taken KC Wolf in for show and tell when they were in kindergarten. I enjoyed watching their faces as I took the costume off in front of their classmates and introduced myself not as KC Wolf but as their daddy. I was the coolest dad at school back then, but like all dads my coolness dropped off when they graduated to junior high.

Over the years my kids have changed, as have I. The one thing that hasn't changed is my love for them and my commitment to them. I like being a mascot. I LOVE being a dad. It is my passion. I'm convinced one of the most important roles God has given me is my role as a dad. Clarence B. Kelland once said, "My father didn't tell me how to live; he lived, and he let me watch him do it." I'm grateful God blessed me with parents who not only taught me what was important in life, but also demonstrated it to me by the way they lived. I want to be the same kind of role model for my children.

Above the dresser in Aaron's bedroom is a picture of him and KC Wolf both dressed as Superman. The original photo was taken at a basketball game I worked in Dodge City, Kansas. Aaron was four years old at the time, and he performed a halftime Superman skit with me. This is one of my favorite pictures of us together. A friend of mine borrowed the photo and made a colored pencil sketch which he framed for me. The framed sketch still hangs in Aaron's bedroom. Every night before Aaron goes to bed I go into his room, pray for him and kiss him goodnight. Each night when I look at that picture, I smile because it reminds me of three very important truths:

#1: I have a son who looks up to me and is watching how I live my life.

#2: I'm no Superman. KC Wolf has 85 inch hips. I'm not faster than a speeding bullet, and I'm definitely not stronger than a locomotive. I can't even leap tall buildings in a single bound. Bottom line is that I am no Superman.

#3: I've come to realize that my son doesn't need another superhero in his life. What my son really needs is a dad who loves Jesus, who loves his mother, and who loves him. I want to set an example for my son and my daughters by living a life that demonstrates my faith and my family are my two greatest passions. As parents we have to remember that someday our kids will follow our example instead of our advice. I'm not a perfect father. My kids know this very well, but I am committed to giving them my best. I'm committed to living my life in such a way that if someone tells my kid they remind them of me, they will stick out their chest and not their tongue.

Cam and I want our home to be a place where our children can grow to become all God intended them to be. We believe each of our kids deserves "Triple A Treatment: Attention, Affection and

Affirmation." By demonstrating this kind of treatment it reminds our kids they are loved and encourages them to be their best. Just like many businesses write a mission statement to define their purpose and the reason they exist, Cam and I also developed one for our home and family.

Meers Family Mission Statement:

"To establish a home which is a lighthouse for Christ, full of love and laughter and rich in respect. A home where each member is valued and encouraged to reach his full potential and where we strive to be optimistic, grateful, faithful and content."

We also have a family Bible verse upon which our mission statement is based.

"You are the light of the world. A town built on a hill cannot be hidden. Neither do people light a lamp and put it under a bowl. Instead they put it on its stand, and it gives light to everyone in the house. In the same way, let your light shine before others, that they may see your good deeds and glorify your Father in heaven" (Matthew 5:14-16).

Every year the Kansas City Chiefs have a goal of winning the Super Bowl. Every year I also have a goal I consider to be even more important than a Super Bowl trophy. My goal is to make my home a lighthouse for Christ where my kids feel loved and encouraged to become all they were meant to be.

God has truly blessed my life with three great kids who deserve a great dad. Being a dad to Mycah, Aaron and Mallory truly is THE GREATEST JOB IN THE WORLD.

6

A Character
with Character

"A hundred years from now it won't matter what my bank account was, the sort of house I lived in, or the kind of car I drove...but the world may be different because I was important in the life of a child."
Forest E. Witcraft

Early in my Chiefs career, I made a goal to actively promote KC Wolf in the community. The character was less than two years old and even though the fans who attended Chiefs games knew KC Wolf, there were still many people in Kansas City and the surrounding areas who were unfamiliar with the character. It was obvious that KC Wolf was not a household name because when I went out to do community appearances people would often refer to me as "The Chiefs' football mouse" or my personal favorite "Chuck E Cheese." My challenge was to figure out a way to educate the public about KC Wolf.

Since the local elementary school programs were becoming very popular, I knew this could be a great way to introduce the young people of Kansas City to KC Wolf. What I didn't realize at the time was how well those elementary school students would educate their parents.

In 1991, I spoke at 139 elementary schools within about a three hour radius of Arrowhead Stadium. After every program I gave an 8x10 colored picture of KC Wolf to each student. Although some of those pictures got dropped in school parking lots or left on school buses, many students managed to get their souvenir picture home and talk to their parents about KC Wolf's visit to their school. I knew my strategy was working when parents came up to me at appearances and told me my picture was hanging on their refrigerator at home. I figured if every family member saw me each time they opened the refrigerator, they would definitely get to know me. The best part was I absolutely loved speaking at the elementary schools.

During my first four years as KC Wolf I spoke at 480 elementary and middle schools throughout the Midwest. As the popularity of the programs increased, so did the distance I traveled. My appearances began in mainly Kansas and Missouri schools, but quickly spread to Oklahoma, Arkansas, Illinois, Iowa, South Dakota and Nebraska. I even spoke to several groups in River Falls, Wisconsin, when the Chiefs traveled there for training camp.

When I prayed God would allow me to use my mascot platform to make an impact in the lives of young people, I never dreamed how He would answer my prayer. Between 1990 and 2015, I delivered more than 2,800 school programs. That number doesn't include all of the other opportunities I had speaking at churches, libraries, summer camps, Boy Scout groups, Vacation Bible Schools and countless other events.

I was taught growing up that you may not be able to change the world, but you can change the corner where you live. My prayer was that God would allow me to be a positive influence in my little corner of the world, and after a while I noticed He slowly began to give me a bigger corner to influence. Every year I drove thousands of miles in my company car doing programs and assemblies. Even though the driving was monotonous, the time I spent with the kids was a very rewarding part of my job. I contacted principals at the beginning of every school year to inform them about KC Wolf's "Edutainment" programs. I knew edutainment wasn't a real word, but I created it to promote the fact that KC Wolf programs were designed to be both educational and entertaining. I never enjoyed boring school programs when I was a kid, so I made up my mind that KC Wolf programs were going to be exciting. My goal was to promote the idea that learning should be fun.

Just like Cam and I had developed a mission statement for our family, I also wrote a mission statement for KC Wolf. "**A CHARACTER WITH CHARACTER MAKING AN IMPACT IN THE LIVES OF OTHERS**" was the statement taped to the wall above my desk at Arrowhead. It was a reminder of what I was really trying to accomplish.

First I wanted to be a character, a great mascot who was entertaining and made people laugh. Mascots are supposed to be fun, and I wanted to make sure I was doing that part of my job with excellence. Not only did I want to be a great mascot, I also wanted to do it with character. Both in and out of costume I wanted to conduct myself as a positive role model. My ultimate goal was to make an impact in the lives of others. I knew the best way to do that was with encouraging words, helpful actions and a positive attitude.

Most KC Wolf school programs were about 45 minutes long. I put on the costume, and as the students walked into the gymnasium I ran around greeting them and giving out hugs and high fives. When all the students were finally seated, the principal would stand up and try to get the kids quiet. This was sometimes difficult because by this point many of the students were already worked into a frenzy.

When the principal introduced me, I slowly stuck my human hand out from inside the costume to create suspense. The students would then try to figure out who was dressed up as KC Wolf. Often times they would begin shouting out a teacher name, thinking it was a member of the school staff dressed in the costume. When I finally removed the KC Wolf head to reveal my face, the older students clapped and cheered while the kindergarteners just sat with a look of relief on their faces. I quickly learned that the younger students didn't always know there was a man inside the costume. Often times kindergarten students looked nervous sitting on the front row while I was running around in my costume. I'm sure I would have been nervous at that age too if a seven foot tall wolf was running around in the same room as me.

After taking off the KC Wolf head, I introduced myself to the students and asked who thought I looked better in the costume. Apparently I wasn't as cute as mom thought, because about 99% of the kids thought I looked better with the KC Wolf head on. I then showed the students a short highlight video of KC Wolf in action. This music video gave the students an idea of what I did at Chiefs' games. Showing the highlight video also gave me a chance to take off my costume and catch my breath before I had to speak. When the video finished playing, I took the next 15 minutes to talk to the students about whatever topic the school had asked me to speak on.

I had a variety of different program titles and topics from which the school administration could choose:

• **A-B-C of Success**—This was the most popular of all of the programs. It stressed the importance of having good Attitude, Behavior and Character.

• **Don't be a Bully**: **Be a Buddy**—This was an anti-bullying program focusing on treating everyone with respect and kindness despite our differences.

• **Do Your Best**: **Ace Your Test**—This was the most popular school program in the spring because it helped prepare students for the upcoming state standardized assessment tests.

• **Chiefs "Fuel Up to Play 60"**—Focused on the importance of proper eating and exercise for a healthy lifestyle.

• **Being a Winner in Life**—Emphasized self-esteem, hard work and saying no to drugs.

• **Choices**—Focused on believing in yourself, respecting others and giving your best.

• **Read to Succeed**—Encouraged students to read and stressed the importance of learning.

I had so many different programs and spoke at so many different schools that occasionally I got confused. On more than one occasion I had to ask the principal to remind me which program he wanted me to present. I had given each of the programs hundreds of times so I could easily switch topics at the last minute if needed. When I finished speaking on a specific topic, I took the final 15 minutes of the program to show the students the KC Wolf costume and give them an opportunity to ask questions. The young students always seemed shocked by the size of KC Wolf's shoes. They were also surprised to learn that when I dressed as KC Wolf, I could see where I was going by looking through KC Wolf's neck instead of through the eyes.

The question and answer portion of the program was always an adventure. The kids weren't afraid to ask anything that was on their mind. Over the years I learned to think very quickly on my feet.

One of the most frequently asked questions was what happens when I have to go to the bathroom in my costume. I answered that question by asking them a question. I asked them what their parents made them do right before they got in the car to go on a long road trip. They would all yell, "Go to the bathroom." I explained to the students that I always used the bathroom just before I climbed into my costume. Truthfully, I usually sweat so much while dressed as KC Wolf that I never had to worry about using the restroom. Instead of trying to explain the effects of dehydration on the body, I just told the students that if I did have an emergency, I could sneak back to the locker room and go to the bathroom. This answer always seemed to satisfy their curiosity.

One time a little girl asked me about my least favorite appearance. I told her about the time I had to do an outside appearance in the summer time when I had a sunburn and poison ivy. The people at the appearance were great, but the combination of the heat and the itching drove me crazy.

My all-time favorite question was from a little boy who wanted to know if the foot long hotdogs at Arrowhead Stadium were really a foot long. His question made me laugh. Most days I enjoyed listening to their questions as much as they enjoyed listening to my answers.

At the end of every school program I asked for a volunteer. Of course almost every student raised his hand even though he had no idea what I was about to ask him to do. Whenever the volunteer got up on stage, I told the crowd we were going to dress the child up like KC Wolf. Most of the student volunteers were so short that when they put the KC Wolf costume on, the belly would immediately drop to the floor. This gave them the appearance of a Hershey Kiss standing in front of their schoolmates. In about five minutes I had the student looking like a miniature version of KC Wolf. I had the child attempt to walk across the stage, and then we posed for a souvenir photograph.

Over the years I have had my picture standing next to a miniature KC Wolf published in hundreds of school yearbooks and small town newspapers all over the Midwest. Young adults still come up to me and tell me they remember when I came to their elementary school and they got to dress up like KC Wolf. These encounters make me feel old, but they also make me feel good knowing I helped create a memory they still talk about years later.

One of the things I learned about speaking to students was Murphy's Law was always in effect. If something was going to go wrong, it would always happen right in the middle of my program. One day I had the opportunity to speak at an elementary school in Tonganoxie, Kansas. Right after the program began there was a big thunderstorm that rolled into the area. The kids could hear the rain beating on the roof of the gymnasium which meant I had to work extra hard to keep their attention. About 15 minutes into my program there was a huge clap of thunder, and the power went out. As soon as the power went out, the lights went off and it was pitch black in the gymnasium. The kids all started to scream, but unfortunately I was no help because with the power out my microphone no longer worked. As I stood in the dark in front of 400 screaming kids, I thought to myself, "I think I'll let the principal handle this problem." After about ten more minutes of chaos the power came back on, and I finished the program.

Murphy's Law was also in effect whenever a student would get sick, which usually happened several times a year. I quickly learned those students who sat closest to the bathrooms were never the ones who got sick. The kid who started to feel sick and needed to vomit was always the kid sitting right in the middle of the entire student body with no way to escape. I also noticed the students who got sick never got sick at the end of the program. It was always right in the middle of my presentation. Imagine trying to keep the attention of a bunch of elementary students while the school custodian was sprinkling powder over the area where a student had just thrown up. I loved speaking to the kids, but on days like that I just looked forward to getting back to Arrowhead as quickly as possible.

A look in my clothes closet at home would reveal my wardrobe was filled with elementary school t-shirts. After my programs either the principal or the PTA president would usually stand up and thank me for visiting their school and give me a t-shirt with the school name printed on the front. It was nice to be able to drive home in a new t-shirt instead of the one I had just sweat in at the school.

One of my most embarrassing moments happened after a school assembly in Wellsville, Kansas. My program was scheduled for the end of the school day. The principal had heard me speak before, and he knew that after the program the kids would be excited. He liked the idea of loading all those rowdy kids on the school bus and sending them home right after my program. I felt good as I was leaving the elementary school because I had just given the students a great talk about the importance of always making good choices. I was also excited because I was getting out of the parking lot ahead of the school buses which meant I wouldn't get stuck waiting on them. As I was leaving the school, apparently I was driving a little too fast in the school zone because the local police officer pulled me over and gave me a ticket for speeding. As the police officer slowly wrote out my ticket, with the lights flashing on top of his police car, all of the school buses drove past. All I could do was smile and wave while the students all stared out of the bus windows. I must admit I felt like a hypocrite after talking to the kids about making good choices only to get a speeding ticket before I even got out of the school zone.

I had a similar embarrassing moment after a D.A.R.E graduation in Humboldt, Kansas. D.A.R.E is an excellent program that educates students about the dangers of drugs and alcohol. The program usually lasts for about ten weeks and is taught by a local D.A.R.E police officer. At the end of the ten week course the students have a graduation ceremony. I got to know a lot of the area D.A.R.E officers from speaking at many of these graduations each year. This particular graduation was held in the evening. When it was over, I was in a hurry to get back to Kansas City. Apparently I was in too much of a hurry because once again a police officer pulled me over. Luckily, when I told him who I was and that I had just finished speaking at the D.A.R.E graduation, he had mercy on me and just gave me a warning.

I always enjoyed getting feedback letters on my speaking appearances. I was very encouraged by an email I received after speaking at a D.A.R.E graduation in the small town of Iola, Kansas. It was from the Mayor of Iola, who had attended the graduation ceremony. His email said:

Dan,

Good Morning! We met last evening, following your excellent presentation at the D.A.R.E graduation of our fifth grade classes. I just wanted to tell you once again how much I appreciated your presentation. Your energy was just what was needed to capture the attention of those in attendance (adults included), and once you had their attention you used your time well.

You offer an excellent role model for young and old alike. Your discussion about character should be heard by every young person. We home-schooled our four children, and both character qualities and character building were always a priority with academic accomplishments still important, but relegated to second place. Your reference to blessings instead of 'luck' and hope instead of 'woe are we' was refreshing and most welcome! The light of Christ was shone through you brightly, in a public arena, and I just wanted to let you know how much it was appreciated.

God bless you and your family (as I'm sure your traveling schedule must be a sacrifice for them). Keep living with purpose!

Letters like this recharged my batteries because they confirmed to me that I was actually making a difference in the lives of others.

During my career as KC Wolf I spoke to well over one million young people at schools, churches, camps, clubs and a variety of other locations. My goal was to encourage young people to make good choices and strive for excellence in all areas of their lives. I was outspoken about my faith and my desire to be a role model for young people. I was always disappointed to hear about or read stories about famous people that many young people looked up to who were in the news for making bad choices. It seemed like every year there was a list of celebrities and athletes who would get themselves into trouble with the law for everything from drugs and alcohol to violence and unfaithfulness.

KC Wolf was not as famous as some of these Hollywood movie stars. I was not as popular as many professional athletes, but I was very aware that many young people knew me and were watching how I lived my life. I didn't want my name added to the list of people whose reputation was ruined because of a moment of poor judgment. It would have been easy for me to sit back and point fingers and tell myself those things would never happen to me, but I was smart enough to know better. In college my Bible study teacher taught me, "As long as a man possesses the ability to walk he possesses the ability to fall." His words challenged me and reminded me that if I wasn't careful my name could easily be added to that list. The Bible says it this way in 1 Corinthians 10:12 (NLT), "If you think you are standing strong, be careful not to fall."

I was no different than others. The areas that caused other men to stumble and fall were the same areas I often struggled with myself. It would be foolish of me to think a downfall could never happen to me. I once read, "No man falls on purpose, yet men often make seemingly small compromises which slowly, over time, ruin their lives." As a mascot I was committed to being a "Character with Character." As a husband, a father and a follower of Christ I wanted to protect myself against anything that could cause me to fall. I wanted to guard myself against anything that could possibly bring shame to my wife, my kids, my family, the Kansas City Chiefs, and most importantly, my Lord.

One of the decisions I made when I arrived in Kansas City in 1990 was to surround myself with a group of Christian men who would hold me accountable. These were men who were committed to the same principles as I, loving the Lord and striving to be more like Him. My first two accountability partners were Rod Handley and Steve Pelluer. Rod had also just moved to the Kansas City area and was working for the Fellowship of Christian Athletes. Rod's roommate was Steve Pelluer, who was a quarterback for the Chiefs.

Once a week we met at the Denny's restaurant across I-70 from Arrowhead. At that weekly breakfast meeting we prayed for one another and asked each other tough questions. These accountability questions were designed to hold us accountable in those areas of our lives we knew were very important if we wanted to be godly men. Here are our questions:

1) Have you spent daily time in the Scriptures and in prayer?
2) Have you had flirtatious or lustful attitudes, tempting thoughts, or exposed yourself to any explicit materials which would not glorify God?
3) Have you been completely above reproach in your financial dealings?
4) Have you spent quality relationship time with family and friends?

5) Have you done your 100% best in your job?
6) Have you told any half-truths or outright lies, putting yourself in a better light to those around you?
7) Have you shared the Gospel with an unbeliever this week?
8) Have you taken care of your body through daily physical exercise and proper eating and sleeping habits?
9) Have you allowed any person or circumstance to rob you of your joy?
10) Have you lied on any of your answers today?[1]

At first I had difficultly being transparent at our accountability meetings. I found it hard to open up and admit my failures and struggles. Fortunately, I began to realize that these men also had similar struggles, and they loved me enough to hold my feet to the fire. They challenged and encouraged me each week in my walk with Christ.

In the back of my Bible I wrote, "Don't pretend to be what you don't intend to be." This simple quote was a reminder to me not to be a phony. Fake diamonds aren't worth nearly as much as the real thing, and I knew the same was true in my life. Being a fake wasn't nearly as valuable and attractive as being authentic. I knew if I really wanted to make an impact in this world, I needed to be real. I had a strong conviction to live an authentic life, and I knew I could only accomplish that with the help of my accountability partners. I made a commitment to be open and honest with these men, and this type of accountability began to radically change my life.

Steve Pelluer left Kansas City to play for the Denver Broncos in 1992, but Rod and I have continued meeting together once a week for more than 25 years. We have added several more guys to our group over the years including our current members: William Hanna, Fred Olson, Mike DeBacker, Bruce Rehmer and Travis Bourbon. These men have played a crucial role in my life. They have walked with me during the good times and the bad. They know my strengths as well as my struggles. They pray for me, and they challenge and encourage me to be all that God intended me to be.

When I was growing up my Dad use to say that the most important thing you possess is your name. Scripture confirms this:

"A good name is more desirable than great riches; to be esteemed is better than silver or gold" (Proverbs 22:1).

Having accountability in my life has helped me protect my name and keep me on the straight and narrow. The men I surround myself with not only love me, they also love my family. As a result they don't allow me to become lazy as a husband, father or as a follower of Christ. I once read, "Reputation is what men think you are; character is what God knows you are." Accountability helps build my character. It is a weekly reminder that I need to make my character and integrity a priority. I learned that when I take care of my character, my reputation takes care of itself. If I live my life for the approval of God, then I don't need to be disturbed by the opinion of others. Living a godly life of character is essential if I truly want to make an impact in the lives of others.

Although my time spent in schools has been very rewarding, I have also spent many memorable days speaking at prisons, churches and nursing homes. I will never forget the first time I spoke at a prison. The prison was located in Ellsworth, Kansas, and the chaplain asked me to come in dressed as KC Wolf to speak at a chapel service for the inmates. Since this was my first time to speak at a prison, I was a little nervous and unsure what to expect. I was comfortable speaking to cute little elementary school children who enjoyed giving me hugs, but these were grown men with a criminal history and numerous tattoos. When I walked into the prison courtyard, I had to laugh. It reminded me of a Catholic school I had spoken at earlier in the week because everyone was dressed alike. At the Catholic school everyone wore blue shirts, but apparently bright orange was the popular color for prisoners.

Before arriving at the prison, I prayed for courage to express God's love to the prisoners. I really wanted the chapel service to be a fun and relaxed atmosphere for these men. As I walked toward the group of prisoners who were gathered for the chapel service, I immediately went to the biggest guy with the shaved head and began shining his bald head. I wasn't sure if it was the smartest thing to do, but it definitely broke the ice and the inmates all seemed to get a laugh out of it. I'm sure if I had attempted to shine his head without wearing the KC Wolf costume, I would have been carried out of the prison on a stretcher.

I really enjoyed my time with the prisoners, who were very appreciative of my visit. It was a privilege for me to share with these men that although we all make mistakes, thankfully, we serve a God who forgives and offers us a second chance. I knew I needed God's forgiveness just as badly as any of the prisoners. I shared with them that we can't undo a single thing we have done in the past, but we can begin today by accepting God's forgiveness and striving to live for Him.

I loved the opportunity to meet with prisoners and spend time praying with them during chapel services. Although I enjoyed these visits, I must admit when it was time to leave I was always thankful I was just a visitor and not a permanent resident.

I also had many opportunities to share God's love with people in homeless shelters, soup kitchens and hundreds of churches all across the United States. One Sunday evening while I was on a flight returning home, I decided to make a list of all the states where I had spoken at churches dressed as KC Wolf. My list included: Missouri, Kansas, Oklahoma, Arkansas, Kentucky, Illinois, Iowa, South Dakota, Ohio, Indiana, Michigan, Wisconsin, Minnesota, Texas, New Mexico, North Carolina, Virginia, and Hawaii. When I finished my list, I felt like an evangelist with fur. Billy Graham and I shared the same "Good News" message. He just spoke to larger crowds and dressed much nicer.

I was definitely not your typical preacher. I arrived at the service dressed as KC Wolf, and after I took the costume off, I usually gave the message dressed in shorts and a sweaty t-shirt. I was blessed to meet many wonderful preachers and make many lifelong friends as I traveled around the country sharing my faith. I also enjoyed eating many delicious potluck dinners. I'm still thankful for all the wonderful cooks who put a smile on my face by putting a meal in my belly.

Besides schools, prisons and churches, my other favorite places to speak were nursing homes. The best thing about nursing home visits was that no one was ever in a rush, and they were always excited to see KC Wolf. The worst thing about nursing homes was it always felt like the temperature was set at about 90 degrees to make sure all of the residents were comfortable. The thermostat probably wasn't set on 90 degrees, but when I was running around in the KC

Wolf costume, I felt incredibly hot. When I spoke at nursing homes, my number one goal was to encourage the residents and make them laugh. Many of these senior adults were very lonely, and I tried to be a bright spot in their day. It's amazing how a simple smile and a hug not only brightened their day but made my day better as well.

I also loved hanging out at nursing homes because some of the best stories, greatest advice and funniest jokes I've ever heard came from senior adults. One older gentleman told me a joke about a little boy named Johnny. Little Johnny's neighbors had a new baby. Unfortunately, the baby was born without ears. When the mother brought the new baby home from the hospital, Little Johnny's family was invited over to see him. Before they left their house, Little Johnny's dad had a talk with him and explained that the baby had no ears. His dad also told him that if he so much as mentioned anything about the baby's missing ears or even said the word "ears" he would get the spanking of his life when they came back home. Little Johnny told his dad he understood completely. When Little Johnny looked into the crib, he said, "What a beautiful baby." The mother said, "Why thank you, Little Johnny." Little Johnny said, "He has beautiful little feet and beautiful little hands, a cute little nose and really beautiful eyes. Can he see?" asked Little Johnny. "Yes," the mother replied, "We are so thankful. The doctor said he will have 20/20 vision." "That's great," said Little Johnny, "Cuz he'd be outta luck if he needed glasses."

Every day I meet a wide variety of people who have helped make my job very interesting. From young kids to senior adults and from pastors to prisoners, I am grateful for each of them because they have enriched my life. As I expressed a genuine interest in others and tried living my life as a Character with Character, I discovered that I was making a lot of friends along the way. Those friendships were what made my mascot days so special.

[1] These ten questions became the basis for Rod Handley's book *"Character That Counts: Who's Counting Yours?"* This book is available through www.characterthatcounts.org

7

Dumb
and Dumber

"You only get one body; it is the temple of your soul. Even God is willing to dwell there. If you truly treat your body like a temple, it will serve you well for decades. If you abuse it you must be prepared for poor health and a lack of energy."
Oli Hille

The most challenging but probably the most important part of my job as a professional mascot was the conditioning. Wearing 30 pounds of fur, along with a five pound Wolf head, was very physically demanding. The costume originally weighed closer to 40 pounds, but in 2002 I discovered the "Mesh Body," which I am convinced added many more years onto my mascot career.

The main part of the KC Wolf costume was a fat body suit covered in fur. In 2002, the costume designer I was working with in Canada began to make mesh bodies. Since KC Wolf almost always wore sweatpants and a Kansas City Chiefs jersey, we eliminated the fur hidden beneath the Wolf clothing and replaced it with mesh. The company designed a new KC Wolf body for me that was fur from the armpits down to the paws and from the knees down to the ankles. When I tried the new suit out for the first time, I was amazed. Not only was the costume 10 pounds lighter, but the mesh also made the suit much, much cooler. The full fur wolf bodies were fine in the winter time, but the new mesh bodies were definitely the way to go in the spring, summer and fall.

Even with the discovery of the mesh bodies, it was still important for me to keep myself in good physical shape. Over the years I had learned from observation that the best mascots in the business were those with the most energy. Nobody wants to watch a guy who just stands on the sidelines and waves. In the mascot business we called those kind of mascot performers "dudes in a suit." Anybody could stand in a costume on a street corner and wave to cars. The Chiefs didn't hire me to be a dude in a suit. They wanted a performer. I wanted the fans to see KC Wolf as a mascot who was very high energy, full of mischief, and always on the move. In order to achieve that persona I knew I had to keep myself in good shape.

On an average Chiefs' game day I would typically be in costume between four to five hours. A typical NFL football game lasts about three hours. The additional time was spent running around at pregame tailgate parties and postgame events. Even though I was able to take occasional breaks, five hours is still a long time to run around in fur.

People often asked me which game was my favorite of the season. I must admit that playing our two biggest rivals, the Oakland Raiders and Denver Broncos, was always fun, but even more important to me than the opponent was the weather. If the weather at the game was cold and I could see my breath, it was a great day to be a mascot. If the weather was hot, those games were much more challenging. I loved December football and tried to survive the August preseason games.

One of the hottest games I ever performed at was on September 3, 2000, at the Chiefs' regular season home opener against the Indianapolis Colts. The weatherman predicted temperatures between 100-105 degrees, not counting the heat index. The Chiefs had additional medical staff on hand to handle the increased heat related illnesses. The game turned out to be the greatest one day weight loss of my life. I dropped a total of 11 pounds in water weight. After the game I went to the Chiefs' training room and received two IV's filled with sodium hydrochloride (salt water) to help stop my muscle cramps. It was easy to see who wasn't a football player in the training room that day. The players were great big muscular guys getting tape cut off their ankles while I was a tall skinny guy laying on a table, drinking Gatorade with a needle stuck in his arm. I was obviously the team mascot.

The other two factors that determined if a game was enjoyable for me were overtime and rain. By the end of the fourth quarter mascots are ready to end their day. In all my years as a professional mascot, I have never met another mascot who enjoyed working overtime. Mascots are paid by the game, not by the hour, so overtime just meant an extended work day. The worst part was that no extra pay was received for working overtime. I don't know of anyone who enjoys working overtime without getting paid extra. Rain was the other factor that made being a mascot much more difficult and less enjoyable. It made the costume feel twice as heavy. Besides the added weight, I walked around smelling like a wet dog and looking like a drowned rat.

I will never forget a game the Chiefs played against the Seattle Seahawks on Sunday night, October 4, 1998. Ask any Chiefs' fan who attended this game, and I guarantee he will remember it well. Despite numerous tornado warnings, hail and torrential rain all day long, 66,418 people came out to Arrowhead Stadium to get wet. The heavy rains caused mini waterfalls to form down the steps at the stadium. The game ended up lasting almost four hours, including a 54 minute suspension of play for lightning. At one point the water-logged Chiefs ran 23 running plays in a row because passing was nearly impossible. Many die-hard fans stayed to the end and were rewarded with a 17-6 Chiefs' victory. After the game I hung up the KC Wolf costume in my changing area at the stadium where it took three days to finally drip dry.

One of the things I love about Chiefs' fans is their die-hard loyalty. Rain or shine they showed up excited and ready to cheer on the Chiefs. I considered myself fortunate to be able to perform for some of the greatest football fans in the NFL. On October 13, 2013, at a home game against the Oakland Raiders, Chiefs' fans broke the world record for the loudest crowd roar at an outdoor stadium. The Guinness Book of World Records measured the crowd noise at 137.5 decibels. I was thankful I had a Wolf head on that day to help protect my ears. Unfortunately the record was broken several weeks later by Seattle Seahawks fans at CenturyLink Field. Chiefs' fans took great pride in making Arrowhead Stadium one of the loudest in the NFL. Seahawks fans may have been a little louder on that day, but I guarantee they don't know how to tailgate as well as Chiefs fans.

Anyone who has ever attended a Chiefs' game knows it is an all-day affair. Fans arrive hours before kickoff equipped with their coolers and grills ready to enjoy the day. By about 10:00 a.m. the smell of BBQ and clouds of smoke hang over the parking lots. Most Chiefs' fans tailgate before the game, and then, win or lose, they tailgate again after the game. In all my years as KC Wolf I have never met anyone who went home hungry from a Chiefs game.

I have made hundreds of appearances at tailgate parties dressed as KC Wolf. The most memorable was on January 7, 1996, which just happened to be my 29th birthday. On this day the Chiefs had a home playoff game against the Indianapolis Colts and I visited 52 tailgate parties. I started doing tailgate visits two and a half hours before kickoff and finished just in time to get on the field for my pregame skit.

Many Chiefs fans remember this game for an entirely different reason. The Chiefs had gone 13-3 in the regular season and had clinched home field advantage throughout the playoffs. Chiefs' fans were very optimistic that this was going to be our year. Unfortunately, the Chiefs lost to the Colts 10-7 in what many still refer to as "Lin Elliot's Ice Cold Nightmare." The temperature that day was brutally cold, and our field goal kicker Lin Elliot missed three field goal attempts during the game. Sadly for Lin, it was the last game of his NFL career. Earlier that morning I had sat next to Lin at the Chiefs' pregame chapel service. Looking back I should have laid hands on him and prayed for him because after the game there were a lot of other Chiefs' fans who wanted to lay hands on Lin for a different reason.

Lin Elliot was actually a really nice guy who had kicked well in his time with the Chiefs, but unfortunately he picked the worst possible time to have a bad game. Everyone occasionally has a bad day at work, but for poor Lin his bad day was broadcast on national television for the whole country to see. The good thing about being the team mascot was that while I never got credit for the victories, I never got blamed for the losses either. My job was just to make people smile, regardless of whether the Chiefs were winning or losing. Any mascot would tell you that the job is much easier when your team is ahead.

Occasionally when I visited an elementary school, a student would ask if I ever worked out with the Chiefs' football players. I always found that question humorous because just by looking at me most people would wonder if I had ever spent time in a weight room in my life. Let's just say I wasn't exactly built like an NFL football player. Most football players train for strength and for speed. As a mascot I didn't need to be strong or fast, I just needed to be able to dance and entertain for long periods of time without getting tired. Although I lifted weights, I tried to stick to using lighter weights and doing more repetitions. I also spent a lot of time doing pushups and sit-ups. The best exercise I found for getting in shape for football season was stationary biking. I started keeping a record of how many miles I biked each year beginning in 1996. My New Year's resolution that year was to bike across America. People thought it sounded really exciting and adventurous until I told them I was doing it on a stationary bike sitting in my basement.

Prior to 1996 I used to workout at the Chiefs' weight room facility at Arrowhead, but after my first child Mycah was born in March 1996, I started working out in my basement so I could be at home with my family more. Every day I tracked my mileage on the bike. I kept a United States map hanging on my basement wall, and at the end of every month I would use a push pin to update how far I had traveled across the country. I stationary biked 3,500 miles that year which averaged out to a little more than 9.58 miles per day. I accomplished my goal for that year and was in the best shape of my life.

I'm convinced the many hours I spent peddling a stationary bike were what helped me to have such a long professional mascot career. During the 18 year period between January 1996 and December 2013, I biked 37,382 miles on three different Schwinn Airdyne stationary bikes. When I wore out one bike, I threw it away and bought another. Over that 18 year period I averaged 2,076 miles per year.

I developed a habit of exercising my mind at the same time I was exercising my body. I had a reading stand attached to my stationary bike, and over the years I became really good at reading and biking at the same time. I read a lot of great books which helped break up the boredom of peddling a bike while staring at a basement wall.

Since I worked hard to stay in good shape throughout the year, during the summer I liked to attempt outdoor adventures that would test my endurance. Luckily my younger brother joined me on these great adventures. In the summer of 2003, Dave and I rode our bikes along the Katy Trail in Missouri. I knew this would be a great way to check my endurance and see if I was in shape for the upcoming football season. The Katy Trail is an old railway line converted into a bicycle trail which starts in Clinton and stretches 225 miles across the state to our hometown of St. Charles. Dave and I thought biking the Katy Trail sounded like a real adventure. Our wives thought we were going through a mid-life crisis.

Dave and I spent two months planning the trip and discussing the details. The planning was probably just as much fun as the trip and definitely a lot less painful. Dave drove his family to my house in Kansas City to spend the night. Early the next morning our wives took us to Clinton and dropped us off at the start of the Katy Trail. They then drove across the state to St. Charles and spent three days relaxing while Dave and I biked our way across Missouri. Our goal was to bike about 75 miles each day and finish our great adventure in three days.

Dave and I both pulled bicycle trailers filled with supplies behind our bikes. We loaded our trailers with a tent, sleeping bags, food, water, toiletries (including toilet paper) and anything else we thought we might need on the trip. Our wives suggested we stay in a bed and breakfast each evening instead of carrying so much extra baggage. We had to explain to them that "real men don't stay in bed and breakfasts" when they are out on a "Big Adventure." Real men, like the Meers brothers, live off the land and stay in tents. It's a guy thing!

The Meers brothers' big adventure started on the morning of Friday, June 20, 2003. We arrived in Clinton, and as we were preparing to leave, I realized I had left my bicycle helmet at home. After two months of planning and making lists, I managed to go off and forget my most important piece of safety equipment. Instead of driving 75 minutes back to Kansas City, I made a quick trip to the local Walmart and purchased a helmet. The Clinton Walmart didn't carry a large selection of bike helmets in my size so I ended up buying one that was a bright, shiny silver color. My head looked like it was wrapped in aluminum foil, but luckily I was 36 years old and really didn't care what other people thought. I was actually hoping the helmet would take the focus off the tight black spandex biking shorts with the padded rear that I wore.

The first day on the road Dave and I were full of energy and excitement. We biked 75 miles and arrived in Boonville just as the sun was setting. We peddled past a sign that said Harley Park where there was a little league baseball game going on so we decided to stop. We ate dinner and enjoyed relaxing on the bleachers, which felt much more comfortable than our bicycle seats.

We introduced ourselves to a local police officer who was at the park watching the baseball game and told him about our adventure. The officer was very nice and informed us that the park was scheduled to close at 11:00 p.m., but he said we could camp in the park as long as we promised to behave ourselves. I think he could tell by looking at us that we were in no shape to stir up trouble. Dave and I set up the tent and crawled into our sleeping bags. It didn't take long for us to fall asleep after biking 75 miles.

By the end of that first day we both agreed that if your rear end is 18 inches wide and your bike seat is only six inches wide, a little discomfort is to be expected. By the end of the third day we learned a whole lot of discomfort is a certainty. Fortunately, we had remembered to pack a very important item—Gold Bond medicated powder. It came in very handy on those hot and sweaty 12 hour days while we were peddling and wearing tight fitting bicycle shorts.

Early the next morning after a breakfast of bananas, granola bars and ibuprofen we set off once again. The second day of our big adventure was the most scenic and also the most challenging. Much of the day was spent biking along the Missouri River enjoying the beautiful view. Even though I had a flat tire, we managed to bike 90 miles and spent the night in the city park in Hermann. The best thing about the Hermann city park was the public restrooms had showers. After 36 hours on the trail, a shower sounded really good. Body odor doesn't usually bother mascots, but I must admit even I wasn't looking forward to sharing a tent with my smelly brother. After dinner and a shower, we once again had no trouble falling asleep.

I woke up sore in Boonville, but my soreness there was nothing compared to how I felt waking up that morning in Hermann. Every muscle in my legs screamed at me, and by the way Dave was hobbling around I think he felt the same way. Once again we ate a big breakfast, downed some more ibuprofen, and set out to finish the last 60 miles of the trip.

The last leg of our big adventure didn't exactly go smoothly, thanks to me. I had three flat tires in a 21 mile stretch. Luckily, we discovered a bicycle shop in Marthasville where I bought a brand new set of tires. The new tires were a good investment because I finished the final 40 miles of our journey with no more flats.

As we approached the finish line in St. Charles, we noticed a group of people standing and holding a bed sheet that said "Welcome Home." Cam, Stacey and the kids, along with our parents, were waiting at the finish line to cheer us on. They made us feel like two soldiers returning from war even though we had only been gone for 55 hours. Dave and I had finished the big adventure but not without pain. Dave finished with a big blister where the sun don't shine. Several weeks after the ride the toenail fell off of my big toe. Despite the injuries, it was a great trip because we made a memory we still laugh about today. We vowed to never bike that far again. But guess what? Three years later, Dave and I packed up the bikes and rode the Katy Trail all over again.

By 2008 we decided it was time to try another big adventure. Since we had already proven to our wives that we were tough enough to conquer the Katy Trail twice, we decided we would try something different. I had heard about an annual canoe race called the Missouri River 340, a race that started in Kansas City and once again conveniently ended in St. Charles. The race was exactly 340 miles long down the Missouri River. Along the course, each team had to sign in at nine checkpoints. Failure to reach each checkpoint by a given time disqualified a team.

When I went on the website to get information, I knew this was going to be the perfect adventure because the top of the webpage, in big bold letters read:

"This ain't no momma's boy float trip."

I laughed when I read the statement because, more than once, our wives had teased Dave and me about being momma's boys. This was our chance to prove them wrong. Once again we took about two months planning and several weeks gathering our supplies: life vests, sun screen, emergency whistles, first aid kit and of course more

Gold Bond medicated powder. We assumed if biking in sweaty spandex shorts was uncomfortable, then sitting in a canoe wearing a wet
swim suit all day would be even worse. The smartest thing we did
in preparing for the Missouri River 340 was convince our dad to be
our ground support for the race. Dad's job was to drive ahead and
meet us at each of the nine checkpoints along the river. At each stop
he gave us a fresh cooler filled with food, Gatorade and water. In
exchange we gave him our bag of trash out of the canoe.

Each team competing in the Missouri River 340 had to come up
with a team name. Our wives decided if we were going to paddle
340 miles down the Missouri River, in the middle of July, our team
name should be "Dumb and Dumber." Father's Day was about a
month before the race. For a Father's Day gift our wives bought us
matching t-shirts that said "D, D and D." We assumed it stood for
Dan, Dave and Dad, but they informed us that it stood for Dumb,
Dumber and Dumbest.

The Missouri River 340 began at 8:00 a.m. on Tuesday, July 15.
When we arrived at Kaw Point near downtown Kansas City around
6:00 a.m., I could tell we were competing against some serious canoe
racers. Almost every other team had racing canoes while Dave and
I had a canoe I had bought years earlier to take my kids out on the
lake. The racing canoes were long and skinny. Our canoe was short
and chubby. This was our first canoe race and nobody had told
Dumb and Dumber that skinny canoes glide through the water
more easily. We looked like an elephant racing a bunch of cheetahs.
The competition didn't seem to be intimidated by our matching
Dumb and Dumber t-shirts either.

The starting gun sounded at 8:00 a.m. and we started paddling.
About a quarter of a mile into the race my paddle slipped out of my
hands, and Dave had to turn us around to go get it. With the canoe
race only five minutes old we were already toward the back of the
pack, paddling the widest canoe on the river.

The first checkpoint was 51 miles down the river in Lexington.
We arrived at 3:24 p.m., took a short 12 minute break, and hopped
back on the river. We reached the second checkpoint in Waverly at
6:39 p.m. and took a 17 minute break to eat dinner. By the time we
arrived at checkpoint three in Miami, we had paddled 105 miles and
were exhausted. It was midnight and thankfully my dad had already

set up our tent. After just four hours sleep we were back on the river. As we pulled out of Miami at 4:16 a.m., I began thinking maybe Dumb and Dumber really was an appropriate team name. I already had five blisters, and the special canoe gloves I purchased had a hole in them. Besides that, the Gold Bond medicated powder wasn't working as well as it had on the bicycle trips.

We arrived at checkpoint four at 10:08 a.m. on Wednesday morning and ate several chocolate donuts to give us a jolt. It wasn't exactly the breakfast of champions, but it was the breakfast of choice for Dumb and Dumber.

The fifth leg of the trip was by far the most difficult. It was a 56 mile stretch of river, which took us almost 10 hours to complete. We were paddling into the wind for the first part of the day, and by dusk we were miserable and exhausted. We arrived at Cooper's Landing at 8:26 p.m. and took an hour long supper break. Although our bodies were telling us to sleep, we decided since the sun was down we would keep paddling in the cool of the night. We also noticed the wind had died down significantly, and the river was relatively calm. At 9:24 p.m. we pushed our canoe back into the river for a late night paddle.

One of the things we learned that night was that with our bodies sleep deprived, we started to see things in the river that weren't really there. About 11:30 p.m. I saw a huge snake heading straight toward our canoe. My heart was racing. As I was about to club it over the head with my paddle, I realized I was seeing a ripple in the river current.

An hour after seeing the snake, Dave spotted a hippopotamus with its head sticking out of the dark waters near our canoe. We frantically paddled to get away from it, but the hippo continued to follow us down the river. We were pretty sure there weren't any hippos in the Missouri River, but we didn't want to take any chances. Thankfully, as we were trying to escape from sure death, we realized that the hippo was just a tree stump floating down the river. Finally, about 2:00 a.m., we decided it was time to give our minds and our bodies a little break. Since we were still 10 miles away from the next check point, we found a sandy river bank and lay down to sleep.

We still laugh about what happened next. Unknowingly, we had made our camp about 100 yards from a highway train crossing. Just as we had fallen into a deep sleep, a train came roaring down the tracks and blew its train whistle. Dave and I both shot straight up, terrified. At first I thought a plane was crashing on top of us, then I thought the hippo had returned and was about to kill us. Finally, it dawned on me; the noise was just a train. We lay back down with our hearts still racing and eventually fell back asleep. About 45 minutes later another train came roaring down the tracks with its whistle blowing. Once again we woke up terrified. Apparently, our camping spot was a hub for late night train activity because about an hour later a third train came screaming through.

Since three separate trains had interrupted our sleep in two and a half hours, we decided to just get back in the canoe and head downstream. The snake, the hippo and the three trains had combined to make that night one of the most terrifying of my life.

At 7:11 a.m. we finally arrived at checkpoint six in Noren, thrilled to see the sun coming up. For breakfast we decided to eat some donuts and drink several Mountain Dews. By this point we didn't care about nutrition. We wanted sugar and caffeine. By the third day I had a whole new appreciation for the men who took part in the Lewis and Clark expedition. I was tired of paddling, and I kept wishing I had a skinnier canoe and a skinnier brother.

Day three was a very long and grueling day on the river. We managed to paddle for 16 hours and 33 minutes and ended up at checkpoint eight in Weldon Springs at 12:44 a.m. Dad had our tent set up so we walked straight in and collapsed on the sleeping bags. We slept without any interruptions for four hours and were back on the river at 5:22 a.m. to finish paddling the final 19 miles. We called our wives and told them we would be arriving around 8:15 a.m. and asked if they would pick us up so we could go to Dave's house to shower and sleep. As we paddled into the final checkpoint in St. Charles, we were greeted by the same crowd of people holding another bed sheet. It read: "WELCOME HOME DUMB and DUMBER." Once again our beautiful wives, wonderful kids, and supportive parents were there to cheer us on at the finish line.

By the time we finished the race, my hands were wrapped up like a boxer's. I had Band-Aids, athletic tape, duct tape and canoe gloves wrapped around them. When I finally removed everything, I counted 18 blisters on my hands. The experience was painful but well worth the cost. Dave and I had paddled 340 miles down the Missouri River in the middle of July without killing each other. It took us 72 ½ hours from start to finish, and we finished 59th overall out of 149 total teams. Not bad for a couple of rookie racers in a chubby canoe.

I once had a KC Wolf appearance at Gail's Harley Davidson in Grandview, Missouri. Painted on the wall in their showroom was this quote, "Life should not be a journey to the grave with the intention of arriving safely in a pretty and well preserved body, but rather to skid in broadside in a cloud of smoke, thoroughly used up, totally worn out, and loudly proclaiming 'WOW! What a Ride!'"

As painful as the Missouri River 340 was, I would do it all over again. Dumb, Dumber and Dumbest still laugh about the longest 72 ½ hours of our lives. During that adventure we were fully alive, and the journey drew us closer together. I don't want to live my life recklessly and out of control, but I also refuse to live my life taped up in bubble wrap trying to avoid all pain and discomfort. At the end of my life I want to be able to look back and say, "WOW! What a Ride!"

Life is a gift from God, and I want to live every day to the fullest. I don't want to miss out on the adventure because I was afraid of pain, failure or what others might think. I choose to live confidently today because I know who I am, but most importantly, I know whose I am. I am a child of God (John 1:12) and knowing this truth has made all the difference in my life. Some people would say paddling 340 miles down the Missouri River in July was stupid. Others, like Dave and me, call it an adventure. All I know is that it's a memory I will cherish for the rest of my life.

8

Mascot
and Minister

*"Your walk talks and your talk talks, but your walk talks
louder than your talk talks."*

By 2005 Cam and I had been members of the First Baptist
Church in Raytown, Missouri, for several years. We loved this
church because we were actively involved in a Sunday school class
with many other couples our age. Like us, these couples also had
small children and knew both the joys and challenges that come
with being parents. It was a blessing to be a part of a Sunday school
class that prayed for and encouraged each other as we journeyed
through life together.

When our kids were young, it was my responsibility to drop
them off at the church nursery along with the diaper bag. The first
time I checked them into the nursery I laughed because above the
nursery door was a Bible verse that read: "We will not all sleep, but
we will all be changed" (1 Corinthians 15:51). I was encouraged to
know the nursery workers had a sense of humor and that when I
picked my child up at least they would be in a clean diaper.

After I had been attending the church for about a year, I was
asked to volunteer in the church nursery. After my first Sunday in
the nursery, I realized why that Bible verse hung above the nursery
door. I've sat through some long sermons in my life, but none felt as
long as my shifts in the church nursery. I was convinced the pastor
saved his longest sermons for those weeks when he knew I would
be working with the little ones. Since my kids were nursery age, I felt
guilty if I didn't help out occasionally, but I definitely didn't want to
get on the weekly schedule. There were many great ministries at the
church, but I was 100% sure my calling was not changing diapers. I
was changing enough of those at home with my own kids.

My wife was active in the church choir and loved to sing. I had sung in the choir during junior high school, but that had been many years ago. While I enjoyed singing occasionally in the shower, I was sure the choir director didn't want me bringing my joyful noise to the church choir. Other than teaching Sunday school once in a while and occasionally working in the nursery, I wasn't sure where I should be serving in the church.

In the spring of 2005 I received a call from our pastor inviting me to lunch. He mentioned he had something he wanted to talk to me about. Now I really don't like meetings, but I do really like food. Since he was my pastor, and since it was a lunch meeting which involved food, I accepted his invitation. When I got off the phone, I began to wonder what in the world the pastor wanted to talk to me about. I immediately started thinking the worst. My best guess was the church needed more fathers to help in the church nursery. Since nobody else would volunteer maybe he was going to give me a promotion and ask me to start working twice a month. If our meeting wasn't about a church nursery promotion, maybe he was going to talk to me about sleeping during his Sunday evening sermons. I admit that occasionally I nodded off on Sunday nights, especially after Chiefs' games. When the Chiefs played a home game that kicked off at noon, I was unable to attend Sunday morning services. For a noon kickoff I arrived at Arrowhead by 8:30 a.m. to begin my day. Since church didn't start until 9:30 a.m., I missed our morning worship services. I made a commitment to my family that if I had to miss on a Sunday morning due to a Chiefs' game we would go together to the Sunday evening service. I tried to hurry home after the game, but no matter how hard I tried, I would always get stuck in traffic. As soon as I arrived home, I ran upstairs, took a shower, ran back downstairs for dinner and then hopped in the car to race to church.

My pastor was a good speaker with very good sermons. However, I struggled to stay awake on Sunday nights because I was always exhausted after spending hours running around in a mascot costume in the hot sun. In addition I ate a big dinner and then sat in a comfortable pew in the air conditioned church sanctuary. This made my struggle to stay awake that much harder. I was usually fine during singing, but about 10 minutes into the sermon Cam would begin giving me the elbow to the ribs to wake me up.

When I fell asleep I didn't snore; instead my tendency was to drool and nod. Whenever I fell asleep at church, I tried to look like I was praying with my eyes closed. It was hard to convince people because when I opened my eyes I had a big wet spot on my shirt collar. My other problem was that when I began to fall asleep, my head nodded which woke me up and caused me to jerk my head back up like I was having a seizure. People naturally looked at me to make sure I was okay. Maybe the pastor was going to ask me to sit in the back row of the balcony during the evening service so I wouldn't be a distraction to others.

When the day arrived for our lunch meeting I was actually a little nervous. When we sat down, he smiled at me and said, "Dan, I would like for you to consider a new position on our church staff as the part time men's pastor." His words caught me off guard because they were not what I was anticipating him to say. He understood I would be gone some Sundays during the fall because of the Chiefs' schedule, but the staff was willing to work with me. I told him I was flattered by the offer, but I would first need to pray about it and talk with Cam.

When I shared the news with Cam, she was excited and said she would support whatever decision I made. Cam and I share a passion for marriages and families. We both feel one of the big reasons for the breakup of many families is the fact many men aren't stepping up and being the husbands and fathers they are called to be. I know countless men who live their lives more concerned with convenience than with commitment. I believe men are called to live lives of commitment: to God, to their wives, and to their children.

As I was praying about whether or not to accept the position, I found a quote I had written down years earlier. "God didn't put us on this earth to make a living; He put us here to make an impact." I had written this quote in my Bible the summer I worked as a counselor at Kanakuk Kamp. In college I felt God telling me to use my mascot platform to make an impact in the lives of young people. Now 15 years later, I realized God was giving me another great opportunity to make an impact in the lives of men, men who hopefully would in turn have a godly influence on their families and in their homes.

I called the pastor the next day and told him I would love to take the job. In June 2005, I officially became bi-vocational. I was a full time NFL mascot and a part time men's minister. I was getting ready to enter the busiest season of my life because I quickly learned there is no such thing as part time ministry. Serving as both a mascot and a minister during football season was not only busy but fun. One Sunday I would be dressed in a suit and tail dancing in front of 78,000 people, and the next Sunday I would be standing in the pulpit in a suit and a tie preaching a sermon. I was a very unique combination. I didn't know of any other mascots who were ministers, and I didn't know any other preachers who were mascots.

One Sunday a man from my church, who was a Chiefs' season ticket holder, came up to me and gave me a huge compliment. He said, "You're a pretty good dancer for a Baptist." I just smiled and said, "I know. That's because I grew up a Lutheran."

Several months after joining the church staff, I was asked to preach at the Sunday services. The pastor was going to be out of town and needed someone to fill the pulpit. He thought it would be a good opportunity for the church to get to know the new guy on staff. Honestly, I was scared to death. I felt like Moses when God asked him to lead the Israelites out of Egypt, not exactly sure I was qualified for the task. I had spoken many times in my life but never in this setting. My sermon was going to be the televised Sunday morning sermon in front of over 2,000 people at my home church. Surely the pastor could see my face was built for radio and not television. The good news was I had a month to prepare. As I was gathering materials for my sermon, I read this quote, "Football consists of 22 men on the field who are desperately in need of a rest being watched by 75,000 people in the stands who are desperately in need of exercise." I laughed because this quote also reminded me of our church. It appeared to me that a small percentage of very dedicated people desperately in need of rest were doing all the work while everyone else seemed content just to sit in the pews and watch from the sidelines.

I decided to preach on the parable of the Good Samaritan found in Luke 10. It's the story about a man who was traveling from

Jerusalem to Jericho and on the way he is beaten up by a gang of thieves, which stole all of his belongings and left him along the roadside half dead. Three men passed by, a priest, a Levite and a Samaritan, but only one of them stopped to help the man. The compassionate man who stopped to help was the Good Samaritan. As he was traveling by on his donkey, the Samaritan was the only one willing to stop and get involved.

My goal was to encourage the congregation to be like the Good Samaritan and be willing to get involved and make a difference in the lives of others. My wife accused me of selfishly trying to make others feel guilty so they would start volunteering to help in the church nursery. I told her that if God convicted some to get involved by helping in the church nursery, I would be more than happy to give up my monthly shift changing diapers.

As I was thinking about a catchy title for my sermon, a title came to my mind in what I'm convinced was a moment of divine intervention: "GET OFF YOUR DONKEY." It was the perfect title for my message. For a moment I considered preaching out of the King James Version of the Bible and calling it "GET OFF YOUR ASS." After giving the idea more thought I decided that probably wasn't a good title for the new pastor's first sermon. I was also pretty sure the head pastor wouldn't let me print "GET OFF YOUR ASS" in the church bulletin. So I decided to preach from the New International Version and stick with "GET OFF YOUR DONKEY."

Apparently my sermon didn't offend too many people because I was invited to preach several more times over the next two years. I enjoyed preaching from time to time, but I knew I didn't want to be a lead pastor because of the pressure to come up with a new sermon every week.

The other big news that happened during the summer of 2005 was the addition of the newest Meers family member. Rusty Meers was born on May 27, 2005. He was the new family dog, purchased for $400. I didn't realize at the time, but he would cost me a lot more money over the next 10 years. Rusty is a Golden Doodle, a mixture of Golden Retriever and Poodle. He was one of the happiest dogs I'd ever been around. Although he had a great personality, he was dumb as a rock. The first thing we did after getting Rusty was spend $75 on dog obedience classes. It became obvious very quickly, I had wasted my money on Rusty's higher education because he was not the sharpest dog from the litter.

Shortly after we got Rusty, we noticed some stray dogs roaming around in our backyard. I didn't recognize the dogs from the neighborhood so I called the local animal control agency and assumed animal control would send someone over immediately. I was wrong.

The following day Cam made a quick run to the grocery store, and when she returned home, she noticed Rusty was missing. She had tied him up in the backyard under the shade tree and left him food and water. After frantically searching the neighborhood for Rusty, she found a note stuck on our front door from the local animal control officer saying they had Rusty at the dog pound. Apparently he had managed to wrap himself around the tree and couldn't get back to his water bowl. When animal control showed up 24 hours after my stray dog report, they found Rusty in a dangerous situation and hauled him in. When we called to explain what had happened they said we could come down and get him from the pound, but we needed to bring $25 to get him back.

I confess even though I was a minister I was thinking some very unkind thoughts towards my local animal control officers. I was frustrated knowing I was the one who had called animal control, and they came to my house and took my dog. I was even more frustrated knowing it was going to cost me $25 to get my dog back. I was beginning to realize dogs can be very expensive pets. Since Rusty wasn't smart enough to keep from wrapping himself around the tree, we invested in a wireless electric fence. Once again I watched several hundred dollars leave my bank account. Even though Rusty wasn't very bright, he was smart enough to understand that when his new shock collar beeped he should quit walking. Unfortunately, Rusty was also smart enough to figure out that when the battery went dead on his shock collar, he was free to leave the yard and roam the neighborhood without fear of pain. We discovered his shock collar was no longer working because when we took Rusty out for a walk everyone we passed seemed to know him by name. The reason he was so well known was that his name was on his collar, and when we left our house in the morning, Rusty roamed the neighborhood making new friends. He would have been a good politician or a Walmart door greeter with his great people skills.

Rusty had a way of making me feel special every time I came home. Whether I was gone for three days on a work trip or for 10 minutes to the grocery store, when I returned home he ran to the car, jumped around, and acted like he hadn't seen me in a month. Rusty didn't lead a real exciting life, but he sure seemed to enjoy the life he had.

Psalms 118:24 (NASB) says, "This is the day the Lord has made; Let us rejoice and be glad in it."

Rusty lived that Bible verse out better than most people I know. He was an expensive pet, but I learned some valuable lessons from him. Maybe that dumb dog wasn't so dumb after all.

Serving as men's minister at Raytown First Baptist was one of the most challenging and rewarding experiences of my life. Our purpose as a men's ministry was to encourage, equip and challenge men to be bold men of integrity who were dependent on God, and who were making an impact for Christ in their home, church, community and world. I often got a chance to pray with men and encourage them to strive to become the husbands, fathers, friends and servant leaders God had called them to be. There were many times when I felt very inadequate and under qualified as the men's minister.

I kept a quote on my desk at church by author E.M. Bounds, which says: "God does not need great talents or great learning or great preachers, but people great in holiness, great in faith, great in love, great in fidelity, great for God—people always speaking holy words, living holy lives. These can mold a generation for God." This quote encouraged me because it reminded me I didn't need a seminary degree to make a difference in the lives of others. I loved the group of men at church and we became known as the B.I.G. D.O.G. MINISTRY.

B – BOLD	D – DEPENDENT
I – INTEGRITY	O – ON
G – GUYS	G – GOD

I wore a t-shirt around church which read, "If you're going to run with the BIG DOGS, you have to get off the porch." This group of men decided life was too short to sit on the sidelines. They wanted to make a difference in the lives of others. "NO MORE COUCH

POTATOES AND NO MORE PEW POTATOES" was their motto. I was extremely proud to be associated with this group of guys.

Hanging on the wall in my church office was a poster one of the men gave to me. It was a reminder of the type of men we were striving to become. It read:

The World Needs Men …
* Who cannot be bought
* Whose word is their bond
* Who put character above wealth
* Who possess opinions and a will
* Who are larger than their vocations
* Who do not hesitate to take chances
* Who will not lose their individuality in a crowd
* Who will be honest in small things as in great things
* Who will make no compromise with wrong
* Whose ambitions are not confined to their own selfish desires
* Who will not say they do it "because everybody else does it"
* Who are true to their friends through good report and evil report in adversity as well as prosperity
* Who do not believe that shrewdness, cunning, and hard headedness are the best qualities for winning success
* Who are not ashamed or afraid to stand for the truth when it is unpopular
* Who can say "No" with emphasis, although all the rest of the world says "Yes"

Those were the kind of men we were striving to become at Raytown First Baptist.

On February 19, 2006, my church officially ordained me as a minister of the Gospel. It was a very exciting day. Several members of my family came to town, including my parents. I felt extremely honored and humbled as I stood before them and my church family. As an ordained minister I could now officially "Marry and Bury" people. After my ordination I didn't feel any smarter, and I still did not have a seminary degree like other ministers, but that was just fine. I had learned God was less concerned with a degree hanging on my office wall than He was with my willingness to step out in love and serve others. I was still just Dan Meers, an ordinary guy committed to God and committed to making an impact in this world. I was reminded once again that all God really wanted from my life was for me to love Him and to love others (Matthew 22:36-40).

In June 2006, Cam started back to college to get her master's degree in Marriage and Family Therapy. She had always dreamed of being a marriage and family counselor. Since our youngest daughter Mallory was ready to start kindergarten, we decided this would be an ideal time for her to get her degree. The next 12 months proved to be the busiest year of my life. I was still working full time as KC Wolf, averaging about 325 appearances a year. I was also continuing to work many hours as the part time men's minister. Many nights I would arrive home just as my wife was heading out the door for school. Since I wasn't a very good cook, and I was usually exhausted by the end of the day, I would load the kids in the car and we would go out for pizza. That year we spent many nights eating at Pizza Street. It probably wasn't the healthiest year of their lives, but my kids loved it because the restaurant had an ice cream machine, and I taught them how to make ice cream cones for desert.

As the year dragged on, I realized I could no longer live my life at the pace I was living it. I had too much on my plate, and I knew it. I was so busy I felt like I was failing at my most important job of being a husband to my wife and a father to my kids. One day as I was reading a devotional, I came across this quote: "The urgent things in life are seldom important and the important things in life are seldom urgent." I knew it was time to make a change. My busy schedule was having a negative effect on the people I loved the most. As much as I loved working at the church I knew it was time to step down as the men's minister. It was a very tough decision, but as I prayed about it I knew it was the right decision.

In June 2007, two years after I had started as the men's minister at Raytown First Baptist, I stepped down from the position. These years had been two of the greatest years of my life, and I had learned a very important lesson: "God wasn't so much interested in my ability as He was in my availability."

9

Game Day

"The reason women don't play football is because eleven of them would never wear the same outfit in public."
Phyllis Diller

A typical Chiefs' game day for KC Wolf was long and exhausting but lots of fun. By the time I arrived back at home after the game I was ready to collapse. Game days reminded me of taking my kids to Disney World. There were always large crowds and everyone was fired up and excited about being at the Magic Kingdom. All day long my kids smiled, laughed and had a great time, but by the time we came back to our hotel they were completely wiped out and ready for bed. That was exactly how I felt after every Chiefs' home game.

I was thankful the Chiefs only played once a week. As a mascot I couldn't imagine having to perform a doubleheader. This was one of the big reasons I switched from being Fredbird to KC Wolf. Professional baseball mascots perform at 81 home games each season, and many of those games are during the summer. Football mascots only have 10 home games each year, and most of those games are during the cooler weather in the fall and early winter. Since the Chiefs only played one game a week, I could go all out on Sundays because I had the rest of the week for my body to recover. Baseball mascots have to pace themselves because they have to wake up the next day and head back to the ballpark for another game.

During my years in Kansas City I became good friends with Sluggerrr, the mascot for the Kansas City Royals. I liked to give Sluggerrr a hard time whenever possible. Every year I called him around the middle of September and pretended I was upset that I still had seven home games left on the schedule. I never got much sympathy from him because even though we both had seven home games remaining by mid-September, he had already performed at 74 games, while I had only worked three.

Most Chiefs' home games kicked off at noon on Sundays. On game day I arrived at the stadium around 8:15 a.m. The gates leading into Arrowhead usually opened around 8:30 a.m., so if I arrived before then I could enter the employee early arrival entrance and avoid the traffic. If I arrived late, I had to sit in traffic like everyone else.

When the gates opened at Arrowhead the scene reminded me of what the Oklahoma Land Rush of 1889 must have been like. Instead of riding horses to lay claim to their territory, Chiefs fans drove a variety of different vehicles to stake out their tailgating area. Most arrived in cars and trucks, but some fans had special Chiefs buses and RVs painted and designed specifically for tailgating. A Chiefs' game day is an experience like no other, and I truly believe we have the best fans and the best tailgating in the world.

After arriving at Arrowhead, I would enter the stadium on the east side of Lower Lot E. This was the tunnel that led underground from the Chiefs' player parking lot, down to the locker rooms and out onto the field. Like everyone else, security searched my bags. It was always entertaining when a new security guard was working at the tunnel. He unzipped my huge bag and found KC Wolf staring at him.

Most people could easily figure out my alter ego because I was always the guy carrying the large bag into the stadium. I kept one KC Wolf costume in my locker room at the stadium, but I always brought a second costume on game day so I could switch costumes at halftime. It was always refreshing to take off a sweaty KC Wolf costume at halftime and come out for the second half dressed in dry fur.

On game day I also carried a duffle bag filled with extra clothing. It was amazing how much laundry I could dirty up during one football game. Before every game I packed four extra pair of shorts, three pairs of tube socks, 10 pairs of wrist bands and 10 extra dry fit shirts. As much as I perspired, I had to continually change clothes or I would begin to sweat through my costume. I quickly learned nobody likes to hug a soggy wolf who smells like sweat.

After passing through security I headed to my locker room, dropped off my duffle bag and hung up my extra KC Wolf suit. It was important for me to start hydrating early so I grabbed a Gatorade and then walked down to the Chiefs' theatre room. During the week the players used the theatre room to watch game film as a team, but on Sunday mornings it was used for the chapel service.

Since I couldn't attend Sunday morning services at my church, the Chiefs' team chaplain, Mike Lusardi, allowed me and my KC Wolf assistant to sit in on the team chapel. Although the players were not required to attend the service, many of them arrived at Arrowhead early for chapel. Often times local pastors or other guest speakers shared a message. These godly men challenged the players to give their best not just on Sundays when they were in front of a huge crowd, but to also give their best and live out their faith throughout the week when no one was watching.

These speakers not only encouraged the Chiefs to be great football players, but also to be godly husbands, fathers, and role models in the community. I still remember a powerful message from one of our chapel speakers called "Payday is coming." He shared a passage out of the Bible from Galatians 6:7-8, "Do not be deceived: God cannot be mocked. A man reaps what he sows. Whoever sows to please their flesh, from the flesh will reap destruction; whoever sows to please the Spirit, from the Spirit will reap eternal life." He explained that the Bible clearly tells us there will be a payday for everything we do in this life. If we sow to the flesh, we reap emptiness, despair and depression. If we sow to the Spirit, we reap love, joy, peace and abundant life. He left us with this question: "Where are you sowing today?" Chapel was always a great reminder that even though the football game was important, other areas in life are much more important.

The two biggest differences between the Chiefs' chapel services and the Sunday services in my home church were the singing and the dress. It was a good thing the Chiefs knew how to play football because from what I heard none of them had a singing career in their future. We truly made a "joyful noise" unto the Lord during those chapel services. The other major difference was how people were dressed. At church almost everyone dressed nicely. At the chapel services the chaplain and speakers dressed nicely, but everyone else sat around in shorts and t-shirts.

On September 25, 1994, Mike Lusardi asked if I would share my testimony at chapel before the Los Angeles Rams game. I was honored to be asked to speak. I shared how I had committed my life to Christ in high school and the incredible faith journey I had been on since then. I also shared that the joy in my life didn't come from being a mascot; it came from my relationship with Jesus Christ. After the service, I was encouraged by so many of the Chiefs players who thanked me for sharing. The players seemed touched by what I shared, but apparently I didn't inspire them too much because the Chiefs went out and lost 16-0.

The Chiefs' chapel service usually lasted until about 9:00 a.m. leaving me about 30 minutes to stretch out and get ready to hop in my KC Wolf suit. Around 9:30 a.m. I would make my first appearance of the day. I hopped on the back of the four-wheeler, and my KC Wolf assistant, Shawn Emerson, drove me to the Fan Zone, an area set up outside the stadium with music, inflatables for the kids, and other fun activities. I walked around for 30 minutes entertaining the crowd. Most of my time in the Fan Zone was spent posing for pictures with fans. Shawn and I were always surprised by the number of fans who didn't know how to work their cell phone camera. If I got stuck with a fan who couldn't figure out how to work his camera, Shawn stepped in and took the picture.

It was always obvious when my 30 minutes at the Fan Zone was up because at 10:00 a.m. Suzie the cheerleader would come riding up on Warpaint the horse. As soon as Suzie and Warpaint began posing for pictures I sneaked away to the four-wheeler, and Shawn and I would head back to my locker room.

Occasionally I tried to think of creative ways to travel between my locker room and the Fan Zone. In the fall of 2012 I came up with what seemed like a great idea. I called it my "Redneck Waterski." I took an old waterski and mounted my son's skateboard wheels to the bottom of it. I then hooked up a ski rope to the back of my four-wheeler and Shawn pulled me through the parking lots. I learned to waterski when I was seven years old and felt very comfortable skiing on a slalom ski. The major difference was that instead of skiing on water wearing a swim suit and a life jacket, I was now skiing on pavement wearing a giant wolf suit.

The first time using the Redneck Waterski was a memorable experience. I was having so much fun skiing behind the four-wheeler that I told Shawn to keep pulling me around the parking lots because the fans loved it. Everything worked great for the first 25 minutes, but as I was skiing back towards the locker room I experienced a problem. Apparently, the bearings inside the skateboard wheels became so hot from the friction that the wheels began to melt. The problem was that it happened suddenly while I was still traveling at about 15-20 miles an hour behind the four-wheeler. One minute I was confidently skiing through the parking lot waving to the fans, and the next moment the front of my ski was shaking uncontrollably. About two seconds later I found myself flying through the air and landing face first on the pavement.

Since I was wearing KC Wolf, my head was very well protected. I quickly jumped up and climbed onto the back of the four-wheeler for the remainder of the trip. When I got to my dressing room, I noticed I had torn several holes in the wolf suit. I also discovered I was bleeding on my elbow, knees and hand. I made a trip down to the Chiefs' training room so I could get bandaged up before the game. My accident confirmed what I already knew, falling on pavement was much more painful than falling in water. If I was going to get hurt at least I had fun doing it. The blood and the bandages were well worth it because Redneck Waterskiing was a blast.

On most game days I got a short break between 10:00–10:30 a.m. When my break was over, I suited back up, and Shawn drove me around on the four-wheeler to visit many of the corporate tailgate parties. The four-wheeler was an important piece of game day equipment. Driving it made navigating through traffic much easier, which helped us get to our many different appearance locations much quicker.

Corporate tailgate party visits usually took between 45-60 minutes to complete. We tried to make sure we were finished with these visits by 11:20 a.m. because at that point I needed to return to my locker room and get ready for the KC Wolf pregame skit.

Most of the game day activities I was required to attend had a little bit of flexibility on when I could arrive. For instance, if I arrived a few minutes late at the Fan Zone because of traffic, I would just stay a few minutes longer at the end. The pregame skit was the only exception. The start time was very specific, and if I wasn't there on time I was in big trouble. Every Friday before a Chiefs' home game I received the script and time table for the upcoming game. The time table was the most important thing I carried with me during pregame because it informed me what was happening next and when I needed to be ready for my skit. Almost every Chiefs game was televised, and the networks were very strict about the exact starting time for the game. As a result, everything that took place leading up to kickoff also had a specific time.

The pregame skit introduced KC Wolf before every game. The skits usually lasted no more than three minutes and involved several "bad guys." These bad guys were usually friends of mine who were willing to dress up as fans from the opposing team and run out onto the field. As they were running out onto the field I would chase after them on my four-wheeler, and KC Wolf would beat them up. Even though Chiefs fans knew KC Wolf would walk away victorious, they would still yell and cheer week after week.

My friends enjoyed dressing up as the bad guys because it was a one of a kind experience. They also received free tickets and a parking pass for the game. In the top drawer of my office desk I kept a long list of friends who volunteered to be on the KC Wolf pregame skit waiting list. These were friends of mine who were willing to trade a bruise from KC Wolf for a chance to be on the field with me. The only promise they had to make was that KC Wolf would win the fight or they would never get invited back. This is how I went my entire career without ever losing a pregame battle.

Although the Chiefs tried to keep the pregame schedule consistent from week to week, occasionally there would be a special presentation or introduction which would alter the time for my pregame skit. The KC Wolf skit almost always followed Warpaint's introduction. Suzie was one of the Chiefs' cheerleaders and she was also very gifted at riding horses. When Warpaint was introduced, Suzie rode out and circled the field. As Warpaint was exiting the field, KC Wolf was ready to be introduced. As I sat on my four-wheeler in the tunnel waiting for my cue, I would try to rehearse the KC Wolf skit in my mind. I also reminded myself not to run over the horse when I raced out of the tunnel during my introduction. Thankfully Suzie knew it was hard for me to see in the KC Wolf costume, so she rode Warpaint over toward the sidelines until I went racing past on my four-wheeler.

Warpaint and I had a love/hate relationship at first. I loved Warpaint, and Warpaint hated me. Every time I walked past her corral at Arrowhead dressed like KC Wolf, she started snorting like I was a seven foot rat that was unwelcome in her area. After several months Warpaint began to realize KC Wolf was harmless and finally started to warm up to me.

Pregame skits were exciting because I got to be the center of attention for about three minutes. It was also quite challenging to come up with creative skits each game. The NFL league offices released the Chiefs' schedule in late April. As soon as I knew the specific dates for our home games, I began planning the KC Wolf skits. The skits were created based on a number of different factors including date, opponent, current events or outfits.

Some skits were planned according to the date on which we played. For instance, if the Chiefs were playing a game on Halloween, I wrapped KC Wolf up like a mummy for the skit. If the Chiefs' game was in late December I dressed KC Wolf up like Santa Claus and had him beat up the Grinch, who would be dressed in a jersey of the Chiefs' opponent. At other times I planned KC Wolf skits based on the opposing team. If the Chiefs were playing the Green Bay Packers, I dressed two of my friends up in Packers jerseys wearing Cheese Heads and beat them up. The Oakland Raiders had a bad boy image, so when we played them I dressed KC Wolf up in a leather jacket and dark sunglasses and rode out on a Harley Davidson motorcycle to the song "Bad to the Bone." If our opponent was the Chicago Bears, I rented three bear suits at the local costume shop and dressed KC Wolf up like Goldilocks.

Occasionally KC Wolf skits were based on current events. A good example of this was when Mike Tyson bit off a piece of Evander Holyfield's ear in a 1997 boxing match. Since everyone knew about the ear-biting incident, for the next Chiefs game I performed a boxing skit and made a fake wolf ear attached with Velcro. My opponent and I each wore huge boxing gloves and during the fight he bit off my ear. KC Wolf then got upset and proceeded to knock him out. Of course I didn't really knock him out, but my friend was a very good actor.

Using KC Wolf outfits was another great way to create skits. Over the years I developed a large selection of outfits that KC Wolf could wear including Superman, Batman, Spiderman, Elvis, Santa Claus, Luke Skywalker and many others. My wardrobe also included a tuxedo, Hawaiian shirts, and even a red sequin dress that I sometimes wore when I wanted to appear as my identical twin sister, "Lacy Wolf." Occasionally I had my assistant Shawn put on my spare costume and we had KC Wolf and Lacy Wolf appear together.

One of my favorite pregame skits actually involved no outfit at all. As a matter of fact I think many Chiefs fans were shocked because they had never seen KC Wolf without his clothes on. The skit began like many other skits. A friend of mine ran out to midfield pumping his fist dressed like a bad guy in the opposing team's jersey. When he arrived on the 50 yard line, the Chiefs sound man began playing the song "The Streak," by Ray Stevens, over the loud speakers at Arrowhead. When I heard the music begin, this was my cue to come running out of the east end zone tunnel naked, wearing nothing but my KC Wolf birthday suit. I'm sure somebody got upset that KC Wolf appeared naked, but the majority of Chiefs fans got a good laugh out of the skit. I learned I could not possibly make everybody happy so I figured if 99% of the fans were smiling after my skits, I had done my job.

I wish I could take credit for all of the entertaining KC Wolf skits over the years, but in reality there were many people who made me look good on game day. My seamstress, Gayle Foust, designed some great outfits which fit my 85 inch hips and body. The Chiefs' video department made KC Wolf look like he could do just about anything in front of a green screen. The Chiefs' stadium announcer and sound man were critical to making sure the timing worked well during the skits. I even have to give my friends credit for making me look really tough beating them up. They often walked away with bumps and bruises, but they also received a souvenir video of their performance. Someday they will be able to sit down with their grandkids and tell them about the time they were beaten up by KC Wolf in front of 78,000 screaming Chiefs fans.

My goal was to create most of the KC Wolf skits during the off season so I wouldn't have to rush around planning them once the season arrived. Football season was busy with appearances, so it was much easier and less stressful if I had the skits planned out before the season ever began. Each summer I took one evening and invited several of my creative friends over to my house. After feeding them pizza, we sat around and brainstormed skit ideas for the upcoming football season. Those brainstorming sessions were always helpful, but I can tell you my friends weren't always overly concerned with being politically correct. Whenever they came up with a skit idea that I thought might get me into trouble I always cleared it with my boss first. I made sure to get his blessing before attempting anything too controversial.

KC Wolf skits usually ended with me driving off the field on the four-wheeler acting like a hero who had just saved the day. I drove up the tunnel, parked the four-wheeler and then returned to the field for player introductions, the national anthem and the coin toss. Standing on the field at Arrowhead, listening to 78,000 screaming fans and giving high fives to the Chiefs' players during pre-game introductions was always exciting. It was even more exciting when the B2 Stealth Bomber, from nearby Whiteman Air Force Base in Knob Noster, flew over the stadium following the national anthem.

I really enjoyed getting to take a kid out to the center of the field along with the Chiefs' captains for the pregame coin toss. It was fun to watch the little kids' faces filled with excitement while they stood next to the players who were easily four times their size. The Chiefs' captains always introduced themselves and made the kids feel very special.

After the coin toss my on-field responsibilities were over, and I was free to roam the stadium and entertain fans. I tried to stick around on the sidelines for the kickoff and the first few minutes of the game. Midway through the first quarter I usually headed for my dressing room. By this point I needed to change into a dry t-shirt. I also got a drink and headed up into the stands to start delivering birthday and anniversary gifts. Every game I had a list of people who paid to have KC Wolf visit a seat location. These visits were usually arranged to surprise a friend or family member who was having a birthday or anniversary. The surprise visits were fun, but they weren't nearly as entertaining as the marriage proposals.

Over the course of my career I helped hundreds of couples get engaged at Arrowhead. It was a privilege to be a part of their special day. I tried to do these proposals during the first quarter because the guy was usually a nervous wreck, and I wanted to take care of the proposal early in the game so he could relax and enjoy the rest of the day. Most guys called me about a month ahead of time to tell me at which Chiefs' game they wanted to propose. However, it wasn't uncommon for a few guys to wait until the last minute. Occasionally, I would receive a call on a Friday afternoon from a guy in a panic saying he wanted to get engaged at Sunday's game. Last minute requests were always more challenging, but I tried to accommodate them whenever I could.

When I got a marriage proposal call, the most important piece of information was the seat location. I had to find out the exact section, row and seats where the guy and his girlfriend would be sitting. Since I had never met these couples, the only way I could find them was by going to their assigned seats. KC Wolf arrived carrying a large sign with the girl's name printed on one side. As I made my way toward their seats, I could usually tell by the look on the girl's face that she had no idea what was about to happen. When I got right next to the girl, I flipped the sign over and the back of the sign read, "Will you marry me?" with the guy's name printed at the bottom. By the time the girl figured out what was going on, the guy was down on one knee with the ring in his hand. What happened next was always very predictable. The girl started to cry, the couple hugged and kissed, and the entire section began to cheer for the newly engaged couple. My assistant handed me a dozen roses to give to the girl and then he would take a picture of KC Wolf with the newly engaged couple. It was always rewarding for me to know we had pulled off the surprise and made their engagement a very memorable experience.

By the time we finished with all of the seat visits and wedding proposals, the game was usually well into the second quarter. I once again dropped by my dressing room for a dry t-shirt and a drink of water or Gatorade. After a short break I would go back down to the sidelines until halftime.

I always looked forward to halftime because I could take an extended break in my dressing room. I changed into dry clothes and hung my first half KC Wolf costume in front of a big fan so it could begin to air out. While I was getting out a dry KC Wolf costume for the second half, my assistant sprayed down the sweaty suit with a special mascot cologne we called "FurBreeze."

I loved the second half of games because my only responsibility was to go out and entertain the crowd. Everything KC Wolf did before halftime was typically scheduled and planned out, but the second half was all spontaneous. My main goal during the second half was not only to entertain the crowd but to also entertain myself. As a mascot I learned if I was having fun in the costume, the crowd was usually enjoying my performance as well. Having fun also made the time go by more quickly.

I not only enjoyed interacting with Chiefs' fans but I learned the opposing teams' fans were also a lot of fun. During a Monday Night Football game against New England one of the Patriots' fans brought a sign which read: "KC Wolf is really Chuck E Cheese." I thought it was hilarious. I walked over, gave him a hug and we had our picture taken together in front of the sign. I used the picture as the screen saver on my computer because it always brought a smile to my face.

One of my favorite pranks to pull on the fans involved a fake spider and a fishing pole. I purchased a large rubber spider with dangly legs from a Halloween store, then took a fishing pole and attached the spider to the fishing line using a binder clip. I sneaked up from behind fans and slowly lowered the spider over the front of their heads. Watching people's reaction when they were being attacked by a rubber spider was hilarious. Judging by the crowd's response I knew Chiefs' fans loved to watch the fake spider terrorize their fellow fans. Women always had the best reaction. Some jumped up and screamed so loud that they would actually scare others who were sitting around them. I had to replace my spider several times because it took a beating from women who were swinging their arms and kicking their feet in an attempt to escape the spider attack. After scaring someone, I would always hug my victim as my way of thanking them for being a good sport.

The rubber spider wasn't the only bait I used to get a laugh with the fishing pole. Sometimes I brought a box of Twinkies to the game to entertain the crowd. I clipped a Twinkie onto my fishing line and went to the upper deck at Arrowhead Stadium. I then lowered the

Twinkie over the edge like I was fishing for the fans in the lower level. I was always amazed at what some fans would do to get a free Twinkie. I dangled the golden sponge cake over their head but still high enough so they would have to jump to get it. As soon as they jumped up to grab the Twinkie, I would pull it higher so it would stay just out of their reach. I personally found it very entertaining watching a chubby guy who had been drinking too much, trying to jump up and grab hold of a free Twinkie. However, after about four or five jumps I started to feel sorry for him and let him have it.

When I realized how much Chiefs' fans loved free Twinkies, I talked to my friends at Hostess about doing a special game day promotion. I bought a Radio Flyer little red wagon and on the side I hung a sign that said "TWINKIE TIME." At the beginning of the fourth quarter I pulled my little Twinkie Time wagon filled with about 300 individually wrapped Twinkies out onto the sidelines. Apparently Chiefs fans were hungry by the fourth quarter because when I threw the Twinkies into the stands, the fans fought for them like they were $100 dollar bills. I entertained myself during Twinkie Time by picking on the guys in the front row who had been drinking too much. I grabbed two Twinkies out of my little red wagon. The first Twinkie I tossed high into the air and when the guy looked up I would drill him in the stomach with the second one. What Chiefs' fans thought was really funny was that I could toss up another Twinkie and the same guy would look up again and I hit him a second time. I have read research that says drinking too much alcohol can kill brain cells, and I'm convinced that research is 100% accurate. I'm sure there were several men who left Arrowhead with welts on their bellies and creamy white filling stuck to their shirts, never knowing what hit them.

The final game of our season was always Fan Appreciation Day. I loved this game because KC Wolf walked around giving away free items. Since the game was usually around Christmas, I would dress KC Wolf up like Santa Claus. The Chiefs filled my Santa sack with hats, t-shirts, music CD's and a variety of other Chiefs goodies. "Santa Wolf" would then roam through the crowd handing out gifts to all good little boys and girls. The gifts were a great way to pull off a prank.

I would find a group of three fans sitting together and reach into my sack. The fans always got excited because they knew they were about to receive a free gift. I gave the first fan a Chiefs hat and the second fan would receive a t-shirt. As the third fan waited with anticipation, I reached deep into my Santa sack and pulled out a jock strap. It was hilarious to watch the look on their face and to listen to the crowd's reaction. I stuck the jock strap back in the sack, gave them a different gift and then headed off to find another victim.

Most of the Chiefs' games that kicked off at noon would usually finish around 3:00 p.m. At the end of the game I celebrated on the sidelines while the players circled up at midfield for prayer. It was encouraging watching players from both teams huddled together, thanking God for a safe competition. It reminded me that players, coaches and even mascots all receive their talents and abilities from God. At the end of the day we needed to stop and thank Him for the privilege of participating in the sport we love.

When I finally got back to my locker room after the game, I hung up the second half KC Wolf suit to dry and put on fresh clothes to travel home. Before leaving Arrowhead, Shawn and I would always stop by the cheerleader's lunch area because we knew there would be leftover food. After filling our bellies, we walked back to my locker room, grabbed our things and headed for the parking lot. After sitting in traffic I usually arrived back home between 4:30-5:00 p.m. By the time I finally pulled into my driveway I felt like I had put in a full day at work.

I quickly showered, got dressed, ate dinner and headed to the Sunday evening service at my church. After returning from church I would try to stay awake so I could watch the Chiefs' highlights on the local news. Running around in the KC Wolf costume made it very difficult to watch the game so I relied on the evening sportscasters to catch me up on the plays of the day. More often than not, I would miss the news because I had fallen asleep on the couch. Before going to bed I took two ibuprofen and shortly after my head hit the pillow I was sound asleep. Yes, Chiefs' game days were very long and exhausting, but they were also filled with plenty of excitement.

Alongside my brother Dave, my mascot career
began as a lion at age four

My family was like fudge – mostly sweet with
a few nuts

During my days as Truman Tiger, my parents were
my biggest cheerleaders

My 'bird legs' were a perfect fit during my time with the St. Louis Cardinals

Being named the 1989 National Collegiate Mascot Champion at Sea World was one of the highlights during my days as Mizzou's Truman Tiger

Ironically, the first NFL football game I performed at was in a Tiger suit at Mile High Stadium

As a college kid, performing at the Maui Classic basketball tournament in Hawaii was a dream come true

Nine months after the Berlin Wall came down, my dad & I visited the site

My granny wasn't sure what to think when I visited her at the nursing home

My first game with the Chiefs was at Olympic Stadium in Berlin, Germany

Under the mask I didn't look nearly so confident with the Chiefs cheerleaders

Children's Mercy hospital visits were always very rewarding

I'm thankful to Chiefs founder and owner Lamar Hunt because without him there would be no Kansas City Chiefs and no KC Wolf.

The inspiration behind my hip shakes.
Me and The King at the Elvis parade in
downtown Kansas City

After 20 years of
marriage my wife
and I started to
look alike

I was all smiles the night Cam said 'Yes'.
KC Wolf helped with the proposal

My roommate had to pose with Cam as
KC Wolf because I didn't want to have a
Bad Hair Day at my wedding

Beauty and the Beast posing with their new baby girl

My favorite Halloween – Trick or Treating with my Three Little Pigs

When I wasn't running around as KC Wolf my favorite place was spending time with my family

A Christmas picture taken with my good friend Sluggerrr, the Kansas City Royals mascot

I loved using my kids in KC Wolf skits. Here we are getting ready to perform a "Gone Fishin" skit against the Miami Dolphins

The pregame skit for the Atlanta Falcons game was a family affair

This picture hangs in my son's bedroom, reminding me that my children watch and imitate how I live my life

KC Wolf makes a dramatic entrance into
Arrowhead with the help of the
Navy Leap Frogs

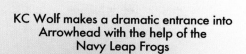

It took several years but I finally got Cam to
perform a KC Wolf skit with me at a Chiefs game

They looked Bad to
the Bone but my
Harley Davidson biker
buddies were very
nice guys

My accountability group makes sure
I'm walking my talk

Elementary school student Andrew Johnson trying on KC Wolf. Years later he became one of my backups.

Dumb and Dumber finishing the Missouri River 340

My raincoat wasn't much help during the Chiefs/Seahawks game in 1998. By the end of the game I felt like a drowned rat.

"Lacey Wolf" and the Lounge Lizards. Occasionally
I would wear a dress to work

The closest thing to Ruby Red Slippers I could find for "Dorothy Wolf"
were my big red Chiefs shoes

My son Aaron joined me as the Dynamic Duo Batman & Robin

One of my all time favorite KC Wolf photos. This picture made the
front page of the Kansas City Star.

It's amazing how much fun you can have with a wagon full of Twinkies

Getting to be a part of the pregame coin toss at midfield was always exciting.

My biggest fear during introductions was tripping a Chiefs player with my big feet.

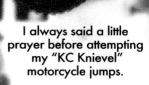
I always said a little prayer before attempting my "KC Knievel" motorcycle jumps.

Cruising through Times Square in New York City on the top of a double decker bus

I wasn't the only one with a large belly in Japan

I met some interesting people at Arrowhead Stadium

Mini Wolf was half my size and half my number

Traveling to the NFL Hall of Fame with the Chiefs cheerleaders was a memorable experience

Receiving the Golden Silly String Award at my induction into the Mascot Hall of Fame

Former Chiefs head coach Hank Stram at his induction into the NFL Hall of Fame

I turned a lot of heads in Jamaica. I'm not sure if it was my hairy chest or my bright red speedo

Making new friends at a Chinese New Year Parade
in Hong Kong

Posing with members of t
Furternity at Aloha Stadiu

The 2013 NFL Mascot Convention at
Lake Louise Inn in Alberta, Canada

Former Chief Tony Gonzalez was one of the greatest
tight ends to ever play the game

Celebrating the wedding of my dear friends
Claud and Jacque Davis

One of my favorite
Chiefs players,
Tony Richardson was
a terrific guy
both on and off
the field

Tony Dungy was one of the classiest coaches and men
I've ever known

This guy was always trying to spoil our fun
at Arrowhead Stadium

Bethany Hamilton was the inspiration behind the movie "Soul Surfer"

Shooting a "Madagascar" movie commercial with actor Ben Stiller

Putting on my size 23 KC Wolf shoes before a game

Dressing up as Alex the Lion allowed me to meet several celebrities, including actor Will Smith

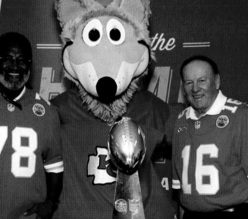

Posing alongside the Superbowl trophy with Chiefs legends Len Dawson and Bobby Bell

Cleveland Browns mascot Chomps and I were two HOT Dogs in the Hawaii sun

Chiefs employees put a lot of love and hard work into building this playground following the devastating Joplin tornado

Appearing with Shaquille O'Neil and Nick Cannon at the Cartoon Network Hall of Game Awards in Los Angeles

Riding on a zip line at Arrowhead Stadium was a thrilling experience

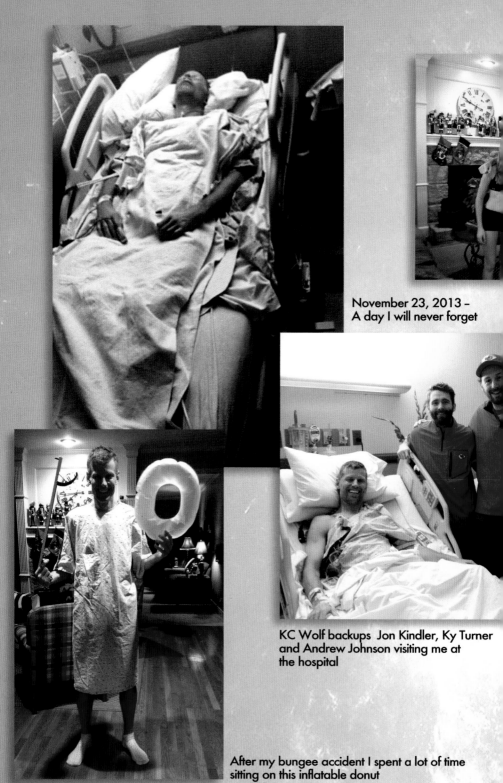

November 23, 2013 –
A day I will never forget

KC Wolf backups Jon Kindler, Ky Turner
and Andrew Johnson visiting me at
the hospital

After my bungee accident I spent a lot of time
sitting on this inflatable donut

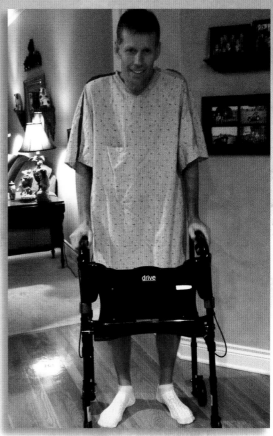

Wearing a back brace and my new Superman boxers, I was able to compete in the 2013 Frozen Bun Fun Run

I never dreamed I would need a walker at age 46

My good friend Blue sent me a Get Well message on national TV during the Chiefs/ Colts playoff game

It was great
to be back at work
after six months
of therapy

My first game back was the start of my 25th season

My greatest passions in life are my faith
and my family

10

Travels

"The world is a book and those who do not travel read only one page."
Augustine of Hippo

I loved to travel, and I enjoyed it even more when someone else was paying my expenses. When the NFL began promoting their games overseas, I was excited because it meant I would get to travel to some very interesting locations. Working as KC Wolf provided me many opportunities to travel abroad and visit places I probably never would have had the chance to see. Some of my most memorable games and appearances were outside the United States, starting with my first Chiefs' game in Berlin, Germany back in 1990.

The Chiefs played their second American Bowl game on August 6, 1994. We traveled to Tokyo, Japan to take on the Minnesota Vikings in a preseason game. The game was played at the Tokyo Dome. My dad had traveled with me to Berlin, but he was very disappointed about the Japan trip. Since Cam and I had married in June 1993, and I was only allowed to bring one guest, she joined me in Tokyo and dad stayed at home.

When we left, Cam and I had our personal luggage and the KC Wolf costume. There was never an easy way to travel with KC Wolf so I would pack him into a huge, black, oversize bag and label it FRAGILE. The costume wasn't exactly fragile, but I thought it might help KC Wolf get better treatment when they were tossing the luggage around in the belly of the plane. Getting into the airport was a challenge because I always had twice as much to carry as everyone else. KC Wolf was like traveling with a small child. I had to carry him everywhere I went. Thankfully I could check him in with our suitcases.

For the Japan trip we parked our car at Arrowhead and rode a chartered bus to the airport with the Chiefs' cheerleaders. The bus ride was extremely loud. I couldn't tell if it was because everyone was excited about going to Japan or because I was riding with a bus load of women. I decided it was probably a combination of the two.

The flight to Japan took 17 hours, and I was thankful to sit next to my wife instead of a Chiefs' player. The football players were very nice guys, but they also took up a lot of room. Punters and kickers weren't bad, but if I got stuck sitting next to an offensive or defensive lineman they usually filled up their seat and also spilled over into mine. I actually felt sorry for some of the guys because I knew they had to be uncomfortable. We flew on a Japanese Air Lines (JAL) Boeing 747 Sky Cruiser. It was the first time I had ever flown on an airplane with two separate levels of seating. Most of the Chiefs' players and coaches sat in the upper level, and the cheerleaders and staff rode downstairs. The Chiefs' management liked to keep the players and cheerleaders separated for obvious reasons.

On the flight I still remember flying over Alaska and seeing the snow covered mountains; it was the first time I had ever seen snow in August. I also remember eating a lot of food on the flight. Professional football players like to eat so whenever I traveled with the Chiefs I never had to worry about going hungry. As soon as one meal was over, the flight attendants were putting another in front of me.

When we arrived in Tokyo, we loaded onto several buses at the airport and drove to the New Otani Hotel. A large crowd was waiting to greet us. The Chiefs' starting quarterback was Joe Montana, and he was definitely one of the crowd favorites. Even though we were all tired from jet lag, we tried to stay awake until evening so our bodies could adjust better to the time change.

Cam and I went up to our hotel room, unpacked our luggage, and took a walk around the streets of Tokyo to help us wake up. We invited Mike and Debbie Lusardi to go along with us. Mike was the Chiefs' chaplain and I figured if we got lost, he would be a good man to have along. After walking for a while, we decided to attempt the Tokyo subway system. I was a little nervous because I couldn't read the name of the streets at the subway station. Every letter of the Japanese alphabet looked the same to me, but I figured even if we got lost, we could always take a taxi back to the hotel. I had grabbed a brochure for the New Otani Hotel and made sure the address was clearly printed on it. I kept the brochure in my pocket just in case.

I considered our first adventure on the Tokyo subway system a huge success. We didn't get lost, and we managed to find our way back to the hotel. Although the streets of Tokyo were very crowded, Cam had an easy time keeping track of me. Most of the Japanese people were short and had dark hair. Since I was 6-foot-3 with blonde hair, I was easy to spot in a crowd.

Cam and I slept very well that first evening, and the next morning the Chiefs arranged for some local tour guides to show us around the city. It was nice to have someone who could explain to us in English what we were seeing. They split us up into several smaller groups and loaded us onto charter buses. We had a great time visiting the Imperial Palace, a Buddhist temple and the local market area. I sampled seaweed at the market and quickly decided American salad bars were much better. When we stopped to use the bathroom, I received quite a surprise. I walked in expecting to find a toilet to sit on and instead was introduced to the Japanese squat toilet. These squat toilets looked more like a porcelain hole in the ground and were a real culture shock for me. After seeing one, I decided to wait until I could find a more traditional toilet. We finished our tour by eating lunch, visiting a Shinto temple and taking a ride on rickshaws through the streets of downtown Tokyo.

As KC Wolf, I attended the American Bowl press conference, along with the cheerleaders and players. Being there was a lot of fun because the Japanese people loved mascots. I posed for lots of pictures with Ragnar, the mascot for the Minnesota Vikings. After the press conference they transported us to the Chiefs and Vikings practice session for another appearance. Making appearances and posing for pictures consumed a large portion of my time in Japan. My favorite picture from the trip was a photo my wife took of two HUGE Sumo wrestlers with KC Wolf. It amazed me that their bellies looked similar to KC Wolf's without the fur.

On Saturday, our final day in Tokyo, we got up very early and made a trip to the Tsukiji Fish Market. This market was filled with thousands of fish, and there were people everywhere. It was fascinating to watch the local fishermen selling their catch. I spent most of my time walking around trying to hold my breath because the smell at the fish market was terrible. I'm sure it was the smell of money to the fishermen, but not to me.

The American Bowl game was a memorable experience. For my pregame skit I drove out on a four-wheeler and tackled a guy dressed in a Minnesota Vikings' jersey. The Japanese fans erupted with applause and laughter. I could tell I was going to enjoy performing for such an enthusiastic crowd. Once again I spent much of my time during the game walking around in the crowd, posing for pictures. The Japanese fans all seemed to have personal cameras, and they loved to take pictures. Although baseball was definitely the most popular sport in Japan, the fans appeared to enjoy their introduction to NFL football. The Chiefs ended up losing to the Vikings 19-7, but it was a preseason game so nobody seemed too upset. After the game I packed a sweaty KC Wolf costume into the large black travel bag, and our group headed for the airport. The trip back to Kansas City seemed to go by much more quickly because, exhausted from the game, I slept most of the flight home.

Two years after our trip to Tokyo, the Chiefs played in another American Bowl game in Monterrey, Mexico. The game was a Monday Night Football preseason contest against the Dallas Cowboys, and it was televised back in the United States. In 1994, Dallas had played the Houston Oilers in Mexico City's Aztec Stadium with 112,000 in attendance. This game was being played in Monterrey as part of the city's 400th anniversary, but unfortunately, the local stadium held only 45,000.

Once again, the Chiefs were very generous and allowed me to bring Cam along on the trip. I found it interesting when I asked Cam to go on a trip with me to western Kansas or southern Missouri for an appearance, her answer was usually no. However, when I asked if she wanted to travel overseas or to the Pro Bowl in Hawaii, she was always quick to accept the invitation. Our daughter Mycah was only four months old at the time, so we asked grandma and grandpa to help with babysitting during our trip.

When we arrived in Mexico, I quickly realized I needed to stay well hydrated. Mexico was a tough place to be a mascot in the month of August. The temperatures were extremely hot and even the Chiefs' guests not wearing a furry costume were miserable. I had been warned several times not to drink the water, so the Chiefs made sure I was supplied with a large amount of bottled water.

While in Mexico we toured some beautiful cathedrals and visited several local markets. Instead of eating seaweed and sushi like I had in Japan, I enjoyed tacos and burritos in Mexico. I also felt more at home on this trip because the Mexican toilets looked just like the ones we used in Kansas City. The Mexican people were very laid back, and I enjoyed their relaxed lifestyle.

On the second day of our trip we loaded our tour buses and traveled up into the mountains to eat lunch and see a beautiful waterfall. On our way back we stopped at the Plaza de Toros—San Felipe. This was a bullring arena where we were given a bullfighting exhibition. Thankfully we got the tame version, and the bull wasn't actually hurt during the battle. The highlight of the exhibition was when Chiefs' defensive end Neil Smith volunteered to get into the ring and serve as the matador. His antics were very entertaining, and Neil looked really brave until the bull started running toward him. Neil had more guts than me because I wasn't about to step into the ring.

On Sunday evening we were treated to an incredible Mexican fiesta. The food and entertainment were always first class. The authentic Mexican food was delicious and we enjoyed sitting back and listening to the Mariachi band play. We also enjoyed watching the entertainers with big sombreros perform the Mexican hat dance.

Twenty four hours later, I was the one doing the dancing at the football game. I was excited because I knew the game was televised on Monday Night Football. I had extended family members all over the United States watching the game. I told each family member that if I waved at the camera and wiggled my belly, I was doing it just for them. What I didn't tell them was I had also told a hundred other people the same thing.

During the game I soon realized that 95% of the fans were cheering for the Dallas Cowboys. Texas was closer to Mexico than Missouri, so the Cowboys definitely had the most crowd support. Thankfully, the fans seemed to like KC Wolf even though I was wearing a Chiefs' jersey.

The game in Monterrey was by far the hottest game of the season. The Chiefs played great and won the game 32-6. After the game a happy group of Chiefs' players, staff and guests loaded onto an air conditioned airplane for a very late flight back home.

Apparently someone in the NFL league offices liked the Chiefs because in 1998 the Chiefs returned to Tokyo for another American Bowl game against the Green Bay Packers. We were only going to be staying in Tokyo for a few days, so other than some of our sponsors, the Chiefs only took players, coaches and certain staff members along on this trip. No guests allowed. Of course Cam was disappointed because she was now going to be home with a two-and-a-half year old and a six-month old while I was hanging out in Japan. I promised to bring her a souvenir, but she still thought I was getting the better end of the deal. I agreed.

The funniest memory from this trip occurred when we arrived at the airport in Tokyo. After getting off the airplane, we were instructed to load onto chartered buses which would take us to the hotel. As I was walking toward the bus, I found myself surrounded by a group of fans taking my picture and wanting me to autograph footballs and other items. Many of the Japanese fans who had gathered to welcome the Chiefs thought I was one of the football players.

As I was going to breakfast the next morning my boss handed me a copy of a Tokyo newspaper written in English. I knew something was up because when he handed me the paper he had a huge smile on his face. When I opened it, there was a picture of me surrounded by a group of Japanese fans. The caption under the photo was the best part. It read: "Chiefs' quarterback Elvis Grbac shares a smile with a Japanese fan while signing his autograph on a football at Narita International Airport." The Chiefs' staff found it very amusing that I was mistaken for Elvis Grbac. I told my boss I wished the Chiefs would get Elvis and I confused the next time they handed out paychecks as I was pretty sure the starting quarterback for the Chiefs was getting paid more than the starting mascot.

From our previous trip I knew how much the Japanese people loved mascots and how they were fascinated with cameras, so I brought along a special prop for the game. I found an old Polaroid camera that was hollowed out and was designed to shoot silly string, the perfect prop to pull a practical joke on the Japanese fans. I walked around in the stands letting the fans take my picture. After they took my picture, I motioned for a group of Japanese fans to get together so KC Wolf could take their picture. As soon as they were all huddled together and smiling, I got up really close and surprised them by spraying them down with silly string. The fans loved it, and I also got a good laugh. I don't know if I have ever performed for a group that was more appreciative than the fans in Japan. The Chiefs ended up losing to the Packers 27-24 in overtime. Once again we hopped on the plane and made the long trip back to Kansas City. We were 0-2 in games played in Japan, but at least we were undefeated in Mexico.

Another exciting Chiefs' trip was much closer to home. We traveled to Canton, Ohio, on August 1-4, 2003. Hank Stram and Marcus Allen were both being inducted into the NFL Pro Football Hall of Fame. KC Wolf and the Chiefs' cheerleaders were invited to take part in the festivities. Cam and I had been married for 10 years, and apparently, she trusted me because I was traveling with a group of all females. There were 36 Chiefs' cheerleaders, the cheerleader director and her assistant, plus two makeup/hair stylists and me. When you added it up I was outnumbered 40:1. I was smart enough to know that if I was surrounded by 40 females I was just going to quietly sit back and go with the flow.

One of the reasons I was looking forward to this trip was because it was the 40th anniversary of the NFL Hall of Fame. All of the living Hall of Fame members had been invited back to take part in the ceremony. It would be a great opportunity to see many of the great football players I had grown up watching as a kid.

We flew into Cleveland on Friday evening and took a bus to our hotel in Canton. Since I was the only male traveling with the cheerleaders, I had a room all to myself. Saturday was the NFL Hall of Fame Parade, and KC Wolf rode in a convertible with one of the Chiefs' cheerleaders. When the parade was finished, I changed back into my regular clothes, and we toured the NFL Hall of Fame building. I spent several hours walking around looking at the displays and reading the history of the National Football League. Since I had grown up loving football, this building with all its history was a fascinating place for me. While I could have spent several more hours looking at all of the exhibits, the cheerleaders were ready to go. Since I was significantly outnumbered, I decided it wouldn't be a good idea to make a fuss.

The enshrinement ceremony took place on Sunday afternoon. I was excited to attend the ceremony without having to wear the KC Wolf costume. This meant I would be free to carry my camera and take pictures of all the Hall of Famers. I purchased an NFL Hall of Fame miniature football helmet at the gift shop and carried it with me, along with a sharpie marker. My goal was to get a couple of autographs on the helmet. There were 115 "Homecoming" Hall of Famers in attendance. It was hard to contain my excitement. There was only one other person who could truly appreciate how meaningful this day was for me, and that was my brother Dave. We had grown up together watching these football players so I called him to tell him how much fun I was having.

About an hour before the ceremony, God sent an unexpected blessing my way. The sky opened up, and heavy rain began to fall. Since the ceremony was outside, when it started to rain many of the Hall of Fame members were escorted into the basement of the Hall of Fame to stay dry. Since I was with 36 Chiefs' cheerleaders who were trying to keep their hair from getting wet, I was also escorted into the basement. I sat there for about five minutes before I realized I had a great opportunity; I was stuck in the basement with every living member of the NFL Hall of Fame. I had my camera, along with my miniature football helmet and a sharpie. I put a smile on my face and started introducing myself to some of the greatest players to ever play in the NFL. By the time the rain stopped I had managed to squeeze 15 autographs onto my miniature helmet. My biggest disappointment was not spending the extra money to buy a full size helmet because I could have gotten many more autographs.

My NFL Hall of Fame helmet is one of my most prized possessions. I received autographs from Hall of Famers Joe Namath, Mean Joe Greene, Bob Griese, Don Shula, Bobby Bell, Billy Shaw, Mike Ditka, Ken Houston, Gale Sayers, Steve Van Buren, Merlin Olsen, Dan Fouts, Don Maynard, Mel Blount and Art Shell. I have never been so thankful for a rainstorm in my entire life.

The next day the Chiefs played the Green Bay Packers in the Monday Night Football Hall of Fame game. Once again it started pouring down rain, but I wasn't nearly as thankful this time because I was running around in the KC Wolf costume. It was a miserable night to be a mascot. I found it ironic that the game was played at

Fawcett Stadium because the rain felt like it was coming from a faucet. With 5:49 remaining in the third quarter, the game ended due to severe lightning, with the Chiefs ahead 9-0. After the game I loaded a very soggy KC Wolf back into his travel bag and headed to the airport for another late night trip back to Kansas City.

It was a trip I will never forget. I had traveled with 40 women, gotten autographs from 15 of my NFL Hall of Fame heroes, and just about drowned in a wolf suit on Monday Night Football. Life doesn't get any more exciting.

In May 2009 I took another trip with the Chiefs' cheerleaders. I almost felt guilty because it was such a relaxing work trip. The Chiefs' cheerleaders went to Jamaica to shoot the Chiefs cheerleader calendar. I went along because while they were in Jamaica, the Chiefs' video department wanted to shoot a video skit of KC Wolf hanging out on the beach. It was a four-day trip to paradise and while there I spent less than four hours in my costume. The rest of the time I spent by myself lying on the beach at an all-inclusive resort. While the cheerleaders were out shooting their calendar pictures, I was back at the hotel relaxing in the sun. Jamaica is the most laid back place I have ever visited. I would love to return and shoot more video skits on that beautiful island.

I didn't always get to stay at all-inclusive resorts and first class hotels when I traveled. On one of my trips to northern Iowa to speak at schools, I could only find one motel in the town. After checking in, I walked into my room and noticed a sign hanging over the bathroom sink that read: "Please don't clean your birds in our sink." Apparently the pheasant hunters who visited that area had a bad habit of bringing their dead birds back to the motel. I could tell right away that I wasn't staying at the Ritz-Carlton.

One of the most exhilarating trips I took was a short eight mile journey from Arrowhead to south Kansas City. What made this trip so thrilling was I traveled in a hot air balloon. The Chiefs were celebrating Red Friday and decided KC Wolf floating in a hot air balloon, waving to people during morning rush hour, was a great way to kick off the day. It was an incredible experience which I was able to mark off my bucket list. Many of my coworkers wanted to join me on the ride but, unfortunately, since KC Wolf has 85 inch hips, there was only enough room in the basket for me and the balloon's pilot.

During my mascot career I received several trophies and awards. The three trophies I received as Truman Tiger at the National Collegiate Mascot Championships were very meaningful. However, I received my most satisfying mascot award on August 15, 2006 on a trip to Philadelphia, Pennsylvania. The Mascot Hall of Fame committee nominated six mascots for potential induction. KC Wolf was one of them. There was a 30 day online voting period. At the end of the 30 days, the three mascots who had received the most votes would fly to Philadelphia for induction into the Mascot Hall of Fame. The Hall of Fame had begun in 2005, and the inaugural induction class included the Famous Chicken, the Phillie Phanatic and the Phoenix Suns Gorilla.

When I called my mom and dad to tell them about the contest, my mom took it upon herself to make sure I got enough votes to win. She comes from a large family, and before I knew it she had my aunts, uncles and cousins logging onto their computers and voting for me each day. She also recruited her friends and coworkers to vote for me. I felt like a politician with my mom as the world's greatest campaign manager. One month later I got a call congratulating me on being selected for the Hall of Fame, along with Clutch the Bear (Houston Rockets) and The Jazz Bear (Utah Jazz). I felt honored to be selected as the first NFL mascot inducted into the Mascot Hall of Fame.

The induction ceremony was held at Love Park in Philadelphia. About 50 other mascots, all dressed in costume, were there to cheer as we received our award. The trophy they presented to the inductees was called The Golden Silly String Award, and I still have it proudly displayed on my book shelf at home. My mom probably deserves the trophy more than I do, because without her help I never would have received enough votes for induction. She screamed when I won the National Collegiate Mascot Championship in 1989, and she screamed again 17 years later, when I was inducted in the Mascot Hall of Fame.

I was proud of my accomplishments as a mascot because I had worked very hard to achieve them. The trophies and awards were nice, and the trips I took were always a lot of fun, but the people I met along the way were what made being a mascot most rewarding.

11
Friends, Celebrities and the "Furternity"

"Our greatest wealth is not measured in terms of riches but relationships."

The quote above describes perfectly the greatest benefit and blessing of being a professional mascot. I'm sure there were other careers I could have pursued which would have paid more money, but very few occupations provide such a wonderful opportunity to develop so many lifelong friendships. The most rewarding part of my job as a mascot wasn't the travels, the trips or the trophies but the friendships I developed over the years.

Two of those friends were Claud and Jacque Davis. I first met Claud when he called me at Arrowhead Stadium. Claud was 59 years old and had fallen in love with his sweetheart Jacque Massey. I can't mention how old Jacque was because I would get in big trouble. Claud wanted to propose to Jacque the next evening at the Hereford House restaurant in Leawood, Kansas. Jacque was a huge KC Wolf fan, so Claud devised a plan to have me help with the engagement. He had arranged with the restaurant manager to reserve a booth near the front door at Hereford House. Claud left the engagement ring with the manager, and when I arrived the manager gave me the ring before I dressed as KC Wolf. Claud told me that he would be the older, chubby, bald man sitting in the booth near the front door. Since I had never met Claud, I had the restaurant manager quietly point him out in case I rounded the corner and found two chubby, bald guys staring at me.

I changed into KC Wolf in the back of the restaurant and walked around to the front, holding tightly onto the ring. When I came busting through the front door at the Hereford House and sat down next to Jacque, the look on her face was priceless. Her excitement grew even greater when I handed her the small box containing the ring. When Claud got down on one knee and proposed, it was easy to see that Jacque was one of the happiest women in Kansas City.

Six months later Jacque called to ask if KC Wolf would be part of their wedding day. Jacque's father had passed away years earlier, and she wanted me to walk her down the aisle and give her away to Claud. I told her it would be an honor. This would be the first time I helped a couple get engaged and then also played a part in their wedding ceremony.

The wedding was held on May 6, 2000, exactly one year and one day after the engagement. Claud and Jacque's wedding was one of the most unique and fun weddings I have ever attended. It was an outdoor wedding in Paola, Kansas, and they set it up like a Chiefs' game day experience.

As the wedding guests arrived, parking lot attendants directed them to their parking spots. The guests were then escorted to their seats by ushers who were walking around handing out peanuts and popcorn. For those wedding guests who were thirsty before the ceremony there was a beer/soda vendor dressed in a striped referee jersey handing out drinks. Another usher walked through the crowd yelling, "Program, get your program here." This activity all took place before the wedding began.

Since my appearance was a surprise to the wedding guests, Jacque and I stayed hidden in a building on top of a hill where the crowd couldn't see us. The DJ began playing the Chiefs' fight song, our cue to come running out. Jacque and I came breaking through a large paper Chiefs banner like one sees at a high school football game. The crowd was stunned to see KC Wolf escorting Jacque down the aisle. We slapped high fives with the wedding guests as we made our way up to the front.

Claud and the minister were waiting at the end of the aisle underneath a goal post that Claud had constructed out of PVC pipe. The wedding party consisted of Claud and Jacque's nieces, nephews and grandkids. The little bridesmaids were dressed as Chiefs' cheerleaders and the groomsmen (groomsboys) were dressed in Chiefs shirts. The only adults in the wedding ceremony were Claud, Jacque, the minister and KC Wolf. As soon as the minister pronounced the happy couple as man and wife, Claud kissed Jacque and fireworks exploded overhead.

The local Paola newspaper printed a full page story filled with wedding photos. For a wedding present, I wrapped up one of my old KC Wolf shoes. On the toe of the shoe I wrote: "To Claud and Jacque, Thanks for letting me be in your wedding! What a special day. I pray that God gives you many happy years together. KC Wolf."

After their honeymoon, Claud and Jacque sent a note to Lamar Hunt thanking him for letting KC Wolf be a part of their wedding. They were shocked when they received a letter back from Lamar. It didn't surprise me at all. Lamar Hunt was that kind of man.

Claud and Jacque's wedding was an unforgettable day. It stands out as one of the most enjoyable appearances of my life. Claud and Jacque were just two of many dear friends I made during my career.

I had another memorable wedding experience in July 2011, when I participated in the Krause wedding in Independence, Missouri. This one was a small wedding in which I played two different roles. When the bridal march began, I escorted the bride down the center aisle of the church while all the guests stood. When we reached the front of the sanctuary, the minister asked, "Who gives this woman to be married to this man?" Since KC Wolf does not speak in costume I just raised my hand. At that point the groom took the hand of the bride, and I stepped over and became the best man for the remainder of the wedding.

After the ceremony the bride and groom walked down the aisle, followed by KC Wolf and the maid of honor. At the back of the church the bride, groom and KC Wolf took pictures with each of the wedding guests as they left the church. Once again it was a day I will never forget, not only because of the friendships I made, but also because I received a speeding ticket on my way home. I never realized how many speeding tickets I've had during my career until I started writing this book.

Another friendship I developed was with a Missouri Highway Patrolman named Kyle Cullifer. As you can probably tell by now, most of the patrolmen I met during my mascot days introduced themselves by asking to see my driver's license and vehicle registration, but Kyle was different. I met Kyle in Macon, Missouri, at an elementary school where I spoke. Kyle knew I was a Christian and invited me to be the speaker at the Crossroads Christian Church annual Wild Game Feed.

Macon is a small community, but that evening there were about 500 people in attendance. I found it humorous that the room was filled with hunters and sportsmen, and the committee asked a Wolf to be the guest speaker. As a joke I wore a bright orange vest over my Chiefs' jersey to make sure I didn't get shot.

Whenever I spoke at banquets I would often get invited to stick around and eat dinner afterwards. I ate at hundreds of banquets, but the Wild Game Dinner in Macon had the most unique menu. Smoked bear, fried pheasant, elk meatballs, fried alligator, duck jambalaya, buffalo meatloaf, grilled deer, frog legs, spoonbill, and turkey fries were just a few of the meats on the menu. Emu was the mystery meat for the evening. I had no idea what turkey fries were so I asked a committee member. With a big smile on his face, he leaned over to inform me that turkey fries come from male turkeys. He said they are like Rocky Mountain Oysters, just on a smaller scale. Since I had already eaten several, I quickly lost my appetite and decided to just stick with dessert.

Kyle and I are still close friends. Occasionally, we go out to lunch when I have appearances near Macon. Whenever we have lunch, I make sure we eat at BBQ restaurants that serve beef and pork. Kyle knows the only fries this Wolf will eat are french fries.

Claud and Jacque Davis, the Krause family and Kyle Cullifer are just a few of the friends I have made at some very interesting appearances. It has been fun to have such a wide variety of friends scattered all over the country and occasionally reconnect with them during my KC Wolf travels.

The old saying is true: "A friend is someone who thinks you're a good egg even though you're slightly cracked." I am thankful for the many friends who love and accept me despite my imperfections.

During my time as KC Wolf I also had an opportunity to meet some famous folks. Some of these were athletes and coaches who became even more popular after I knew them. Bill Cowher, Tony Dungy and Mike McCarthy were former assistant coaches for the Chiefs under Marty Shottenheimer, men who were all hired later as NFL head coaches and went on to win Super Bowls.

During the 1996 season, when Mike McCarthy was the quarterback's coach for the Chiefs, he asked me to make an appearance at his daughter's birthday party. It was a fun party even though a few of the young birthday guests were afraid of the Wolf. Fortunately Mike's daughter was not one of them, and she was thrilled to have KC Wolf as her special party guest. I hadn't seen Mike for several years, but I crossed paths with him and his family at the 2012 Pro Bowl. Mike introduced me to his daughter who was now in college. When she realized who I was we had a good laugh reminiscing about her party.

The Pro Bowl was also a good place to meet both former and current NFL players. Over the years I posed for photos with Peyton Manning, Aaron Rodgers, Matt Hasselbeck, John Lynch, Warren Moon, Tony Gonzalez, Trent Green, Tony Richardson, Will Shields, Harry Carson and many other NFL greats.

My favorite Pro Bowl picture is from 2012, and it wasn't even taken with a football player. The NFL invited Bethany Hamilton to speak at the NFL sponsored luau. Bethany was a professional surfer who is known for surviving a shark attack in which she lost her left arm. Her story was the inspiration behind the movie *"Soul Surfer."* Bethany shared a very inspirational message at the luau, stressing the importance her faith and her family had played on her road to recovery. I didn't know it at the time, but less than two years later, I would be the one relying on faith and family to help with my recovery. When she finished speaking there was a long line of football players and mascots waiting to have their picture taken with this amazing Christian woman. I was one of them.

In February 2013, I had my picture taken with the tallest celebrity I've ever met, with the biggest feet I've ever seen. The Cartoon Network invited KC Wolf to participate in the *Hall of Game Awards* in Los Angeles. I competed against three other professional mascots for the "Most Awesome Mascot Award." The host for this televised *Hall of Game Awards* show was Shaquille O'Neal, who was 7-foot-1 and weighed 325 pounds during his NBA playing days. When I met Shaquille, it was obvious that he hadn't shrunk, and I was amazed at his size 23 tennis shoes. Shaq was the only person I ever met who had the same size shoe as KC Wolf.

During my travels I met such a wide variety of athletes, musicians, celebrities and movie stars that I began to keep a Famous Folks photo album, an album filled with my photos with famous people. My list of famous folks in the album included: Lynn Swann, Papa John, Curly Neil, Billy Ray Cyrus, Bo Diddley, David Cook, George Brett, Will Smith, Ben Stiller and many more.

In 2009, I shot a television commercial with Ben Stiller, but I wasn't dressed as KC Wolf. I received a call from DreamWorks Animation asking if I would dress up as Alex the Lion from the movie *"Madagascar."* Ben Stiller was the voice of Alex the Lion, but a mascot was needed to wear the costume. Since the commercial was being shot at a Walmart in Bentonville, Arkansas, they were looking for a professional mascot from the Midwest to fill the role. Since Kansas City is only a four hour drive from Bentonville, I was asked to make the trip.

My kids owned the *"Madagascar"* animated movie so I watched it several times to get an idea of the personality and mannerisms of Alex the Lion. I figured if I was going to dress up like Alex, I wanted to do it right. I felt like a football player studying film before a big game. I drove down to Bentonville and met Ben Stiller in the Walmart employee break room before the video shoot began.

Filming took several hours, but the commercial shoot was a lot of fun, and Ben Stiller was great to work with. I brought along DVD's of *"Madagascar"* and the movie *"Night at the Museum,"* which Ben autographed for my kids. When I returned home, my kids thought it was really cool that Dad had hung out with a "real live movie star" for the day.

Alex the Lion was also my ticket to getting a picture with movie star Will Smith. DreamWorks Animation once again hired me to dress up as Alex the Lion at a Walmart convention held at Bartle Hall in downtown Kansas City. DreamWorks was at the convention to promote the *"Madagascar"* movie, which had just been released on DVD. Will Smith was in town, along with his wife, Jada Pinkett Smith, who was the voice of Gloria the Hippopotamus in the movie. In my Famous Folks photo album I have a great picture of me dressed as Alex the Lion standing alongside Will Smith and the four penguin characters from *"Madagascar."* I had a great time at the

Walmart convention, and once again I walked away smiling because I was getting paid to have fun.

Apparently the people at DreamWorks Animation liked my work because after appearing as Alex the Lion, I received another call the following year to appear at the same convention dressed as Shrek the green ogre. I was beginning to feel like a real animated movie star. I appeared on stage with Jeffrey Katzenberg, who had cofounded DreamWorks with Steven Spielberg. Once again I dove into my kids' movie collection and watched both *"Shrek"* movies to study the big green ogre's personality and mannerisms.

As soon as I put on the Shrek outfit, I could immediately tell it was the nicest and most expensive mascot costume I had ever worn. The costume was in such great condition I almost felt bad sweating in it. Shrek was also different from other costumes because he had no eyeholes to allow the wearer to see. DreamWorks had the costume designed with small video cameras mounted inside each of Shrek's eyeballs. Inside of the costume was a small video monitor I watched to see what was in front of me. Everything was fine as long as no one covered up Shrek's eyes. If that happened, the video monitor inside the costume went completely black. Since the monitor served as my eyes to the outside world, it took me a while to get comfortable using it. Eventually, I got the hang of it and over the next three days of the convention I posed for thousands of pictures. Shrek was definitely the most popular costume character I had ever worn.

Since I was a full-time NFL mascot, the majority of my photo albums are filled with pictures of other members of the "Furternity." The Furternity was the name given to anyone who dressed up in fur and made a living being a mascot. The more familiar term, fraternity, comes from the Latin word "frater" meaning "brother." To a mascot, the Furternity was a brotherhood of other guys who knew both the joys and the challenges of wearing a costume.

Although I knew other professional mascots from the NBA, NHL and MLB, the Furternity brothers with whom I was closest were my fellow NFL mascots. I have never been around a more fun group of guys both in and out of costume. I usually saw my NFL Furternity brothers a couple times each year. Once a year we got together for an NFL mascot convention held in a variety of locations. Believe it or not, these conventions were very helpful because I usually came away from them with several good ideas to implement with the KC Wolf program. Any time that many creative guys were together in the same room for a brainstorming session, I could walk away with several skit ideas for the next season.

In 2002, our mascot convention was held in New York City. Our meetings were held at the NFL offices on Park Avenue, but we also planned other events to help promote our visit to the Big Apple. Our brief appearance at the MTV studios ended up getting nationwide coverage as we all danced around on the set dressed in our costumes. The other appearance that gained local attention was our trip through Times Square. Our group arranged for a double decker New York sightseeing bus to pick us up and drive us through the heart of the city. Even New Yorkers seemed surprised to see a bus filled with NFL mascots driving through the middle of Times Square.

In 2006, I had an opportunity to travel to Hong Kong with five of my NFL Furternity brothers. We were invited by the Hong Kong Tourism Board to participate in a Chinese New Year parade. I've never been involved in a more exciting parade with people from all over the world participating. Before I suited up as KC Wolf, I walked around and had my picture taken with people from about 25 different countries. We all spoke different languages, but I was quickly reminded that everyone smiles in the same language. A simple smile communicates friendship no matter where you live.

One day during our trip we ate lunch at a small Chinese restaurant that didn't have pictures on the menu. This presented a small problem because no one in our group could read Chinese. Since mascots are risk takers by nature, we decided to each just point at something on the menu. The deal was no matter what the mystery dish was on the plate, you had to eat at least three bites. When the meal was delivered, everyone else was relieved to get a plate filled with rice and topped with either beef, pork or chicken. I wasn't so lucky. My meal arrived in a bowl and it looked like "Fish Ball" soup. From what we could tell it was made of ground up fish, bones and all, patted into fishy meatballs, and tossed into a soup broth. I gagged down three bites and then walked across the street to Burger King and ordered a Whopper.

My all-time favorite NFL Mascot convention was at Lake Louise in Alberta, Canada in 2013. The local hotel and ski resort agreed to host our conference if the NFL mascots would compete against each other in a mascot ski race. They wanted to use the video footage from the race to promote their ski resort. The NFL Furternity saw it as a great opportunity to have our convention in a fun location.

Mascots always have a hard time sitting still for more than a few hours, so our conventions usually consisted of meetings for half the day and then play time for the remainder of the day. We spent our first day in Canada having meetings until noon and then going out to the ski slopes. Some mascots like Miles, the horse from the Denver Broncos, had an advantage because they lived near the mountains and snow skied on a regular basis. Other mascots, like Swoop from the Philadelphia Eagles, Rampage from the St Louis Rams, and TD from the Miami Dolphins hadn't seen a snow covered mountain in years. We all decided that a half day of skiing without costumes was probably a good idea before the race.

Day two of the convention was race day. We arrived at the ski resort, dressed in our costumes and headed up the mountain. The competition was a short downhill run on a green slope. It was a head-to-head competition, with the winner advancing to the next round and the loser being eliminated. My first round opponent was T-Rac from the Tennessee Titans. Even though he beat me down the hill, T-Rac had failed to maneuver around the slalom flags set up on the course so KC Wolf won by disqualification.

My second round opponent was Toro from the Houston Texans. Toro was from a southern state with no snow covered mountains, but I quickly learned he hadn't grown up in Texas and had snow skied often as a kid. When the gun sounded, I got off to a fast start, but half way down the mountain I wiped out, and Toro raced past me for the victory. When the 2013 NFL Mascot Ski Race competition was finally over, Freddie Falcon from the Atlanta Falcons had won the gold medal.

Snow skiing in Canada with the Furternity was great fun, but snorkeling together in Hawaii wasn't bad either. One of the big advantages of being an NFL mascot was that the Pro Bowl was almost always played in Honolulu. I attended eight Pro Bowls during my career, and seven out of the eight were in Hawaii. The only exception was the 2010 Pro Bowl, held in Miami, Florida.

The NFL mascots typically stayed at the Hilton Hawaiian Village in Honolulu for the Pro Bowl, which was located right on Waikiki Beach. The mascots had two large passenger vans we used to travel to our appearances all over the island of Oahu. Throughout the week we made appearances at army bases, schools, hospitals and several other events.

Each time I attended a Pro Bowl we worked hard, but the NFL Furternity also found time to enjoy the island. When we weren't doing appearances, we were either relaxing on the beach or sightseeing somewhere on the island. We visited the USS Arizona Memorial in Pearl Harbor, the Dole pineapple plantation, North Shore and Diamond Head State Monument. My favorite place on the island was Hanauma Bay, a protected marine life conservation area and underwater park located along the southeast coast of the island. Whenever we would get several hours of free time, we would load into the van and take a trip to Hanauma Bay to snorkel. More than 400 species of fish inhabit the bay, as well as a large population of Green sea turtles.

On one of our visits to Hanauma Bay, I was out snorkeling with my friend Freddie Falcon from Atlanta. He motioned for me to look under the water where he was swimming. When I looked, he was slapping the front pockets of his swimming suit and hundreds of fish were swarming around him. He later told me he was tired of swimming around trying to find the fish, so he decided to let the fish come to him. His secret for attracting fish was to stuff his pockets with saltine crackers.

One of my greatest memories from Hawaii occurred at my first Pro Bowl in 2001. As I was hanging out on the sidelines in the third quarter, a presumably beer-goggled spectator ran on to the field. The players stood with their helmets off and watched as several big security guards chased the man around the field. This chase went on for about a minute, as everyone in Aloha Stadium watched the action. I moved closer to the field to get a better view of the shirtless spectator. As the fan continued to elude security, I noticed he was heading down the sideline straight toward me. When the man was about five yards away, I jumped out and tackled him to the ground. The crowd erupted with laughter and applause. As I lay there on top of the drunken fan, all I could think was "How much trouble am I going to get in for that stunt?" Listening to the crowd's response, I knew if I did get into trouble, it would be worth it. The game was a blowout, and the tackle seemed to bring some energy back into the stadium. As security guards hauled the man away in handcuffs, I stood up, took a bow, and walked away like a tough guy. The rest of the game I spent giving high fives to players and fans. After the game several television and newspaper reporters wanted to interview me about "The Tackle."

I was scheduled to fly back to Kansas City the next day. At the airport I grabbed a copy of the *Honolulu Star-Bulletin* newspaper so that I would have something to read on the long flight home. The top of the front page read, "Mascot Makes One of the Best Hits of the Day." When I turned to the article it was titled "Biggest Hit Didn't Come from a Player." The first part of the article read:

> "The best, most entertaining tackle at yesterday's Pro Bowl at Aloha Stadium was not delivered by Ray Lewis of the Baltimore Ravens or Junior Seau of the San Diego Chargers. It was applied by Dan Meers of the Kansas City Chiefs. Haven't heard of him? Probably because he's the team mascot."

I turned around, walked back into the airport gift shop and bought four more copies of that newspaper. I wanted to make sure each of my brothers received a copy so they could read the headlines about KC Wolf's big tackle at my first Pro Bowl.

I had a similar tackle six years later at Arrowhead Stadium. The Chiefs were playing the Minnesota Vikings in the home opener. Once again an intoxicated fan ran out onto the field. When I saw what was happening, I immediately gave chase. With the help of two security guards, I wrestled the unruly fan to the ground. The crowd loved my takedown and the next day KC Wolf's picture was in the *Kansas City Star,* belly flopping on the out-of-control fan.

Whether I was in Hawaii, Hong Kong or somewhere in between it was always fun to sit around and exchange mascot "war stories" with other Furternity members. These stories reminded me of fishing stories because they seemed to get bigger and more exaggerated every time you listened to them. One of the classic mascot stories happened to my friend Rowdy the Dallas Cowboys mascot, a cowboy character with a big goofy grin on his face. Several years ago Rowdy was at an appearance where he changed into costume in the back of his conversion van. Many mascots drive conversion vans with tinted windows and use the back of the van as a dressing room.

When Rowdy was in his costume and ready to go, he jumped out of the back of the van, where he surprised a mounted policeman on horseback. The horse was so startled that it kicked Rowdy in a very tender spot with its back hoof. No one knew Rowdy was hurt because the costume still had a big goofy grin plastered across the face. Rowdy fell to the ground and then crawled back into the van. He made one of the shortest mascot appearances ever because he immediately drove himself to the hospital to get stitches.

KC Wolf was never kicked by a horse, but I was bitten by a dog. Luckily, the dog got all fur and no flesh. On another occasion I made an appearance at a little boy's birthday party, a football themed party with KC Wolf as the special guest. When I arrived at the party, the little boys were extremely excited and wanted KC Wolf to play football with them. I was chosen to be the designated quarterback for both teams. After about 15 minutes of football the birthday boy's mother called everyone over to take a group picture. As I was listening to find out where she wanted me to stand for the photo, a little boy threw a pass that I didn't see coming. The football hit KC Wolf in the eye and the eyeball on my costume shattered in several pieces. The mother felt terrible, and attempted to tape the Wolf eye back together with no success. The following week I received a "thank you" note from the mother with a group picture from the birthday party. The picture made me laugh because KC Wolf looked like a pirate with only one eye and no eye patch to cover it up.

Another funny story took place at a charity event I attended that was held outside on an extremely hot day. Knowing I would have limited access to water, I used a camel back to keep hydrated. A camel back is a hydration water pouch, carried on the back like a school backpack. Mine held about 50 ounces of water and had a long tube that stretched from the water pouch over my shoulder and into my mouth. I loved the camel back because I could easily hide it under my costume. To get a drink all I needed to do was bite down on the mouthpiece that was attached to the end of the tube. I thought it was the perfect way to stay hydrated on those really hot days. I could get a drink without having to find a place to take off my KC Wolf head.

Everything worked well until halfway through my appearance. I bit down to get a drink, and the camel back mouthpiece fell off inside my mouth. I quickly spit it out and started biting the tube to stop the flow of water. As I was walking back to my dressing area to fix the problem, a little boy ran up to get a hug. I bent down to hug him without realizing what was about to happen. When I bent over to hug the little boy, the back of the costume pressed down on the pouch causing the water to come shooting out of the tube. I quickly tried to stand up but it was too late. The little boy went running away yelling, "Mom, KC Wolf just slobbered on me."

I experienced another awkward mascot moment when I showed up at an appearance without the KC Wolf head. I remembered the rest of the costume, but somehow I managed to leave the head in my garage at home. Fortunately the people who had scheduled the appearance were nice enough to let me start my appearance 30 minutes later which gave me time to rush home and get the head. I remember as a kid my dad telling me I'd forget my rear end if it wasn't attached, and sure enough on that day I forgot my head because it wasn't attached. I know many mascots who have experienced what it feels like to show up at an appearance missing a glove, paw or shoe. I think I'm one of the few who actually arrived without his head. A mascot can still go out and perform without a glove for his costume, but without the head, he's up a creek.

Looking back, I realize the friendships I've made are what give my job meaning. The famous folks I've met make my job interesting, and my Furternity brothers with all their crazy stories are what make my job fun. Together these friends, celebrities and fellow mascots have combined to make my journey very exciting.

12

Memorable Moments

"Great moments make great memories; so be you, be
great and make great memorable moments."
Ricardo Housham

In 1992 I began keeping a journal. My wife calls these notebooks
my diaries, but I like to refer to them as journals because it sounds
manlier. Diaries are for girls. Real men write in journals. Regardless
of whether they are journals or diaries I'm very glad I took the time
to record what was happening in my life. I don't write in my journal
every day, but I do try to write in it whenever I have a life experience or a memory I don't want to forget. My goal is to have as many
memorable moments in life as possible.

One of my first journal entries summarizes how I want to live
my life. It reads, "Don't let life pass you by Dan! Get involved, get
dirty, take your bumps and bruises, but don't let life just pass on by.
BE A PARTICIPANT IN LIFE, NOT A SPECTATOR!"

A few years later, I read Tim Hansel's book *"You Gotta Keep*
Dancin." In his book Tim says, "I don't know how much string is left
on my ball of twine. There are no guarantees as to how long any of
us will live, but I know full well that I would rather make my days
count than merely count my days. I want to live each one of them
as close to the core of life as possible, experiencing as much of God
and my family and friends as I am capable. Since life is inevitably too
short for all of us, I want to enjoy it as much as I can, no matter what
the circumstances. It's been said that the older we get, we don't
regret the things that we did do, but only those things that we failed
or forgot to do." Tim's words stirred me and I went on to write in
my journal, "Lord, I want to begin to celebrate life more. Not just

existing but taking the time to truly enjoy life. Start living Dan! Push life to a new level." I want to live a life of no regrets.

As I read back through many of my journals I realize some of the most memorable moments I've had as a mascot fall into one of four categories: frustrating, funny, frightening or fabulous. One of the things I love about being a mascot is the low stress. A mascot's job is to have fun, not to walk around stressed out like so many others in this world. When I did encounter stress at work, it was usually the result of my travels. One of my journal entries recorded a frustrating trip I took to South Dakota.

"I'm sitting on an airplane in Sioux Falls, South Dakota. Yesterday was one of the longest and most frustrating days of my life. I was scheduled to fly out of Kansas City at 11:00 a.m. so I raced to get to the airport on time. I later found out that I didn't need to rush because we sat in the airplane for an hour before taking off. When I arrived late into Minneapolis, I learned I had missed my connecting flight to Sioux Falls. I was rebooked on another flight leaving an hour and a half later.

When I boarded my flight, another 45 minutes passed before takeoff. I finally arrived in Sioux Falls about 4:30 p.m. I was scheduled to speak in Winner, South Dakota that evening to about 200-300 people at a ministerial alliance outreach event, and the town was over a three hour drive. I rushed to rent a car and then waited for my luggage only to find out that my luggage (KC Wolf costume) hadn't made it. My costume was stuck in Minneapolis and wouldn't arrive until 8:30 p.m. By this point it was 5:00 p.m. so I jumped in my rental car frazzled and frustrated and drove about 80-85 miles per hour to Winner. I felt guilty speeding while going to share my faith. After a short detour due to road construction, I finally reached Winner at 7:45 p.m., only 15 minutes late. Five minutes after arriving, I began my talk. Unfortunately, I wasn't dressed as KC Wolf like originally planned.

The people I spoke to were very understanding, and afterward I enjoyed dinner with the local ministers at McDonalds. Upon arriving at McDonalds I couldn't find my wallet. I thought it had been stolen, but I later found it buried in my carry-on bag. I left Winner at 10:00 p.m., driving back to Sioux Falls. At 11:30 p.m. I was pulled over by a cop in Platte, South Dakota, for driving too fast in a work zone. Since there were no workers present the officer gave me a verbal warning which was the best thing that happened to me all day. I finally arrived back in Sioux Falls at 2:15 a.m. and found a hotel. My alarm rang at 5:45 a.m. to wake me for my 7:00 a.m. flight. The KC Wolf costume was waiting for me when I checked in at the Sioux Falls airport."

Another frustrating moment I recorded occurred at a Chiefs' game. The Chiefs work very hard to make sure our game day presentation to the fans looks polished and well organized. Like any great organization, our goal is to strive for excellence. During one of our games we arranged for a very unusual pregame entrance. With the help of the Navy Leap Frogs, KC Wolf was going to parachute into Arrowhead Stadium. I had two costumes which we dressed to look identical. Since I had never parachuted before, I decided trying to land in a stadium filled with 78,000 people probably wasn't a good idea, so a Navy Leap Frog made the jump for me.

The plan was for him to jump out of the airplane dressed as KC Wolf. I would be dressed in the other costume waiting in the tunnel at Arrowhead so the fans couldn't see me. When KC Wolf landed and waved to the crowd, he would run up the tunnel. As soon as he was up in the tunnel I would run back down the tunnel onto the field. We were hoping Chiefs fans wouldn't realize the first KC Wolf was an imposter.

The cameras zoomed in on KC Wolf floating through the sky as the parachute approached Arrowhead. When they showed him on the giant video boards the crowd erupted. Waiting in the tunnel, I was getting excited just listening to the crowd's reaction. I was anticipating a huge cheer when KC Wolf finally landed on the field. Unfortunately, the big entrance never happened. The winds suddenly shifted and the Navy Leap Frog ended up landing in a nearby parking lot close to the Royals' baseball stadium. Our dramatic KC Wolf entrance definitely didn't go as planned.

The Navy Leap Frogs attempted a similar parachute jump four different times during my career. On two occasions they made successful landings on the field. The other two jumps weren't so successful. Besides the parking lot landing the other unsuccessful attempt happened during a practice jump. Thankfully the stadium was empty at the time. When the Navy Leap Frog jumped from the plane he encountered a small problem; KC Wolf's head blew off. He floated to the ground and landed on the 50 yard line as planned, but the head was missing. It came off 5,000 feet in the air. We immediately started looking for the head, but it was nowhere to be found. The next day I received a phone call at Arrowhead from a father saying he had KC Wolf's head. The family lived near the stadium and his kids had found it in a tree while they were playing. I was relieved to get the head back, and we rewarded the family with tickets to the next Chiefs' home game.

My most frustrating and disgusting mascot moment, however, came at an appearance on a hot July afternoon. As I was driving to the appearance, I noticed my costume smelled exceptionally bad. A foul odor coming from my costume bag wasn't unusual, but on this day it seemed to be worse than usual. When I arrived at my appearance and started to get dressed, I quickly discovered the source of the odor. Apparently my neighbor's cat had come into my garage, where I kept my costume, and used the KC Wolf costume bag as a litter box. Since then I have never been fond of cats.

Reading my journals also reminds me of many funny memories. One year for the Denver Broncos game I found a two-person horse costume which was supposed to resemble a bronco. I was going to use the horse costume in the pregame skit. My friend was going to dress up in a Bronco's jersey and a cowboy hat and walk onto the field leading the horse. Once they arrived at midfield, KC Wolf was going to race out of the tunnel on a four-wheeler, pretend to beat up the cowboy and then punch the horse in the mouth. Two of my friends volunteered to be the cowboy and the front of the horse, but I was still searching to find someone to be the other half of my horse. Jokingly, I called my brother and said, "Dave, I really need a 'horses rear' and your name came to mind." After promising to give him tickets and a parking pass, Dave agreed to help and the skit went great.

Several years later I used my father-in-law in a skit. We performed to the song "YMCA" dressed as the Village People. KC Wolf was dressed as a cop and my father-in-law danced around dressed as a soldier. Needless to say the entire family got a good laugh, and that skit is a memory I will never forget.

Another funny moment occurred at the grand opening of a grocery store where I was appearing. I spent the morning running around the store entertaining the shoppers. I tried to hang out in the frozen food aisle because I knew it was cooler in that part of the store. An older lady pushing a shopping cart was walking toward me so I began to shake KC Wolf's belly. She began to smile and laugh. As she walked past she leaned over to me and whispered, "You know they make an ointment for that." I'm sure she heard me laughing as I continued down the aisle.

Another of my most memorable KC Wolf moments was a frightening one. I had traveled to Sioux City, Iowa, to perform at an Arena League football game. The Sioux City Bandits were owned by a man named Bob Scott. I met Bob at an FCA event where I spoke, and we became good friends. Every year Bob invited me to perform at a Bandits football game. The games were very exciting, and I always had a lot of fun.

The games usually ended around 10:00 p.m. Since Kansas City was over four hours away, Bob reserved a room for me at the local hotel. My costume was always sweaty after the game, so I would bring it into my room and hang it up for the night. It made the room smell like a locker room, but at least the costume had a chance to dry out.

On this particular trip I woke up in the middle of the night confused because I was in an unfamiliar place. When I looked around trying to figure out where I was, I saw a big body and a set of eyes staring at me. I started to breathe heavily, and my heart started to pound in fear as I got ready to fight off the intruder. Finally, it dawned on me where I was. When I flipped on the light, sure enough my friend KC Wolf was looking at me. I got up, turned the head around so the eyes would be facing in the opposite direction and went back to bed.

Thankfully my frightening experiences are few compared to the many fabulous moments I've had as KC Wolf. My journal entry from February 7, 2004, recorded one of those times. "This morning I had the privilege of speaking at the Pro Bowl Military Prayer Breakfast. Aeneas Williams of the St. Louis Rams, Peter Boulware of the Baltimore Ravens and Coach Tony Dungy of the Indianapolis Colts also spoke. What a thrill to share the stage with these three men who also have a love and a passion to follow Christ. Lord, thanks again for the opportunity to share my faith."

Being a mascot has helped me create many special memories with members of my family as well. I mentioned earlier that I helped my brother Dave get engaged to his wife Stacey at a Mizzou basketball game in 1989 when I dressed as Truman Tiger. What I did not mention is 25 years later I helped my nephew Blake (their oldest son) get engaged at a Chiefs' game dressed as KC Wolf. It made me realize I've been blessed with a long mascot career.

KC Wolf also helped me create many special moments with my own kids. I took my oldest daughter, Mycah, on a work trip with me to Chicago. I spent three hours running around dressed as KC Wolf at a convention, and then Mycah and I spent three days running around Chicago making memories.

Another time, my youngest daughter, Mallory, took a trip with me to Grand Lake in Oklahoma. The Chiefs were creating a video for me to show at schools, and I arranged to shoot some video footage of KC Wolf parasailing. On that hot summer day I spent 30 minutes in a furry costume flying high above the lake. When I was finished, Mallory and her friend Ellie DeBacker went up for a ride. We shot some great video footage, but more importantly, I made a memory with my youngest daughter that I will have for the rest of my life.

On July 9, 2012, my son Aaron and I experienced one of the greatest father/son moments of all time. KC Wolf had made an appearance for ESPN in New York City earlier in the year, and as a thank you they were kind enough to send me two tickets to the 2012 MLB All-Star Game Home Run Derby. The All-Star Game was being played in Kansas City which made it even more exciting. It was a beautiful evening, and we arrived early so we could eat snacks and drink Gatorade at the ESPN VIP party. When we checked in, we also received a 2012 All-Star Game baseball glove as a souvenir. Our tickets were located in the right field seats so we began cheering for all the left handed hitters, hoping we could catch a ball. However, catching a ball didn't look promising because most of the batters were right handed and hit their home runs to left field.

Aaron and I were living the dream. We are both big baseball fans and the All-Star Game is about as good as it gets. After watching for about two hours, we got up and stretched our legs and then settled back into our seats for the championship round. Jose Bautista and Prince Fielder were in the finals, and we were cheering for Prince because he is a lefty.

During the championship round, Prince Fielder crushed a ball over the fence towards our seats. Since Aaron was sitting on the aisle, he immediately jumped up and ran toward where the ball was hit. I watched him jump up and come down with the ball in his glove. He turned around with a big smile on his face, and I gave him a big hug. An already great night turned into one of the most memorable nights of his life.

Since the Home Run Derby was being broadcast nationwide on ESPN, my cell phone immediately started to go crazy. Within five minutes of Aaron catching the ball I received 22 text messages and 13 emails from friends congratulating us and asking if it was really us on television. Some might say it's just a coincidence that Aaron caught a home run ball at the All-Star Game. I don't believe that for one second. I once read a quote saying, "A coincidence is something that God arranges, but prefers to remain anonymous."

In my journal later that night I wrote these words, "On the way to the ballpark I thanked God for the tickets and even whispered a little prayer that this would be a special night my son would always remember. Little did I know God had a very, very, very special night planned for us. I'm convinced Prince Fielder didn't hit that home run ball to my son, God sent that home run in Aaron's direction. Tonight, God just decided to bless two of His children with one of the greatest nights of their lives, an experience a father and son will get to talk about for years to come. Lord, I know that everything happens for a reason. As a believer in Christ, everything is just an incident in Your perfect plan. Thank you for being so good."

I didn't realize it at the time, but 16 months later I would experience another memorable moment. This incident, however, wasn't nearly as pleasant; it was much more painful.

13

A Day that Changed My Life

"To realize the worth of the anchor we need to feel the storm."

I woke up early on Saturday, November 23, 2013, excited for the day ahead, not realizing it would be a day that would impact the rest of my life. I began the day by driving 90 miles from Kansas City to Chillicothe, Missouri, for the town's annual Holiday Parade. I had appeared in this parade every year since 2003, and I always looked forward to attending because it was held the Saturday before Thanksgiving when the weather was usually nice and cool.

I was particularly excited for this year's parade because the Chiefs were doing well, and I knew I would be the second most popular guy in town. The Chiefs were 9-1 and tied with the Denver Broncos for first place in the AFC West. When the Chiefs were winning, KC Wolf always seemed to get better treatment. The previous year when the Chiefs were 1-9 after their first 10 games, I had to put up with all kinds of jokes and snide comments at my appearances. This year was different. The Chiefs were on a roll, and I felt as popular as Elvis Presley in his glory years. I knew the only man more popular than KC Wolf at the parade would be the other chubby guy dressed in red—Santa Claus.

It is hard to compete against Santa Claus at a Christmas parade. I noticed Santa always received special treatment. Year after year, Santa always rode in the bucket of the city's shiny red fire truck, waving to his adoring fans. On the other hand, KC Wolf always got stuck behind a bunch of horses with small bladders. I'm not sure what they fed the horses in Chillicothe, but it must have been high in fiber because each year the parade route was like walking through a mine field. KC Wolf wears size 23 shoes, so I had to really watch where I was stepping. Even though I had to use extreme caution while walking the parade route, I always had a great time hanging out with the good people of Chillicothe.

After the parade I walked back to my changing area to get out of my costume. Superman can change in a phone booth, but KC Wolf has 85 inch hips and needs a little more space. Fortunately, in Chillicothe they allowed me to change at the Chamber of Commerce office, which was the perfect dressing room because I had plenty of space. More importantly, the parade committee fed me donuts.

After saying my goodbyes in Chillicothe, I started the 90 minute drive back to Kansas City. I was tired from the parade but also fired up, knowing the most exciting part of my day was about to take place. I had to be at Arrowhead at 1:30 p.m. to practice a wolf stunt I planned to perform the next day in the Chiefs' game against the San Diego Chargers. This skit wasn't going to be just another ordinary KC Wolf entrance on his four-wheeler. It had potential to be the greatest KC Wolf skit ever. The Chiefs were celebrating Military Appreciation Day so we wanted to do something very special to honor the brave men and women of our Armed Forces. One of the many things I appreciated about the Chiefs' organization was their commitment to honoring those in the military and their families who sacrifice so much for our country.

The plan for my pregame entrance was to have KC Wolf, dressed in Army fatigues, jump out of the lights at the top of the stadium and zip line down onto the field. This stunt was by far the most thrilling way to enter Arrowhead in a wolf suit. The zip line attached to the lights above the press box on the south side of the stadium. It then stretched all the way across the field to the north side of the stadium and connected to the huge steel beams that held another bank of lights. The zip line hung 260 feet above the field. Since it remained in place during the game it needed to be high enough not to interfere with the punts.

I initially received permission to perform this stunt in August 2013 and was thrilled when I heard the news because I had been wanting to do it for several years. I knew that since Arrowhead Stadium opened in 1972, no man or mascot had ever performed such a stunt. Even though I was a little nervous, I was also very excited. Neil Armstrong might have been the first man to walk on the moon, but Dan Meers was going to be the first mascot to zip line over Arrowhead.

Military Appreciation Day was actually going to be the second time for me to zip line into Arrowhead. The first time had been for the Chiefs' 2013 home opener against the Dallas Cowboys. I will never forget the feeling I had that day, flying over 200 feet above 78,000 screaming football fans. It was truly an unforgettable experience. Two of the fans at the opening day game were my mom and dad. I got them tickets because they were always my biggest supporters, and I wanted them to be able to witness KC Wolf's big entrance. I also knew they would be praying for me, and I wanted all the prayers I could get. On that day the Chiefs beat the Cowboys 17-16. We received such great feedback on the zip line entrance that we decided to do it again later in the season. After much discussion, we decided Military Appreciation Day would be the perfect time for a repeat performance.

My goal as a mascot was to try to keep my pregame entrances from becoming too predictable. Since KC Wolf had zip lined into the stadium against Dallas, I decided to add a little surprise for the crowd by bungee jumping out of the lights and then zip lining by hanging at the end of a 20 foot bungee rope. I had always wanted to bungee jump, and I also knew the thrill of flying into Arrowhead attached to a zip line. I thought this was going to be the greatest KC Wolf stunt I had ever performed, and I couldn't wait to listen to the crowd's reaction the next day.

When I finally arrived at Arrowhead from Chillicothe, I rode the elevator up to the press box. Since the press box is the highest floor reached by the elevator, I then walked up a staircase to get to the roof. It was very cold and windy while I waited for the rigging crew to finish doing safety checks and put the final touches on the equipment. The view from the top of Arrowhead was amazing with the sun shining and very few clouds in the sky. From where I stood I could easily see Royals Stadium and the Fellowship of Christian Athletes National Headquarters to the north and the downtown Kansas City skyline to the west. While the rigging crew completed their work, I went back down into the press box to warm up and put on my zip line harness.

While putting on my harness I remember thinking to myself, "I am the luckiest man alive. I make a living having fun and performing crazy stunts. Most people have to pay money if they want to bungee jump or ride on a zip line, but not me." I was doing both for free and getting paid for it. With a smile on my face and adrenaline pumping through my body, I headed back to the roof ready to experience the thrill of my first bungee jump. I was excited knowing there was plenty of time for me to practice the stunt several times. Riding the zip line at Arrowhead was fun, and I wanted to get in as many practice rides as possible.

My first attempt was going to be without the KC Wolf costume so I could get a feel for the bungee jump without any restrictions from the costume. I was then going to put the KC Wolf suit on for several more practice runs until I felt comfortable for show time the next day.

When the rigging crew was finished, they secured the bungee rope to the zip line and attached my harness to the bungee rope. They gave me the thumbs up and told me I could jump at any time. As I stood in the lights preparing for my big jump, I remember thinking, "Wow, this is really scary."

I thought back to when I was a kid standing on top of the high dive at the swimming pool, afraid to jump. Everyone below me was either trying to encourage me or yelling at me to hurry up. What I remembered from that childhood experience was the longer I stood on the diving board looking down at the water, the harder it was to take the plunge. Now, 40 years later, I was having the same feeling standing in the lights at Arrowhead Stadium. As I stood staring at the Chiefs logo painted on the 50 yard line 260 feet below, I decided I'd better go ahead and jump or else I was going to wet myself. I counted, "1...2...3" and made the leap.

What happened during the next 10 seconds is still a blur. Everything happened so fast, and I was in so much pain, I struggle to remember the details. What I do know is that the stunt didn't work as planned. I was supposed to free fall about 20 feet, and then the bungee cord would bounce me back up, and I would begin to zip line out over the football field. However, instead of falling 20 feet, I fell 75 feet and crashed into the upper level seats at Arrowhead Stadium. I hit the seats so hard that I knocked two of them out of the concrete where they were mounted (Section 324, Row 34, Seats 22-23). After hitting the seats, I immediately went into shock. I was dazed but alert, and my body was shaking uncontrollably. All I wanted to do was get my feet on the ground, but since the bungee cord was still attached to the zip line, as soon as I hit the seats it pulled me back up, and I went flying over the field. Traveling over 200 feet above the football field, hanging from the bungee cord, I knew something had gone terribly wrong. My body was throbbing, and I was scared. I also knew I was badly hurt. I didn't know what my injuries were, but I knew the pain was far beyond anything I had ever experienced. What scared me most was that I was having a really, really hard time breathing. It felt like someone had knocked the wind out of me, and all I could do was take very short, shallow breaths.

By this time the zip line movement had stopped, and I was suspended high above the field. I hung there like a rag doll and tried not to move because I didn't want to risk damaging my spine. As I hung above the football field trying to catch my breath, I began to pray. A Bible verse popped into my mind that I had memorized 25 years earlier while I was in college. The verse was Isaiah 41:10, "So do not fear, for I am with you. Do not be dismayed for I am your God. I will strengthen you and help you; I will uphold you with my righteous right hand."

I had memorized this verse because I knew it was a promise from God. I also knew God was faithful, and He ALWAYS keeps His promises. I was still very unsure about what was going to happen next, but I had a peace knowing God was by my side. Author John Ortberg once said, "Peace doesn't come from finding a lake with no storms; it comes from having Jesus in your boat." Never in my life was I more thankful to know that Jesus was in my boat and by my side.

I hung in the air for a short time before the rigging crew slowly began to lower me onto the field. Since the weather was extremely cold, the Chiefs' grounds crew had a tarp covering the field to protect the grass. As I inched closer to the ground, I looked down and noticed there was a trail of blood leading from the Chiefs' sideline all the way to midfield. When I looked directly below me at midfield, there was a puddle of blood. Blood doesn't usually bother me because I grew up in a family with three boys, and we used to shed blood all the time. However, when I realized I was the one making the mess on the field, I was concerned. With my body still in shock, I was trying to figure out where all the blood was coming from.

I learned later that when I had smashed into the seats, I cut the back of my leg deeply enough to require stitches. The blood was running down my leg, through my sweatpants and tennis shoe, spilling onto the field. Later at the hospital, I was given two units of blood to help replace all the blood I had lost.

By the time I reached the ground, the Chiefs' personnel and grounds crew could tell by the look on my face and the blood on the field that something was seriously wrong. While someone called 911, others unhooked me from the zip line and laid me down on the field. I was extremely thankful one of the grounds crew members was also an EMT (emergency medical technician). He told me to lie very still, just in case there was damage to my spine. I asked if they could get the zip line harness off my body because I was still struggling to breathe, and the harness was very tight. I had worked closely with the Chiefs' grounds crew for 24 years. They were not just fellow workers but guys I truly considered my friends. They reminded me of a group of Boy Scouts because they were always prepared and willing to help out. This day was no exception.

When I asked to get out of the harness, they immediately started pulling out pocket knives and scissors to cut it off my body. To control the bleeding, they also cut the leg off my sweatpants and applied pressure to the cut on my left leg. Since my body was shaking from shock and the cold weather, the grounds crew gave me a pair of gloves to wear. They also found towels and coats to cover me with until the ambulance arrived.

Lying on the football field buried under coats, in extreme pain and struggling to breathe, I began to wonder if the ambulance was ever going to arrive. As I waited, a man came over, knelt down beside me, and asked if he could pray for me. It was the first of thousands of prayers that people prayed for me over the next seven months. I'm convinced God used this man to remind me He was still by my side and still in control.

When the ambulance arrived, it backed down the underground tunnel that leads to the field on the southeast corner of the stadium.

The paramedics placed a neck brace around my neck and strapped me onto a back board to stabilize my spine. I could wiggle my fingers and toes, which I knew was a very good sign. After loading me into the ambulance, the medics checked my vital signs, hooked me up to an IV, and started the trip to the hospital.

Even though this was one of the worst days of my life, I got to do something that had always been on my bucket list. I rode really fast in an ambulance with the sirens blaring; we even ran a bunch of stoplights without getting a ticket. I decided if I ever had another chance to ride in an ambulance, I wanted to be the guy sitting in the driver's seat instead of the guy laying in the back hooked up to an IV.

Racing to the hospital in an ambulance seemed really exciting when it was on my bucket list, but the "real life" experience ended up being extremely painful. Just before we arrived at the emergency room, I asked the paramedic if he thought I would be spending the night in the hospital. He laughed and said, "Yes, Mr. Meers, I'm pretty sure you're going to be staying overnight." He was right; I was getting ready for an extended stay in the hospital. I think he already knew what I suspected. The injuries I suffered from my bungee jump were very serious.

14

Surgery and Scars

*"Scars show us where we have been; they do not
dictate where we are going."*
David Rossi

When I arrived at Centerpoint Medical Center in Independence,
the paramedics rushed me into the emergency room where at least
six or seven doctors and nurses were waiting. It seemed to me like
each of them had a big needle and was looking for a spot on my
body to stick it. The main emergency room doctor was a small lady
with a soft voice. After she took a few X-rays and examined me, I
saw her huddle up with a few of the other doctors and nurses. I was
hoping that she was going to tell me to take an aspirin and go home
and sleep it off. Unfortunately, that was not the case.

She slowly walked over to me, leaned down, and in a very serious voice said, "Mr. Meers, I'm afraid I've got some bad news. We've
discovered that you have a pneumothorax." I couldn't believe what
I was hearing. I thought to myself, "NO, NO, NO—NOT A PNEU-
MOTHORAX! I'm still so young."

I silently said, "Lord, PLEASE......ANYTHING BUT A
PNEUMOTHORAX!"

The doctor said, "Mr. Meers, do you know what a pneumothorax is?"

I said, "No, but it sounds REALLY BAD." I told her it sounded
like something out of a Dr. Seuss book. I was doing my best to keep
my sense of humor because I'd always heard laughter was the best
medicine. At the time laughter didn't seem like such good medicine
though, because every time I laughed it really, really hurt.

The doctor smiled and informed me a pneumothorax was a collapsed lung. She said when I fell and hit the seats, I had broken seven
ribs which was why it hurt so badly when I laughed. She also told

me that the collapsed lung was why I was having such a difficult time breathing. As soon as they finished stitching up the cut on my leg, she said they would insert a tube into my chest cavity to help me breathe more easily. While the doctors finished stitching up my leg, I began to think about the chest tube. I don't know much about the human body—most mascots weren't pre-med in college—but I did know there was no easy access route to get a tube into my chest cavity. In my calmest voice I asked, "How do you go about that procedure?" With great confidence, the doctor responded, "We will stick you with a needle just under your armpit to numb the skin. Once you're numb, we will cut a small incision and then slowly feed the chest tube into your chest cavity." With a straight face she said, "You may feel a 'little pressure.'"

One important lesson I learned the hard way was that if a doctor says you may feel "a little pressure" right before he sticks a tube in your body, get ready for a very unpleasant experience. It happened to me twice during my hospital stay. The first was when they inserted the chest tube into my chest cavity. The second was when they inserted a catheter somewhere else. During both procedures, I thought my eyes were going to pop out of my head.

As the doctor began inserting the chest tube, it quickly became apparent that her idea of a "little pressure" was totally different from mine. What I thought was going to be a small little tube being inserted into my chest cavity felt more like a garden hose being shoved between my seven broken ribs. The procedure was extremely painful!

Although the doctor was wrong about how much pressure I would feel during the procedure, she was right about how much more easily I could breathe. When the chest tube finally reached my chest cavity, my lung slowly began to inflate. For the first time since my fall I was able to breathe somewhat normally.

After getting the chest tube, I overheard two of the nurses talking. One of them walked over to me and said, "I remember you. You came and spoke at my elementary school." I wanted to laugh, but I just smiled because laughing hurt too much. What crossed my mind was that I had better do a good job at my school programs because some day those same kids may be working on me at the hospital.

The nurse told me several friends from Arrowhead were waiting out in the emergency room lobby. They had witnessed my accident and had come to the hospital to check on me. Since the chest tube was in, I told the nurse to let them come in. I appreciated their concern. One of the reasons I love working for the Chiefs is the people I work with, who are not only my coworkers but also dear friends.

As I was visiting with my coworkers, two of my favorite people in the whole world arrived. My wife Cam and daughter Mycah had been at a Christian music concert. As they were leaving the concert, they received a phone call from my friend Mike DeBacker telling them I had been in an accident. I didn't want the emergency room nurses to call Cam because I knew a call saying I had been rushed to the hospital would upset her. Instead, I waited until my chest tube was in place and called Mike to explain what had happened. Mike then contacted Cam and let her know that I was going to be fine, but she should come to the hospital. I didn't want Cam to be alarmed, so I had Mike tell her I "might" have to stay overnight. I intentionally tried to downplay my condition to put her mind at ease. Cam and Mycah raced across town and when they walked in the door of the emergency room, I could see the concern reflected on their faces. As a husband and a father, I didn't like seeing my girls upset. I tried to convince them that I was fine. I assured them everything was going to be okay, but I think they could tell by my appearance that this was more than just a few bumps and bruises. Cam and I were supposed to go to a 50th birthday party for a friend that evening, but obviously I had messed up our Saturday evening date plans once again.

The nurses let us visit for a few minutes and then informed me that I still had one more stop to make. They wheeled me into a room where there was a large machine that took CT scans. The doctor wanted to see if I had any more injuries so she ordered scans of my head, cervical spine, chest, abdomen and pelvis. Several nurses lifted me off the stretcher and slid my body into a large tube. They told me to lie very still, though by this point I was so exhausted and in so much pain that I didn't want to move. After the CT scans, they lifted me back on the stretcher and wheeled me up to the hospital room that would be my home for the next nine days. As I lay in my hospital bed, I thought back on the day and my brush with death. I had read stories about people who had a near death experience, get knocked unconscious, see a bright light and hear some soft peaceful harp music. My near death experience was much different. I was awake and conscious the entire time and never saw a bright light. Besides that, all I remember hearing was some lousy rap music blaring from Arrowhead's loud speakers. As I waited on the doctor, I quietly said a little prayer thanking God. I realized I had come within inches of losing my life, and the fact that I was still alive was truly a miracle. I was a survivor of a bungee jump accident, and I knew this made me part of a very small group of people.

As I visited with Cam and Mycah, our friends Mike and Darla DeBacker arrived. I was relieved when I saw my other two children, Aaron and Mallory, walk in with them. Since my accident had really upset my wife and kids, I was relieved to finally have the whole family together. Even though I looked terrible, it was good for my kids to see that daddy was going to survive. My kids stayed for about an hour, during which I did my best to assure them I was going to be fine. On their way out the door I wanted to hug them, but because of my pain, I settled for a kiss on the cheek. I was very emotional as I kissed them and told them how much I loved them. My accident reminded me of what was truly important in my life and how often I took my family for granted.

Shortly after my kids left, a new doctor came into my room with a serious look on his face. I was quickly learning that a serious look usually meant bad news. After looking at the CT scans, they determined that my fall had shattered my tailbone and cracked my sacrum. The good news was my shattered tailbone was like my appendix, I didn't really need it. The bad news about my tailbone was the recovery was going to be extremely painful, and there was nothing he could do to make it feel better. He said the only thing that would relieve the pain was time. I was discouraged to learn I would probably have discomfort in my rear end for at least nine months. I was used to being a pain in the rear, but I wasn't looking forward to having a pain in the rear. The doctor then gave me more bad news. The CT scans also revealed I had a fracture of the T-12 vertebrae in my back. He explained I would need to have back surgery the next morning, where he would place two titanium rods in my back to stabilize my spine.

When I heard I would be having back surgery, I finally started to realize the severity of my injuries. Originally, I thought I would need a few stitches and a week of rest. I was now beginning to understand I would be hospitalized for several more days, and my recovery would require several months of physical therapy and rehab. The news was depressing, but I did my best to stay positive.

I told the doctor if he was planning to cut on me with a knife the next morning and insert two titanium rods into my back, I would appreciate it if he would go home and get a good night's rest. It was a Saturday night, and I told him I definitely didn't want him going out drinking. The doctor laughed and promised he would go straight home and go to bed. On his way out the door, the doctor paused and turned back to look at me. He said, "Mr. Meers, I hope you realize you are a very lucky man. If you fell 75 feet today, you are lucky to be alive and lucky that you are not paralyzed." His words were very sobering and reminded me how blessed I was to still be alive.

As the doctor left my room, I realized the day could have turned out a lot worse for me. However, I didn't really believe that I was lucky to be alive. When I became a follower of Christ in 1985, I quit believing in luck. I didn't even believe my fall was an accident. I once read a book that said, "There are no such things as accidents, only incidents in God's perfect plan for my life." I believe this statement with all of my heart. In the Bible, God made me a promise. I knew God's promises were just as true during the difficult times of life as they were during the good times. In Jeremiah 29:11, God says, "I know the plans I have for you declares the Lord, plans to prosper you and not to harm you, plans to give you hope and a future."

What had happened earlier in the day was no accident because God knew it was going to happen to me before I was ever born. While obviously I would have never wished for this to occur, I fully believed God could cause something good to come out of my pain. My friend Dan Erickson always says, "There is only one word not in God's vocabulary and it is the word 'Oops.'" His quote reminds me that God doesn't sit in heaven and say, "Oops, I didn't intend for that to happen." I knew God was a sovereign God who knew the day I would be born, and He knows the day I will die. God also knows everything that will happen in my life between those two dates, and nothing happens accidentally.

Psalm 139:16 (NLT) says, "You saw me before I was born. Every day of my life was recorded in your book. Every moment was laid out before a single day had passed." I took comfort in knowing God knew this day would happen, and I knew He would give me the strength to get through this situation. Some people might question why an all-powerful God would allow something like this to happen to one of His children. Did it mean God didn't love me because He allowed something awful to happen in my life? I knew the answer was "No."

My pastor used to say that sometimes God allows negative things into our lives because He wants to get our attention, or because He has something He wants us to learn. I would soon find out for myself there are many valuable lessons in life which can only be learned through pain and adversity. While lying in that hospital bed, I did not like that I was going through suffering, but I tried to remind myself of another one of God's promises, found in Romans 8:28: "We know that in all things God works for the good of those who love Him, who have been called according to His purpose." Like many of God's promises, I found them easier to believe when everything was going well in my life. Now that I was facing adversity and pain, I knew my faith would be tested. I just never dreamed how much.

My first night in the hospital was one of the longest and most miserable nights of my life. Even though the nurses were coming in every few hours to give me pain medication, I was still hurting. Cam was by my side all night, but neither of us were able to get much rest. My back, tailbone, ribs, and chest tube were hurting terribly, and I couldn't sleep because I couldn't get comfortable. Since my lung had collapsed, the nurses placed two small clear tubes up my nose to help me to breathe pure oxygen. Due to the surgery scheduled for the next morning, I was not allowed to eat or drink anything after midnight, which only added to my misery. I was miserable not only because of the pain, but because I was completely dried up. The pain medication was drying me up, the oxygen tubes up my nose were drying me up, and to make matters worse I wasn't allowed to drink anything. I tried to lick my chapped lips, but doing so was no help because my tongue was completely dry. A nurse gave Cam a cup of water and a plastic stick with a sponge on the end of it. It was the only thing that provided any relief. When my mouth got so dry that I couldn't take it any longer, Cam took the sponge, dipped it in the cup of water and wiped it on my lips. This routine went on all night long. About every 15 minutes, I asked Cam to wet my lips because I was so dry and thirsty. By about 2:30 a.m. all I could think about was my pain. I tried not to complain, but in my mind I was having a pity party. I had never felt so miserable in my entire life. I was in pain, I was discouraged, and I was lying there feeling sorry for myself. It was one of the lowest points in my life.

What happened next can only be described as a "God moment." It quickly put an end to my pity party and caused me to realize how blessed I was. My lips were once again dry, and I asked Cam if she would wipe them with the sponge. As she held the sponge to my lips, it dawned on me there had been another man who had been thirsty and asked for a drink, and they also offered it to Him on a sponge.

The story is found in the Bible in John 19:28-30. Jesus was hanging on the cross and He said, "I am thirsty." The soldiers at the foot of the cross took a stick with a sponge on it, soaked it in wine vinegar, and lifted it to Jesus' lips. And the Bible says, "When He had received the drink, Jesus said, 'It is finished.' With that, He bowed His head and gave up His spirit."

At that moment, tears began filling my eyes as I was reminded of a very important truth. Just as it was no accident I was lying in a hospital bed because this was part of God's plan for my life, it was also no accident Jesus hung on a hard wooden cross. The suffering Jesus experienced on the cross was also part of God's plan. The cross was God's plan for restoring sinful mankind (Dan Meers) back into a right relationship with a holy God. God used my dry lips and a wet sponge to encourage me and to remind me He knew what I was going through. Jesus had endured even greater suffering than me while on this earth. I knew everything was going to be okay.

I was very thankful to see the sun come up the next morning. The night had felt like it would never end. At 6:00 a.m. there was a knock on the door, and in walked my mom and dad. Cam had called them the night before and told them about my injuries. They knew I was scheduled to have back surgery at 9:00 a.m. and wanted to arrive before I went into surgery. They had left their house in St.

Charles about 11:30 p.m. and had driven through the night. At 3:00 a.m. they arrived in Kansas City, slept in a hotel for a few hours, and then came to the hospital. It was nice to visit with them before I went in for surgery.

It felt strange knowing the Chiefs were getting ready for a noon kickoff. This would be the first Chiefs' home game I had missed in more than 23 years. I had dressed as KC Wolf for 248 consecutive Chiefs' home games, but my streak was about to end. Fortunately, I felt like lying on an operating table, knocked out and getting two titanium rods placed in my back was a good excuse for missing work. Two of my backup KC Wolves, Shawn Emerson and Andrew Johnson, worked the game for me. When I awoke from surgery, the first thing I remember was a nurse telling me the Chiefs had lost to the Chargers 41-38 in the last minute of the game. I was disappointed, but I was also so groggy that all I wanted to do was sleep.

When I got back up to my hospital room, my brother Dave and his wife Stacey had arrived from St. Charles. Once again I was reminded of how blessed I was to have a family who loved me and was always there during my time of need. We visited briefly, but before long I was sound asleep. Downstairs in the hospital chapel a group of 25 family and friends gathered to pray for me. This prayer gathering was very encouraging for Cam and my kids, letting them know they were surrounded by so many caring people.

I spent Monday visiting with my family and taking several naps. My hospital room began to look like a small floral shop. I received flowers and candy arrangements from friends, family and even businesses with whom KC Wolf worked during the year. My friends at HyVee, the Kansas City Symphony, the Platte City Police Department, Midwest Dairy Association and several other companies sent cards and flowers that helped brighten up an otherwise dull looking room.

As we watched the news that evening, I was surprised to see the local news stations airing stories about KC Wolf's accident and injuries. I smile to think I was important enough to get news coverage on all four major stations at 5:00, 6:00 and 10:00 p.m. I felt like a celebrity, but I also realized it was probably a really slow news day if they were reporting on mascot injuries.

When I woke up on Tuesday, November 26, I was excited because the nurses told me I could get up and try to walk later in the day. They told me the sooner I got up and walked, the quicker I would heal. I was already tired of lying in a hospital bed and wanted to get home as soon as possible. That afternoon when they sat me up on the edge of the hospital bed, my body was throbbing, but the worst part was my head. My head was spinning, and I was extremely nauseous. After about 20 minutes, I was finally able to take about six steps with a walker and sit in a chair. I sat on a stack of pillows because my shattered tailbone caused extreme pain. I sat in the chair for a few minutes and then headed straight back to bed. I was encouraged that I could walk, but I was surprised by how exhausted I felt after going just a few steps. I was used to wearing a 35 pound KC Wolf costume and running around for five hours at Chiefs' games. Now, after taking just a few steps with the help of a walker, I was collapsing back into bed completely fatigued.

As I was lying in bed trying to regain my energy, I received a phone call from Clark Hunt, the owner of the Chiefs. I knew Clark was a very busy man during football season, and so his call meant a lot to me. After we had visited for several minutes, I thanked him and joked that I would try to get off the injured reserve list as soon as possible. I think we both knew I was going to be on the PUP list (Physically Unable to Perform) for the rest of the season.

Wednesday was another day filled with visitors. I was excited to see my brother Honey, who had made the trip across the state to visit me. I also received a visit from Chiefs' president Mark Donovan. The Chiefs were having a great season, so I told Mark to remember me if the Chiefs made it to the Super Bowl. He promised if the Chiefs made the Super Bowl, they would take me along on the trip.

That afternoon the nurses told Cam I was seeing too many visitors and needed to get more rest. I knew the nurses were right, but I had trouble turning away visitors because they relieved my boredom and helped to keep my spirits up.

Thursday was Thanksgiving Day, and it was the first time I had ever spent Thanksgiving in a hospital. In many ways it was one of the best Thanksgivings of my life. Instead of just sitting around watching football games and overeating like I had done so many times before, I actually took time to reflect on the many things for which I was thankful. The fact I was still alive was at the top of my list.

My doctor had good news and bad news on Thanksgiving Day. The good news was my collapsed lung was healing well so the doctor was going to remove my chest tube. The bad news was while one tube was coming out another tube was going back in. Earlier in the week the doctor removed my catheter but unfortunately my bladder was not emptying properly so he reinserted another one. They had inserted the first catheter during my surgery, but this time I was going to be wide awake. Needless to say, I was not excited.

Other than having the catheter inserted, Thanksgiving ended up being a good day. I was able to get up and take several walks which made me feel productive. I felt like a little old man as I shuffled down the hallway holding on to my new walker. Occasionally, I battled discouragement because I always returned from my walks feeling exhausted. I had spent countless hours on a stationary bike getting in shape for football season. Now after less than a week in the hospital, I felt like I had lost all my stamina.

Whenever I caught myself having a pity party, I discovered the best thing to do was go visit other patients. Many patients on the floor didn't seem to get visitors, so I decided while I was out shuffling up and down the hallway with my walker, I would smile and try to make a few new friends. I once heard, "Friendship doubles our joy and divides our grief." This reminder was just what I needed during my time in the hospital. When my friends visited they were always a huge encouragement and a bright spot during my day. I hoped to be the same for other patients on my floor.

My nurses were another huge encouragement. Even though they stuck me with needles several times each day, they also took great care of me. I developed a tremendous amount of respect watching how these nurses helped others on a daily basis. They were constantly dealing with patients who were struggling with pain and often times not pleasant to be around. Yet the nurses continued to serve with a loving heart. I once read, "Greatness is not measured by how many servants you have but by how many people you serve." The nurses at Centerpoint Medical Center were truly great people.

The day after Thanksgiving I spent some extended time with my in-laws, Jim and Nancy Cochran. They came up to stay with me while Cam went home for some much needed rest. I always got along very well with my in-laws, and since I had missed Thanksgiving, I enjoyed getting some one-on-one time with them. Back at home the support we were getting from our family, friends and fellow church members was amazing. Many of the neighbors in our subdivision dropped off meals for Cam and the kids. Other friends helped watch our kids and tried to keep their lives as normal as possible. My doctor said we should find a recliner for me to sleep in for several weeks because of my shattered tailbone and back surgery. Since Cam and I didn't own a recliner, our friends Mike and Darla DeBacker were kind enough to deliver their loveseat recliner to our house.

My wife was working behind the scenes to make sure everything was ready for me when I came home from the hospital. She knew I desperately wanted to get back home. My doctor wanted me to remain in the hospital through the weekend, but he said if everything continued to heal properly I could go home the following week.

I spent the weekend watching football on television and walking the hallways to regain my strength. I figured the more the nurses saw me up and walking, the better my chances were of getting to go home. Each time I passed a nurse I would stand up extra tall and try to look strong and healthy. Even though my body was still in a lot of pain, I was now taking my pain medications in pill form instead of intravenously. I knew this was a good sign, because I could take pain medication at home just as easily as I could at the hospital.

Saturday afternoon my accountability partner Rod Handley and his family stopped by to pray for me. Rod and I had been meeting together weekly for almost 25 years, and have prayed together hundreds of times. I was very thankful for the deep friendship we shared. As the Handley family left my room, I once again thanked God I was not traveling this difficult road alone. Later that evening I watched my beloved Missouri Tigers beat Texas A&M to win the SEC East Crown, an exciting way to end an otherwise boring day at the hospital.

Sunday was an eventful day. Early that morning I received a visit from my friends Kelly Kennedy and Steve Crum, who live near Wichita, Kansas. They were in town for the Chiefs' game against the Broncos and had arrived early so they could come to the hospital and see me. Laughter was good medicine that day because I was feeling much better by the time they left.

The best part of my day was when my son Aaron and several of his friends came to the hospital after church to watch the Chiefs' game with me. I had been in the hospital for over a week, and I really missed getting to hang out with my kids. Even though the Chiefs ended up losing, I had a great afternoon with my son and his buddies.

Just when I thought my day couldn't get any better, the nurse came in with some very exciting news. My bladder had healed and the doctor was going to remove my catheter. She also informed me that I should take my walker and get into the shower because I would be leaving the hospital the next day. I was thrilled with the news that I was heading home.

I slowly climbed out of bed and went to the bathroom to get cleaned up. It was the first time I had showered in nine days. The shower was much more refreshing than the sponge baths I had been receiving. I still had a very long road ahead of me, but at least I would be recovering at "Home Sweet Home."

15

The Frozen
Bun Fun Run

"It's not how far you fall, but how high you bounce that counts."
Zig Ziglar

On Monday, December 2, 2013 at 1:00 p.m. I was released from
Centerpoint Medical Center. I returned home for the first time since
I had left for my appearance in Chillicothe the morning of
November 23. I was excited to go home but sad to say goodbye to
the hospital staff who had been so good to me. I stopped by the
nurses' desk to give hugs and thank them for all they had done for
me. They sent me home with a very important going away present.
It was a pillow I would end up sitting on for the next six months
while my very sore, shattered tailbone healed.

By the time I arrived home I was exhausted and ready for more
pain medications. I headed to the recliner and fell asleep until my
kids got home from school. That evening I was encouraged just to
be able to sit and visit with my kids. The past nine days had been
hard on the entire family, and it was good to be together again.

Darla DeBacker helped organize meals which were delivered to
our home each night. Many of these meals came from our friends at
Lee's Summit Community Church. The support we felt was a huge
blessing to our family. So many people signed up that we received
meals for over a month. The food was not only delicious, but it also
played an important role in my recovery because it helped me gain
weight. Having these meals relieved stress for Cam, who was busy
caring for me. While I was in the hospital I didn't have an appetite
and my weight dropped to 168 pounds, not a healthy weight for a
guy who is 6-foot-3. Before my fall my average weight was around
185 pounds, so I knew I needed to gain at least 15 pounds. It took

me several months, but with the help of many delicious meals and a steady diet of high calorie protein shakes, I eventually gained the needed weight.

The Kansas City Chiefs' organization was also very supportive. The staff went out of its way to make sure I had everything I needed during my recovery. Even though my coworkers were extremely busy with the season in full swing, they still made time to check on me and stop by to visit. I was also encouraged to receive several calls and emails from former Chiefs personnel.

On December 2, I received an email from former Chiefs' General Manager Carl Peterson which read:

Dan:

So sorry to hear of your bad accident. I never expected that when we selected you to be our "new" mascot, K.C. Wolf, in 1990, that you would still be doing crazy stunts some 25 years later! Seriously, have the young guys do those, because YOU are the best at what YOU do, and we need to see you HEALTHY!

Thanks for ALL that you did for ME, Lamar, our Chiefs' organization, and hundreds of thousands of kids (and adults). Get well soon, and best to your lovely family. CARL (& Lori)

A week later another former Chiefs' General Manager, Scott Pioli, called to check on me and to let me know I was in his prayers.

The most encouraging email I received was from Lamar Hunt's daughter Sharron Hunt. It read:

Dear Dan,

I was so, so, so very sorry to hear about your accident. I want you to know what an inspiration you have been and continue to be. You have been such a positive, upbeat, happy, energetic person. You have radiated charm, politeness, and goodwill to literally thousands of people in your career; you have communicated hundreds and hundreds of positive messages. I have often thought that I hope my sons grow up to be as polite, convicted, passionate, and impactful as you have been thus far in your career. The Chiefs' organization has been BLESSED to have you as a most important part of our team for soooooo many years.

You are a living example of true grace under extremely trying circumstances. As you mend, please be comforted and lifted up by the multitude of thoughts, prayers and good wishes that are surrounding you. Sending you my unending best wishes, I remain most respectfully yours,

Sharron Hunt

The Chiefs' organization and the Hunt family are a class act, a fact never more apparent to me than during my hospital stay and rehabilitation. Thanks to the support I received from the Chiefs, the only thing I had to focus on during my time off work was recovering from my injuries. There is no other team for which I would rather work.

My biggest supporter during my recovery was my wife. Although Cam never complained, I know she felt like she was taking care of a newborn baby again. Unfortunately for her, I was 47 years old and not nearly as cute as a newborn baby. I was grateful that when we took our wedding vows, we had included "for better or for worse" and "in sickness and in health." I was even more grateful I married a woman who was committed to those vows.

The day after I arrived home I had my first in home physical therapy appointment. My body felt miserable, and the last thing I wanted to do was therapy, but I knew I wouldn't get any better sitting around in the recliner. I determined in my mind to push myself a little harder each day. I didn't realize it at the time, but I would continue doing physical therapy three days a week for the next six months.

My first week at home was a very humbling experience. I literally needed help with everything I did. If I needed a drink, I would ring a bell, and someone would refill my water cup. My kids helped me put on my socks because I couldn't bend over. My wife had to help pull up my pants. I felt helpless, and I began to get discouraged. The doctor warned Cam to watch for signs of depression because that is normal in patients trying to recover from major injuries. The cold weather and the fact that I was confined to the house contributed to my discouragement.

One morning, as I was reading my Bible, I came across this verse. "The Lord hears his people when they call to Him for help. He rescues them from all their troubles. The Lord is close to the brokenhearted; He rescues those whose spirits are crushed. The righteous person faces many troubles, but the Lord comes to the rescue each time" (Psalm 34:17-19, NLT).

God knew my struggles and once again He used others to encourage me just when I needed it most. I began receiving cards and letters in the mail every day. Many days as I sat in my recliner and read these letters I became overwhelmed with gratitude as I realized people all over the United States and around the world were praying for me. Knowing thousands of people were lifting me up and praying for my healing was a huge encouragement.

One day the Chiefs sent a courier to my house. He delivered two tubs filled with hundreds of cards and letters mailed to Arrowhead from Chiefs' fans who were concerned about KC Wolf. Many of these were large envelopes from elementary schools filled with get well wishes from students. Once again, my eyes filled with tears. For 24 years I had traveled all over the Midwest encouraging students to be their best, and now I was the one on the receiving end of the encouragement.

One of my favorite notes was from a little girl named Lauren who had creative spelling and wasn't afraid to say it like it was. On the outside of the card she wrote, "Get Well Soon KC Wolf! Merry Chrismas and Happy Thanksgiving"

The inside of the card read:

"hello KC Wolf my name is Lauren. You came for a asembaley at my school. You probably don't rember but I am from Sterling Elimentry and I am so so sorey and you know what you are so lucey you dident die. That would be sad wouldnent." Merrey Chrismas
Love Lauren

I laughed because she was absolutely right. It would have been sad if I would have died, but thankfully I was still very much alive. I really enjoyed reading the letters from the little kids because they were brutally honest. It was also fun to read their notes and try to decipher some of the creative spellings.

On Wednesday, December 11, I left my house for the first time. Cam drove me to the hospital for an appointment with my back surgeon. He examined me and said everything looked normal. Since the seven and a half inch scar on my back was healing properly, he removed the staples and sent me to get fitted for a back brace, which I wore for the next several months. Even though I still couldn't drive, the doctor said as long as I wore my back brace and promised to be cautious I could venture out of the house. Just knowing I had the freedom to leave the house lifted my spirits. After being stuck in a hospital and at home for almost three weeks with nothing to do, even a visit to Walmart felt like a trip to Disney World.

On Sunday, December 15, I attended church for the first time in a month. I laughed on the way into church because while everyone else was carrying their Bibles into the service I was carrying an inflatable donut to sit on to take pressure off of my tailbone. God must have a sense of humor, because I was trying to gain weight, and at the service our pastor announced he was starting a new sermon series on fasting.

It felt good to be back in church. The service reminded me it was only by the grace of God I was still alive and worshipping with my family that morning. Once again, the tears began to roll down my face. It had been three weeks since my fall and I was still feeling strong emotions. Lots of people came up to me with hugs and handshakes and let me know I was in their prayers. I returned home from church both encouraged and exhausted. I spent the afternoon sitting in the recliner, napping and watching the Chiefs win big over the Oakland Raiders, 56-31. It had been an encouraging day, and God used that Sunday to prepare me for the challenging week ahead.

That week I decided to reduce my pain medications. Although I liked the pain relief, I did not like the many side effects that came with the medicine. One of those side effects was constipation. With a shattered tailbone, a large hematoma under the skin on my upper left leg, and the lingering pain from my back surgery, sitting on a toilet was a painful experience. My doctor warned me that constipation would make the pain even worse. I had no desire to live on pain medications and stool softeners for the rest of my life, so I decided to take action. I thought that if I slowly weaned myself off the pain medications, I would also reduce my risk of constipation.

One night while trying to sleep in the recliner, I could tell I was in trouble. I was starting to get stopped up. While the rest of the family was upstairs sleeping, I searched the internet to see how to avoid constipation. I found an article which said to drink plenty of water and eat foods high in fiber. I immediately drank a big glass of water and started looking through our pantry for the foods with the highest amount of fiber. In the back of the pantry I found a can of kidney beans. I read the nutrition label which said the kidney beans contained 36% of my daily dietary fiber needs per serving. What was really exciting was that each can of beans contained three and a half servings. I opened the can of beans, got out a spoon, and within 10 minutes I ate 126% of my daily dietary fiber. About an hour later, the water and beans worked their magic, and everything was flowing just fine.

As I began to reduce my pain medications, however, my sleeping patterns were disrupted. For several weeks I slept an average of four hours each day. The lack of sleep took a toll on me. I was physically exhausted and mentally worn out. The most difficult time for me was between 11:00 p.m. and 4:00 a.m. while the rest of the family was sleeping. I read, watched movies, prayed and walked around trying to make myself tired. Several mornings I could see the sun coming up before I finally fell asleep.

I kept a journal during my recovery, and many of my journal entries expressed my struggles and frustrations. One week was particularly challenging.

On Sunday I wrote: "God, I'm so tired. I've struggled trying to sleep at night this past month. It's 2:00 a.m. and I'm still awake. Lord, please help me to sleep."

On Monday: "Battling discouragement today. Didn't fall asleep until 4:00 a.m. last night. Slept TERRIBLE. Struggling not to have a pity party today."

On Friday: "It's 6:49 a.m. and I haven't slept all night. Very frustrating and discouraging. This recovery has been emotionally draining. Lord, please give me the strength to continue. Please help me sleep better."

By the end of the week I couldn't take the sleeplessness anymore. I called my doctor, who prescribed some sleep medications to help me get the sleep I needed. Once again I felt like my road to recovery was filled with ups and downs. I was encouraged to be using less pain medication, but discouraged because I felt like I was replacing pain pills with sleeping pills.

I did receive encouraging news on Friday, December 20. My back doctor gave me permission to begin riding my stationary bike and using an elliptical machine. He made me wear my back brace, but he said I could ride for as long as I could tolerate the pain. I knew this exercise would help build up my endurance. I was also hoping it would wear me out so I could sleep better at night. On the first day I biked 15 minutes sitting on a pillow and then walked 20 minutes on the elliptical. It wasn't much compared to the hour I was riding before my accident, but at least it was a start.

The stationary bike was definitely the more painful of the two exercises. Just to be safe I sought a second opinion from my tailbone specialist. He agreed with the back doctor. There was really no way for me to further damage my tailbone because it was already shattered. He agreed that as long as I could tolerate the pain, I should keep on exercising. He told me the additional blood flow would actually speed up the healing process. If riding the stationary bike helped me heal more quickly, I decided I would start riding about four to five times every week. Each time I went downstairs to ride, I brought a thick pillow to sit on to help ease my tailbone pain. I kept trying to remind myself of the old slogan: "No pain, no gain." I could definitely feel the pain, and I was praying for the gain.

On the evening of December 20, I returned to Arrowhead for the first time since my accident for the Chiefs' company Christmas party. It was great to see my coworkers again and say thank you to those who had helped me the day I was injured.

The week surrounding Christmas was just what I needed. All of the parties and activities helped distract my mind from focusing on my pain and struggles. Christmas Day was especially meaningful for me. In our home we have a strange Christmas Day tradition. I'm not sure how the tradition got started, but we call it the "Frozen Bun Fun

Run." On Christmas morning my kids wake up early, and we go downstairs to open our gifts. After we open gifts, we read the Christmas story out of the Bible and pray together as a family. Then while Cam prepares breakfast, the kids and I get ready for the Frozen Bun Fun Run.

This run is something our family looks forward to each year. Every Christmas there is one gift I know my kids are going to get me, and that is a pair of boxer shorts. The boxers are not a surprise because I get a pair every year. The only surprise is what is going to be on the boxers. Over the years my kids have given me boxers with Homer Simpson, Uncle Si from Duck Dynasty, Flash Gordon, and a variety of other characters. Because of my bungee accident a month earlier, my kids thought it would be appropriate to give me a pair of Superman boxers that had a little red cape attached to the back. My son Aaron had also received a pair of boxers. His new Batman boxers had a black cape attached.

As Cam prepared breakfast, the kids and I went upstairs to get ready for the run. I put on my boxer shorts with nothing else—no shirt, no shoes, no nothing. Aaron also put on his boxers, and Mycah and Mallory dressed in shorts and swim suit tops. When everyone was dressed, we met downstairs to compete in the race.

The Frozen Bun Fun Run consists of running one lap around the outside of the house barefoot in the snow. I had never missed a race on Christmas morning, and I didn't want to miss this year just because of my injuries. I figured the doctor probably wouldn't want me to participate in the race this year so I didn't ask his permission. I just did it.

Apparently the kids didn't think I was going to be much of a threat to win because they were very nice to me. They knew I couldn't run, so they let me wear tennis shoes so my toes wouldn't get frostbite. They also allowed me to wear my back brace in case I slipped on the ice in the driveway.

When the race began, the kids were half way around the house before I even got down the stairs off the back deck. I slowly began my very refreshing trip around the house, being extremely careful not to slip. The day was brutally cold, and I felt like I was about to freeze, but as I shuffled my feet through the snow I was a very happy man. I felt fully alive. It was exactly one month and two days after my 75 foot fall, and I was healthy enough to compete in the 2013 Frozen Bun Fun Run. I finished in fourth place and posted the slowest time ever recorded in the history of the Frozen Bun Fun Run, but at least I was alive and able to compete.

Why do I get half-naked and run through the snow every year on Christmas morning? The answer is simple. I do it because my kids think it is fun, and we make memories. I want my kids to know their dad loves them so much that he is willing to get out and run half-naked in the snow with a back brace. Once again, we are making family memories that will last a lifetime.

During the first week of the new year I really began seeing progress on my conditioning. I was now riding the stationary bike for 30 minutes and walking on the elliptical for another 45 minutes. I was exercising for 1 hour and 15 minutes, and I could tell that my legs were getting stronger. Even though it was a challenge, I was getting better at riding the stationary bike while wearing a back brace and sitting on a pillow.

January 7, 2014 was my 47th birthday, and I decided it was the perfect day to really push myself and see how far I could bike. I ended up biking for an hour and went 18.5 miles. When I climbed off the bike, I was super excited and also very tired. It was the best birthday gift I could give myself.

The next day I had another visit with my back doctor. He told me everything looked good and encouraged me to start doing outpatient physical therapy. My friend Barry Kindler suggested I visit Summit Strength Physical Therapy and Rehab in Lee's Summit. He had done his physical therapy there and had nothing but good things to say. Summit Strength was only five minutes from my house so I called and scheduled an appointment.

My physical therapist, Ed Knapp, and his assistant, Chandra Moore, were excellent. I told them on my first visit I wanted them to push me and to challenge me if they ever caught me being lazy during my rehab. Ed promised me that my road to recovery was going to be a long process, but if I was patient and worked hard I would see major improvement.

My first visit to Summit Strength was on January 10, 2014. Ed performed an initial evaluation and told me I was well below where I needed to be in flexibility and strength. The only area where I scored above average was the strength of my stomach muscles.

Over the next five months I came to know the staff and patients at Summit Strength very well. Many of the older patients were there for knee or hip replacement therapy. Some of the younger patients were athletes who had injured themselves playing sports. I was the only guy there who had injured himself doing a bungee jump. As a matter of fact, Ed told me I was the only mascot and bungee jump survivor ever treated at Summit Strength. Ed had a great sense of humor and he informed me that "PT" stood for "Pain & Torture." After my first couple of visits, I believed him. The joke around Summit Strength was the physical therapists should be called the physical terrorists.

One of the first things Ed worked on was breaking up the scar tissue which had developed in the tissue around my spine. I laid face down on the therapy table and Ed dug his thumbs deep into the muscle tissue along both sides of my incisions. This process lasted about 20-25 minutes and was incredibly painful.

During one session while Ed was busy inflicting pain on me, he gave me permission to call him names. I promised I wouldn't say anything bad, but if he continued to hurt me I was going to bite a hole in his therapy table. The next appointment, as Ed was once again delivering pain and torture, I said, "Ed, I'm trying to pretend this is a massage and that you're cute and I'm really struggling with both." He laughed, and I think he realized I needed a laugh to keep from crying. After several weeks of this intense therapy, the scar tissue on my back finally started to loosen up. I was making progress, slowly but surely.

My therapy appointments lasted about two-and-a-half hours. I spent the first hour stretching and letting Ed work his magic on the scar tissue and paraspinal muscles in my back. The second hour was spent with Chandra doing a variety of exercises to strengthen my back, legs and core muscles. The final 30 minutes I worked out on my own doing lunges and other exercises I knew would help me get back into mascot shape. By the time I finished and arrived back home, I was ready for a nap, but I rarely took one because I knew sleeping in the afternoon would keep me from sleeping at night.

On March 26, I traveled to Sioux Falls, South Dakota, to speak at the Western Iowa Dairy Alliance prayer breakfast. The long drive to South Dakota was hard on my tailbone, but it felt good to take a few days and get a break from my physical therapy appointments. Midwest Dairy Association was one of KC Wolf's sponsors, and I always enjoyed speaking at their events. Just knowing I was well enough to go out and speak again lifted my spirits. Having the opportunity to share my story felt like one more hurdle I was clearing on my road to recovery.

At the prayer breakfast I spoke to about 350 people about how God had spared my life. Emotionally, telling the story was very challenging because it caused me to relive the events of November 23, 2013. However, I felt my experience had given me a greater empathy for others who were dealing with both physical and emotional pain. Driving home from South Dakota, I realized maybe God had allowed my painful experience so I could better minister to others who were dealing with pain in their lives.

When I returned home, I began receiving many more requests to share my story. After all the pain and struggles of the past four months, I was encouraged to think that maybe by sharing my experience, I could have a positive impact in the lives of others. The pain was no fun, but God was always faithful in the midst of it. As I settled back into the routine of having therapy three days a week, my road to recovery continued to feel like a rollercoaster. One day I would be encouraged, and the next day I would struggle with disappointment. My journal entries often revealed my emotions and struggles:

"God, I am battling strong feelings of depression and discouragement. I have worked so hard to get stronger and recover from my injuries. There are many days when I still feel like half the man I used to be. My back pain and stiffness drive me crazy and make me angry. When I become angry and depressed, I withdraw and become self-absorbed. My family suffers because of this behavior. I feel like I'm on an emotional roller coaster, and I'm getting very tired of the ride."

In April my NFL Furternity brothers surprised me with a ticket to Seattle, Washington, for a weekend with 12 other NFL mascots. They were all in Seattle to make an appearance at the Multiple Sclerosis Walk. Even though I still wasn't cleared by my doctor to dress up as KC Wolf, I enjoyed watching my Furternity brothers perform.

The Seattle Seahawks mascot Ryan Asdourian (aka Blitz) was diagnosed with multiple sclerosis in 2008. He is one of my heroes. Instead of sitting around and feeling sorry for himself, Blitz used his platform as the Seahawks mascot to help raise money for MS research. In his first four years, Blitz raised over $300,000. As I talked with Blitz about how he had taken his health struggles and used them to make a positive impact in the lives of others, I realized I could do the same thing. I returned home excited about the possibilities that lay ahead. I smiled as I once again remembered Romans 8:28, "We know that in all things God works for the good of those who love Him, who have been called according to His purpose."

Several days later, my longtime friend and accountability partner Rod Handley handed me this quote, "God has a purpose for your pain, a reason for your struggles and a reward for your faithfulness." This quote summarized what God had been teaching me. Rod reminded me what a one of a kind story God had given me. He said, "An NFL mascot who survives a failed bungee jump is a very interesting and unique story." He encouraged me to share my story in the pages of a book. I immediately thought back to a conversation I had with Jack Steadman several months earlier at the Chiefs' Christmas party. Jack had encouraged me to make a bucket list and start working to check things off my list. Writing a book was one of the things on my list, and I realized now was as good a time as any to begin. The thought of writing a book seemed overwhelming, but since I was still off work and not sleeping well at night, I had plenty of time to begin the project.

Rod and I decided *"Wolves Can't Fly"* would be a perfect title for the book since I had proven I couldn't fly during my bungee jump. As I looked through photo albums and journals trying to gather the details of my mascot career, I began to get a vision for what God could accomplish through my story. It was fun to look back and reminisce about the people, places and events I had experienced during my 25+ years in feathers and fur. Doing research for the book also helped to take my mind off my pain.

For the next several months I spent hundreds of hours working on the book. I began to wake up each morning with anticipation and a renewed sense of purpose. Writing down the details of my accident and all the lessons God had taught me became a blessing. I realized there really was a purpose behind my pain, and I made a commitment to use my story to minister to others who are struggling with pain and hurt.

On June 3, 2014, I was finally released by my doctors to return to work as KC Wolf. I was both thrilled and relieved. When I arrived at Arrowhead, a big banner was hanging on the front door that said, "Welcome Back KC Wolf." When I went upstairs, I discovered my coworkers had filled my office with balloons and had streamers hanging from the door. Just outside my office door was a table sitting in the middle of the hallway. On the table was a "Welcome Back KC Wolf" cake. I didn't get much accomplished my first day back, but I did have a great time eating and catching up with friends I had not seen in more than six months.

My first appearance in costume was several weeks later at the Nazarene Church in Chanute, Kansas. I was nervous because I had not dressed as KC Wolf in nearly seven months and wasn't sure how my body would respond. I quickly learned being a mascot is like riding a bike, once you learn to do it you never forget. It didn't take long for me to start feeling comfortable in costume again, and I was very encouraged with my stamina. Apparently the six months of physical therapy had paid off.

I knew my body's biggest test would come on August 7 when the Chiefs played the Cincinnati Bengals in their first preseason game of the 2014 season. I was very excited about this game because not only was it my first game back since my accident, it also marked the beginning of my 25th year as KC Wolf.

As I stood on the field, listening to the National Anthem and staring up into the crowd at Arrowhead, once again I was overcome with emotion. Under the KC Wolf head, where nobody could see me, I had tears of joy running down my face. I was finally back to doing what I love.

16
Lessons Learned

"Success comes in a lot of ways, but it doesn't come with money and it doesn't come with fame. It comes from having a meaning in your life, doing what you love and being passionate about what you do. When you have the ability to do what you love, love what you do and have the ability to impact people. That is having a life of success. That's having a life of meaning."
Tim Tebow

I gave up playing church league basketball in the summer of 2013. Although I loved playing with the guys, it became more and more obvious I needed to step away. Every Sunday afternoon when I drove to the gym, I asked myself if one hour of fun was really worth three days' worth of pain. That was how long it took my body to recover from the beating it took trying to play basketball against the younger guys. I had a big problem with remembering and acting my age. In my mind, I was thinking I was still in my early 20's, but in reality my body was double that age. What my mind thought my body should do, and what my body was capable of doing, were two totally different things.

I was reminded of a story I had read by author Max Lucado. Max talked about the basketball players at his church. He said the players fell into one of two categories, the Flat Bellies and the Fat Bellies. The Flat Bellies were those guys who could touch their toes and touch the rim. The Fat Bellies were the guys who couldn't even see their toes and definitely couldn't touch the rim. In 2013, I finally realized I no longer fit into either category. My belly was still flat thanks to my job as KC Wolf, but I noticed my toes were getting much more difficult to reach and the rim was getting a whole lot harder to touch. Church league basketball was making me feel old so I decided it was time to step away.

As much as I don't like feeling like I'm getting older, in a way I'm thankful for it because the aches and pains remind me that life really is short and I need to make the most of the each day I'm given. Above my desk at Arrowhead Stadium I have a quote which says, "Life is like a coin, you can spend it any way you wish but you can only spend it once, so spend wisely." I love this quote because it reminds me that I get to make choices every day regarding how I will live my life. I get to choose how I spend my coin. I want to spend wisely. I want to live my days on this earth with purpose and passion. Unfortunately, many people today are passionate about things in life that don't really matter, and they are passive about those things that do matter. My desire is to live passionately for the important things in life. As my friend Dan Erickson says, "I don't fear failure; I fear succeeding in life at things that don't really matter." I want to live so that on my deathbed I can look forward with anticipation, instead of looking back with disappointment and regrets.

As I reflect on my career, I realize how blessed I am. I think about all the people I've met and the places I've visited during my 25 plus years in feathers and fur. My journey has been a lot of fun, but more importantly I've learned some valuable lessons along the way. Most of these lessons I learned from reading God's Word and from observing the lives of the many people I've met. I'm thankful to those people who have modeled for me how to live life to the fullest and how to spend my coin wisely.

In the spirit of late night talk show host David Letterman, I have created a Top 10 List. These are the Top 10 Lessons I've learned during my mascot career. I've tried to live according to these principles each day so someday I can look back on my life with no regrets.

Lesson #10 – Live Like a Bee, Not Like a Buzzard

The way we treat others is extremely important. We can learn an important lesson from buzzards and bees. Buzzards and bees both fly around looking for things to eat. While buzzards are out looking for nasty things like dead animals, bees are busy looking for flowers with pollen and sweet nectar. The buzzards and the bees always find what they are seeking. Over the course of my career I've learned the same is true with people.

Some people act like buzzards. They go through life being critical and always looking for the worst in others. Since none of us is perfect, finding fault with others is not hard to do. However, living like this is no way to make friends. People who live like bees never have a shortage of friends. They are encouraging to be with because they have learned to look for the best in others. Who would you rather spend time with? Someone who points out your faults and failures, or someone who encourages you by pointing out your good qualities?

One of the nicest men I've ever known was "Mr. Music" Tony DiPardo. Tony and the TD Pack Band played live music at every Chiefs home game for more than 40 seasons. What made Tony an inspiration to others wasn't just his music, but more importantly, the man himself. Tony DiPardo was a bee. Every time I saw Tony he would give me a hug and an encouraging word. I never heard him say a bad thing about anyone, which explains why Tony had thousands of friends.

Scripture tells us very plainly that we will reap what we sow (Galatians 6:7-8). This principle applies to farming, but it also applies to the way we treat others. A friend of mine once told me, "You can either be a wind in someone's sail or an anchor in their tail." He is absolutely right. You can either go through life building others up or tearing others down. Tony DiPardo was a builder. He realized it is just as easy to look for the good in other people as it is to look for the bad. If you really want to live a life of no regrets, learn to live like a bee and not like a buzzard. Make a habit out of looking for the best in others, and then sow seeds of love, kindness and respect. "Treat others the way you would want them to treat you." The reason it's called the Golden Rule is because it is as good as gold. Try it. It works.

Lesson #9 – Worry Less and Laugh More

I will confess I've spent too much time in life worrying. I've worried about grades, girlfriends, bills, taxes, dentist appointments, rising gas prices, politics, first impressions and even NFL football games. After years of losing sleep, I finally figured out worrying is a waste of time. The only thing worry does is pull tomorrow's clouds over today's sunshine. I once read, "You can't change your past, but you can certainly ruin a perfectly good present by worrying about the future." God's Word tells us not to worry in Philippians 4:6-7 (NLT): "Don't worry about anything; instead, pray about everything. Tell God what you need, and thank him for all he has done. Then you will experience God's peace, which exceeds anything we can understand. His peace will guard your hearts and minds as you live in Christ Jesus." Also, 1 Peter 5:7 (NLT) says: "Give all your worries and cares to God, for He cares about you."

Worry is not part of God's plan for my life, and it only leads to regret. God cares for me, and I need to remember He is in control. I'm not helping God out by worrying about my problems. He wants me to trust Him and enjoy the life He has given me. Life is much more enjoyable when I worry less and laugh more.

Written on a note card taped to my desk at work is the KC Wolf mascot motto: "Laughter is like changing a baby's diaper, it won't change anything permanently but it will sure make things more bearable for a while." I love this motto because it reminds me to take time to laugh every day. Laughter is to life what shock absorbers are to automobiles. It helps me handle the bumps in the road.

I've learned when I look closely there are many things in life that make me laugh. I came across one the other day in a church bulletin. It was a story about a church pastor who was out visiting church members on a Saturday afternoon. He stopped at one house and knocked on the door, but nobody answered. The pastor was a little annoyed because he heard footsteps, and he knew the mother was at home. So he left his business card on the front door and on the back of it he wrote Revelation 3:20, "Here I am. I stand at the door and knock. If anyone hears my voice and opens the door, I will come in and eat with him."

The next day at church as the congregation was leaving, the woman who had refused to answer the door greeted the pastor on her way out and handed him her business card. On the back of her card she had written Genesis 3:10. Later when the pastor got home he looked that Bible verse up and it said, "I heard thy voice in the garden and was afraid because I was naked and I hid myself."

Trust me. Laughter is good medicine even if you're not a mascot. My goal is to laugh a lot during my lifetime so when I'm older all of my wrinkles will be in the right places. The people I know who live life to the fullest are those who have learned to laugh more and worry less.

Lesson #8 – Avoid Busyness and Embrace Priorities

We live in a very busy world. If you're like me, it seems there is always something needing my attention. My grass needs mowed, the car needs an oil change, my kids have ball practice and the list goes on and on. Many days I feel like a tight rope walker struggling to keep my balance. Trying to balance my responsibilities at work and home often times becomes very difficult. The older I get the more I realize that busy doesn't always mean better. I've learned that if I'm not careful, busyness can lead to regrets. I'm speaking from experience because this is one of the lessons I have learned the hard way.

When you stop and think about it, there are two kinds of regrets. First there are those times in life when you do or say something that you wish you could take back. This happens when your mouth speaks before your brain kicks into gear. I refer to this as "Open Mouth and Insert Foot." The second kind of regret involves times when you don't do something and later wish you had. These are missed opportunities that could have been taken, but now the moment has passed. If we are not careful, busyness will cause us to miss out on things we will later regret.

A dear friend of mine once told me, "If the devil can't make you bad, he will make you busy." There is a lot of wisdom in this statement. The Bible tells us the devil is out to destroy our lives. 1 Peter 5:8 (NLT) says, "Stay alert! Watch out for your great enemy, the devil. He prowls around like a roaring lion, looking for someone to devour."

Satan would love nothing more than to take out my marriage, my family and ultimately destroy me. I believe busyness is one of Satan's greatest strategies because he knows when we get too busy we begin to lose our focus. Those things which should be a priority in our life begin to take a backseat. Urgent things begin to replace the important things, and when this happens regret is soon to follow. Let me repeat something I mentioned earlier in chapter 8, "The urgent things in life are seldom important, and the important things in life are seldom urgent." The happiest people I know are those who live for the important things.

My priorities are very simple—my faith and my family. Everything else falls in line after these two priorities. My life is most satisfying when I remember to keep the main thing the main thing. A prayer I wrote in my journal expressed my desire to live my life according to God's priorities. "Lord, help me never to clutter my life with things or stuff that will take my eyes off of You. I don't want the busyness of life to distract me from Your purpose for me. I want to live life according to Your day planner, not mine."

My family is also top priority. My children are growing up very quickly. I only have them under my roof for a short amount of time. I don't want to miss out on dad moments because I'm busy doing less important things. I want my words and my actions to demonstrate to my wife and kids that they are very important to me.

In 2005, I felt a strong conviction that I needed to make my family a higher priority. This was the primary reason I decided to hire my first backup KC Wolf. It was hard for me to admit that work had taken precedence over my family, but it was true. For 15 years I had been the only person to wear the KC Wolf costume. I ran around trying to make every single appearance people requested. In the early years it wasn't too bad because I only averaged 200-250 appearances a year. As the years went on and the popularity of KC Wolf grew, I was making over 350 appearances annually. Even though I still claimed my family was my priority, in reality KC Wolf appearances often trumped family. When my kids started elementary school, I noticed I would often miss their activities because of work.

When I had my yearly review with the Chiefs after the 2004 season, I knew something needed to change. I told my boss that while I loved being KC Wolf, I could no longer be out entertaining other kids while my own children had an absent father. I suggested we hire a backup KC Wolf, which would allow me greater flexibility with my schedule. If my children had a school concert or a sporting event scheduled at the same time as a KC Wolf appearance, I could send my backup to the appearance. It is the best career decision I ever made. I was happier, but more importantly, my wife and kids were happier. As a father I can honestly say I would rather watch my kids play Little League sports than watch an NFL football game any day. And trust me, nobody likes NFL football more than KC Wolf.

Like many men, I admit there have been times during my career where I have allowed my work to interfere with more important things. I regret those times when I have failed, and I've tried to learn from my past mistakes. I once heard a very successful businessman say, "If you are a success in your business but not a success in your home, then you are not a success." I have tried to keep this truth in mind as I strive to give my best at both home and work. I strive for excellence in all areas of my life, but I'm often reminded that I have limitations. If I'm going to be an overachiever, I want it to start in my home first.

Lesson #7 – Don't Be Greedy, Be Grateful

As I was growing up, my mom stressed to my brothers and me the importance of loving others. She taught us that loving people was more important than loving things or stuff. The words were easy to say, but it has been a whole lot harder to live out.

We live in a very materialistic society. If we're not careful, we find ourselves more concerned with our possessions than with the people in our lives. Author Dave Ramsey likes to say, "We often buy things we don't need, with money that we don't have, to impress people we don't even like." This quote may sound cute, but I'm convinced it's true. Advertisers try to convince us to buy the latest and greatest items on the market today. These include everything from the cars we drive, to the clothes we wear, to the phones we use to talk and text. What we want and what we *need* are two very different things. I confess there have been many times in life when I have gotten my needs and my greeds confused.

First Timothy 6:6-7 says, "But godliness with contentment is great gain. For we brought nothing into the world, and we can take nothing out of it." Often I have to stop and ask myself, "What tent am I living in? Content or discontent?" If my answer is discontent then it is time for an attitude adjustment.

On May 24, 2000, I wrote down this quote in my devotional journal. "Contentment is the product of a heart resting in God. It is the soul's enjoyment of the peace that passes all understanding. Contentment is only possible as we maintain the attitude of accepting everything that enters our lives as coming from the hand of Him who is too wise to err and too loving to cause one of His children a needless tear." I concluded my journal entry with this prayer: "Lord, teach me to be content in every situation. Always desiring more, bigger or better is a dangerous attitude to have. Thank you Lord that knowing You is greater than anything this world has to offer."

An important lesson I've tried to teach my kids is learning to be content and grateful. My goal is to set an example for them by being a grateful person myself. I wish I could forget my problems as quickly as I seem to forget my blessings. Living a grateful life doesn't come naturally to me, but I've learned it is definitely worth the effort. The people I've met who seem to enjoy life the most aren't always the ones with the most money. I have met some very rich people who seem absolutely miserable. The happiest people I know are those who have learned the secret of being content and grateful. They are thankful for what they have, and they realize more stuff doesn't mean more happiness. A Benedictine monk once said, "In daily life we must understand that it is not happiness that makes us grateful, but gratefulness that makes us happy." If you want to live a happy life learn to be grateful, not greedy.

Lesson #6 – Avoid Selfishness and Embrace Service

Just like gratefulness makes you happy, selfishness makes you miserable. I have never met a truly happy person who was self-absorbed. It is impossible to enjoy life to the fullest if the only person you're concerned with is yourself. Of all the four letter words, "self" is the worst. I've learned when we become self-absorbed, we fail to connect with those around us. When we begin to focus on ourselves, our world becomes very small. When our world is small, it causes our problems and preoccupations to appear much larger. However, when we turn our focus toward others, our world expands and keeping our own problems in perspective becomes much easier. Philippians 2:3-4 (NLT) says, "Don't be selfish; don't try to impress others. Be humble, thinking of others as better than yourselves.

Don't look out only for your own interests, but take an interest in others, too."

One of the most rewarding KC Wolf appearances I've ever made was on August 23, 2012, in Joplin, Missouri. An EF-5 tornado had devastated Joplin the previous year, and the town was still struggling to recover. The Chiefs took several buses filled with players, coaches, cheerleaders, employees, and me to assist in building a playground for the community. The day was long, exhausting and very hot, but the experience was one I will never forget. After a day spent serving the people of Joplin, I left there realizing my big problems weren't so big after all. Martin Luther King Jr. once said, "Everybody can be great...because anybody can serve. You don't have to have a college degree to serve. You don't have to make your subject and verb agree to serve. You only need a heart full of grace. A soul generated by love." My day in Joplin reminded me of a very important lesson. God measures our service not by our ability, but by our willingness. Joy in this life is found in service to others, not in selfishness.

Lesson #5 – Avoid Compromise and Embrace Character

One thing many Chiefs' fans may not know about me is that I love country music. One of my favorite songs is, "You've Got to Stand for Something" by Aaron Tippin. My favorite part of the song isn't the melody, it's the lyrics. The chorus says:

"You've got to stand for something or you'll fall for anything.
You've got to be your own man, not a puppet on a string.
Never compromise what's right and uphold your family name.
You've got to stand for something or you'll fall for anything."

If you want to live life to the fullest then don't compromise. Stand up for your convictions. Take a stand for your beliefs. One of my journal entries from 1998 reminded me that living a life of character often involves making tough choices. It read, "Today I turned down an appearance at the grand opening of a video store. I was going to make a large amount of money for the appearance, but I turned it down because the store had a small room in the back where they sold adult X-rated videos. The decision should have been easy to make, but like always Satan tried to get me to compromise and rationalize my decision. I know I made the right decision, and I know the Lord will bless that decision. Choices should be easy. There is God's way and there is every other way. DO THINGS GOD'S WAY." Horace Greeley once wrote, "Fame is a vapor. Popularity is an accident. Money takes wings. Those who cheer you today will curse you tomorrow. The only thing that endures is character."

During my Chiefs career one of the players I greatly admired was Tony Richardson. Tony was an undrafted fullback out of Auburn who went on to play 16 seasons in the NFL. Eleven of those seasons were in Kansas City. Tony and I became friends during his time with the Chiefs, and we did numerous charity events together. Tony appeared in four Pro Bowls and is considered one of the greatest fullbacks in NFL history, having blocked for 1000 yard rushers in nine consecutive seasons. He was an incredible football player, but what I admired most about Tony Richardson was his faith and his Christ like character.

I watched how Tony conducted himself both on and off the football field. I learned a very valuable lesson from my observations. "Your reputation is precious, but your character is priceless." In his professional life, and in his personal life, Tony was committed to living a life of character. Tony knew what he believed, and he stood for those beliefs.

Individuals who stand out because of their character have learned not to make decisions based upon what is most convenient or what is popular at the time. Men and women of character make their decisions committed to always doing what is right. There is a great song called, "You Can't Go Wrong Doing Right." This important message is what I try to teach my children. I hope to model the message for them by living a life of character.

Lesson #4 – Fight Fear With Faith

Several years ago I had the privilege of hearing Eric Boles speak at my church. Eric was a former wide receiver for the Green Bay Packers and New York Jets. Eric is now a motivational speaker and the president of Game Changers, a company dedicated to leadership and personal development. During his sermon Eric made this statement: "Fear and faith are both contagious." The more I thought about his statement the more I realized its truth.

Some mornings when I wake up, worries and fears threaten to consume my thoughts and rob my joy. On those mornings I get to make a choice. I can choose to feed my fears, or I can choose to feed my faith. Whichever one I choose to feed is the one that will grow. Either my faith becomes bigger and my fears become smaller, or my problems and fears become bigger and my faith becomes smaller. It's a battle, but I've learned the best way to fight my fears is by putting my faith in a God who loves me and promises to take care of me. God never promised me a life that is free from pain, but He does promise to walk with me through my pain. He promises to join me on my journey.

Have you ever seen a bird having a nervous breakdown? No, the Bible says birds don't fly around with fears and worries because they know God will feed them. Scripture tells us that we are far more valuable to Him than birds (Matthew 6:25-34). We can learn a lot from birds. Fear leads to regret. Faith in Christ leads to hope and security. Fears will cripple you while faith will set you free to live life to the fullest.

Lesson #3 – Choose Joy

I have always been attracted to joyful people because they are more fun to be around. Joy is something I desire in my own life. The Bible says, "The fruit of the Spirit is love, JOY, peace, patience, kindness, goodness, faithfulness, gentleness and self-control" (Galatians 5:22-23, NASB).

I have no interest in being a religious "nut," but I desperately want the fruit of the Spirit to be displayed in my life. Joy seems to be a pretty important quality because God placed it second on the list behind love. I wanted to figure out how I could be a more joyful person.

At one of my appearances at Arrowhead I met an amazing man who taught me a very valuable lesson about joy. His name was Bob Wieland, a Vietnam War veteran who lost his legs to a mortar mine in 1969. After recovering from his injuries, he became a marathon

206 WOLVES CAN'T FLY

participant. Bob is the only double amputee to finish the difficult
Hawaii Ironman race without a wheelchair. He also ran across
America on his hands, taking three years, eight months, and six days
to travel from coast-to-coast. After talking to Bob I was impressed
by all he had accomplished, but I was even more impressed by the
joy that was evident in his life. Bob shared with me, "Joy is a choice."
God offers us joy, but it is our choice to accept it. Bob was obviously a man who chose to be joyful despite his difficult circumstances.
He was an inspiration to me that even on my worst days, I can still
choose joy.

Author Barbara Johnson once wrote, "Some days you're the
pigeon, and some days you're the statue." I'm thankful for men like
Bob Wieland who taught me that even on those days when I feel like
a statue, I can still choose joy.

These eight lessons I've learned have been a huge blessing in my
life. My goal is to live them out each and every day. Life is much
more enjoyable and meaningful when I'm looking for the best in
others and living my days filled with love, laughter, contentment,
character, service, faith and joy. These eight lessons have impacted
me greatly, but the two greatest lessons I've learned I have chosen
to wrap into the next and final chapter, as my story draws to a close.

17

My Two
Greatest Lessons

*"Don't worry what you could do if you lived your life over;
get busy with what's left."*

When I think back on my bungee jump accident and all I've
been through during my recovery, at times I wish I could turn back
the clock. If I could somehow go back to November 23, 2013, I
would have kept my feet firmly planted on the ground. The physical pain and emotional struggles continue to be a source of frustra-
tion. Although I have worked extremely hard to recover from my
injuries, I realize my body, and especially my back, will never quite
be the same. Those who live with chronic pain know how physically draining and emotionally discouraging some days can be.

I am fully convinced God has a purpose behind every trial and
difficulty we face in life. I also believe both the type and the timing
of accidents, or what I call incidents, are under His wise control.
Even though I wish I could have avoided my physical injuries, I am
very thankful for the important lessons God has taught me. Though
life isn't always fair, God is always faithful. God needed to work in
my life before He could work through my life. My bungee jump was
a major wakeup call to show me that life really is precious. In a matter of seconds my life and my perspective on it changed. I quickly
realized I'm not a cat with nine lives; I'm a wolf with one, and my
life came close to ending on that cold November afternoon. Since
then I wake up every morning grateful for another day.

In John 10:10 (NASB), Jesus says, "I came that they may have
life, and have it more abundantly." This is another promise from
God's Word. If God makes me a promise, I intend to take Him up
on it. I don't want to get up every morning and go through the

motions of life. I refuse to live the precious few days I have on this earth just existing. Jesus came to give us life, not just mundane life, but abundant life. He created us to thrive, not just to survive. But He is the door (John 10: 7, 9). He is the way (John 14:6). We have to walk through the door and commit ourselves to Him if we want to experience abundant life. We can't stand with one foot inside the door and one foot out in the world and expect to thrive. I've learned I need to be "all in."

During my career I've observed many sports teams have a large number of fans, but not many fans are true followers. Fans are enthusiastic admirers. They show up on game day, wear their team's jersey, and cheer loudly. But once the game is over they go on with life. For a follower, sports *is* their life.

The same principle holds true in my relationship with Christ. I don't want to be a fan; I want to be a follower. In Matthew 16:24-26 (NLT), Jesus says, "If any of you wants to be my follower, you must turn from your selfish ways, take up your cross, and follow me. If you try to hang on to your life, you will lose it. But if you give up your life for my sake, you will save it. And what do you benefit if you gain the whole world but lose your own soul? Is anything worth more than your soul?" Jesus isn't looking for fans. Jesus wants followers.

I choose to be a follower of Christ because He has given me a life of purpose and meaning. He has changed me so I am no longer the man I used to be. The good you see in me is Jesus, while the bad you see in me is still me. He is slowly changing me into His image. "Anyone who is joined to Christ is a new being; the old is gone, the new has come. All this is done by God, who through Christ changed us from enemies into His friends and gave us the task of making others His friends also" (2 Corinthians 5:17-18, GNB).

I have an indescribable peace knowing I am a friend of God. He has filled my life with love and joy that money can't buy. I wouldn't trade the security and the satisfaction of knowing Christ for anything this world has to offer.

Above my desk at Arrowhead hangs the following quote. It reminds me every day is a gift from God. "This is the beginning of a brand new day. God has given me this day to use as I will. I can waste it, or I can use it for good, but what I do today is important because I'm exchanging a day of my life for it. When tomorrow comes this day is going to be gone forever, leaving in its place something that I have traded for it. I want it to be gain and not loss, good and not evil, success and not failure, in order that I shall not regret the price that I have paid for it."

My accident was a reminder that I have a limited number of days on this earth. How I invest my life each day is important. Life is a lot like finances. We generally do one of two things with our money. We spend it, or we invest it. Money we spend we never see again. Money we invest wisely multiplies and comes back to us. We do the same thing with our lives. We spend our life, or we invest our life. Life spent selfishly is gone, but a life invested in helping others will bear fruit for eternity. I don't want to waste my remaining days. I want to invest them in making an eternal impact. I once heard I can spend my life on temporary pleasures or I can invest in eternal treasures. I want to be an investor. I want to invest my time and my treasures on those things that truly matter to God and nothing matters more to God than people.

My desire is to live my life in a way that others will see Christ in me. Not just in the words I speak, but more importantly in my actions. I want my faith to be more show and not all tell. Words are cheap if they are not backed up with action (James 1:22). When people look at my life, I want them to see a life overflowing with faith, hope and love.

Faith is what gives my life security. I have security knowing God's principles and God's promises never change; they are reliable no matter how severe or painful the situation. My faith gives me assurance that no matter what happens in my life, the good and the bad, it is all part of His plan. There truly are no such things as accidents—they're all just incidents in His perfect plan for my life.

Hope is what gives my life peace in a world filled with pain, suffering and uncertainty. Every four years we have a presidential election in our country, and there is always talk about hope. I laugh at the thought of ever putting my hope in a politician. My hope is not found in the Democrats or the Republicans. It is not found in the donkeys or the elephants. My hope is found in the lamb, Jesus Christ the Lamb of God. It is because of what Jesus, the sacrificial Lamb, did for me on the cross that I can have hope not only today but for all of eternity.

Love is the other quality I want to demonstrate in my life. Love is a verb and should be the distinctive mark of those who are followers of Christ. The opposite of love is not hate. The opposite of love is indifference and apathy. If my life is ever going to make an impact, I need to get out of my comfort zone and actively seek ways to put love into action. I want to speak softly and live loud.

At my funeral I don't want to just be remembered as KC Wolf, the professional mascot. More importantly, I want to be remembered as Dan Meers, the man who lived a life of love. I want people to say Dan Meers was a man who loved God and who loved others. The way I live my life today will determine how I am remembered at my graveside. I desire to live now so the preacher won't have to lie at my funeral.

In Matthew 22:36-39, Scripture makes clear how we should live our lives. It says, "Love the Lord your God with all your heart, with all your soul, and with all your mind. This is the greatest and the most important commandment. The second most important commandment is like it: Love your neighbor as you love yourself." These verses remind me that instead of putting myself in the top spot, I need to make God and others my main priority. My first love needs to be God and second those around me.

The turning point on my road to recovery came on a bitterly cold morning in late January 2014, as I was driving to a physical therapy appointment. I was feeling down and discouraged because once again I was in a great deal of pain and worn out emotionally. As I was listening to the radio, I heard one of the radio personalities say, "Each day we wake up everyone has something to complain about and everyone has something to be thankful for. Whichever you choose to focus on will determine your attitude for that day." As I sat in my car with tears in my eyes, God taught me a very valuable lesson. I learned:

- I could either complain about my seven broken ribs, or I could choose to be thankful for the other 17 good ones, which weren't broken.
- I could choose to complain about my collapsed left lung which still didn't feel normal, or I could be thankful God gave me two lungs and the other was working just fine.

- I could choose to complain about the three new scars I had on my body, or I could be thankful that with my pants and shirt on no one could see them anyway.
- I wanted to complain on that bitterly cold morning that, once again, I woke up with intense pain in my back, ribs and rear. Instead, for the first time since my accident I actually chose to thank God for my pain. I thanked Him because it finally dawned on me that if I couldn't feel the pain, I would either be dead or paralyzed. When I thought about death, paralysis and pain, I realized God had truly blessed me with the best of the three.

Later in the day I read this quote by Mother Teresa, "It's okay to have pain in your life; it's not okay to be one." Her quote made me laugh because I realized it's okay if I have a pain in my rear, but it's not okay for me to be a pain in yours.

I still wake up with pain most days. Each day is a struggle, but I'm learning to thank God for my pain because it is a daily reminder that I have more things in my life to be thankful for than I have to complain about. Although in many ways my body isn't able to do what it used to do, every morning I get to make a choice. I can either rise and shine or I can rise and whine. I consider this the second most important lesson I've learned during my career. Therefore it is #2 on my Top 10 List.

Lesson #2 – Be a Shiner, Not a Whiner

Matthew 5:16 says, "In the same way, let your light SHINE before others, that they may see your good deeds and glorify your Father in heaven." I want my light to shine in my conversations and in my conduct. In my words and actions I want my life to be a sermon in shoes. My life is not attractive to others when I walk around speaking "Whinese." Nobody enjoys listening to me complain about my problems and pains. Laugh and the world laughs with you; complain and you live alone. I've learned if I want to make an impact on others, the choice is clear, I need to rise and shine each day. It's impossible to experience life to the fullest and be a difference maker in this world by walking around with "Stinkin Thinkin," whining to others about your troubles.

My journey as a professional mascot has taught me a great deal about myself. Including my time as Truman Tiger and Fredbird, I have been wearing costumes for almost 30 years! During that time I have made more than 8,000 appearances dressed in feathers and fur. That translates into thousands of hours spent disguising the real Dan Meers. The most important lesson I've learned during my long career as a mascot is a truth I love to share with others.

Lesson #1 – Take Off The Mask

So many times in our lives we act one way on the outside, but we are a very different person on the inside. We walk around trying to portray the image that we have it all together. We try to hide our pain, faults and fears from others. We do this because we are afraid others will see those things as a sign of weakness in our lives. So we continue to wear a mask in order to fit in and find acceptance. Instead of being real with others, we continue to create a facade.

The trouble with wearing a mask is that it leaves us feeling empty. The mask misrepresents us, and what other people see in our lives is a lie. The mask is not who we are or who we were meant to be. We can change our outside appearance by dressing it up with makeup or nice clothes, but even those can't change who we really are deep down inside.

I was finally able to take off my mask when I realized God loves me just the way I am right now. Even with all of my faults and failures, His love for me will never end. God's promises that are true in my life are true for everyone. Romans 8:38-39 says, "And I am convinced that nothing can ever separate us from God's love. Neither death nor life, neither angels nor demons, neither our fears for today nor our worries about tomorrow—not even the powers of hell can separate us from God's love. No power in the sky above or in the earth below—indeed, nothing in all creation will ever be able to separate us from the love of God that is revealed in Christ Jesus our Lord."

I no longer have to wear a mask in order to fit in and find acceptance because I have found my identity and my acceptance in Jesus Christ. C.S Lewis once said, "The more we let God take us over, the more truly ourselves we become—because He made us. He invented us. He invented all the different people you and I were intended to be. It is when I turn to Christ, when I give up myself to His personality, that I first begin to have a real personality of my own." My challenge for you is to trust God enough to take off your mask. Only when we finally remove our mask can God begin to change us and make us more like Himself. He will slowly begin to fix the flaws we have been trying to cover up.

God tells us in John 1:12, "Yet to all who received him, to those who believed in His name, He gave the right to become children of God." Becoming a child of God is as simple as A-B-C.

A – Admit. Admit to God you are a sinner. "For all have sinned and fall short of the glory of God" (Romans 3:23).

B – Believe. Believe in Jesus Christ as God's Son and receive Jesus' gift of forgiveness of sins. "For God so loved the world that He gave His one and only Son, that whoever believes in Him shall not perish but have eternal life" (John 3:16).

C – Confess. Confess your faith in Jesus Christ as Savior and Lord. "That if you confess with your mouth, 'Jesus is Lord,' and believe in your heart that God raised Him from the dead, you will be saved" (Romans 10:9-10).

You can become a child of God with a simple prayer of faith: "Lord Jesus, I believe you are the Son of God. Thank you for dying on the cross for my sins. Please forgive my sins and give me the gift of eternal life. I ask you into my life and heart to be my Lord and Savior. I want to serve you always."

God created you for a specific and unique purpose. He is calling you to become all He wants you to be, and it all begins with a relationship with Him. God's unique plan for my life was to become a professional mascot. It has been an incredible journey. God has an amazing plan for your life as well. Don't miss the journey by hiding behind a mask. I encourage you to give your life to Him today.

Psalm 100:3-5 says, "Know that the Lord is God. It is He who made us, and we are His; we are His people, the sheep of His pasture. Enter His gates with thanksgiving and His courts with praise; give thanks to Him and praise His name. For the Lord is good and His love endures forever; His faithfulness continues through all generations."

I'm thankful the Lord is my shepherd, and I am forever grateful that He chose me to be one of His sheep. A sheep dressed in wolf's clothing.

So You
Want to be a Mascot?

Being a professional mascot is a great job, and I've had a whole lot of fun during my career. People often ask me what advice I would give to someone just starting out and wanting to become a mascot. I wish I could give you a book or a manual to read that would make you a great mascot. No such luck. The only way to become an effective mascot is by experience. Hopping in a mascot costume and performing is the best way to learn.

Below are 10 helpful hints to get you started. I call these the 10 Commandments of Being a Good Mascot. Grab a costume and get ready to have some fun!

The 10 Commandments of Being a Good Mascot

1) **Never Let Them See You Sweat**—In other words, don't let people see you out of costume. It ruins the "Mascot Magic," especially for kids.

2) **Stay in Shape**—Being a mascot isn't all fun and games. In order to be a good mascot you need to stay in excellent physical shape. Endurance is critical if you want to be entertaining for an entire game.

3) **Stay in Character**—Consistency is an important part of being a mascot. One of the first things a mascot should do is decide the personality of his character (fun-loving, mischievous, proud, cocky, tough, wimpy, etc.). The personality of the character often depends on the look of the costume. For example, it's much easier to act tough in a tiger suit than in a kitty cat costume. Once you decide on a personality, stick with it. The same goes for your walk. Whether you strut, bounce or waddle, do it consistently.

4) **Don't Talk**—If you're like me, this is the hardest rule to learn. Not talking is important because it forces you to learn how to communicate your emotions through actions and not words. Though difficult at first, it will definitely make you a better and much more effective mascot.

5) **Be Exaggerated**—Every action in your mascot outfit should be exaggerated enough to be easily seen in the stands. This means every action from walking, to waving, to blowing your nose. A good rule to follow is make sure what you are doing is exaggerated enough for the fan in the top row of the stadium to see.

6) **Don't Be Crude**—A mascot's #1 fans are always kids, and they're always watching. Be sure never to make any crude or obscene gestures during your performance. Not only are you being a bad role model for children, you are also a poor representation for your school or team.

7) **Use Props**—Props almost always add to a mascot's performance. However, make sure the props are large enough so the fans in the stands can easily tell what you are doing. Be creative, and you will begin to see that almost anything can be used as a prop. Some examples of good props include: security guards, vendors, bald heads, baseball bats, cheerleaders, diapers, jerseys, brooms and many, many more.

8) **Be Energetic**—I can't overemphasize how important this rule is to being a good mascot. Nobody likes to watch a mascot just sitting around doing nothing. While you are in front of the fans be energetic and enthusiastic. Of course, you can't keep up a frenzied pace for an entire game without a few breaks. It is okay to take a break when you start to feel tired or need a drink of water. When your break is over and you get back out in front of the crowd, turn on the energy again. Staying energetic and active in costume is what separates good mascots from ordinary mascots. The key to being a good mascot is high energy.

9) **Have Fun**—If you are a mascot and you are not having fun, something's wrong. This is your big chance to get away with all those things you've always wanted to do while nobody knows who you are. Once you put on the costume, really get into it and become your character. Don't worry about feeling goofy. Mascots are supposed to be goofy. A good way to tell if you are really becoming your character is to notice if you catch yourself smiling for pictures even though your mascot head is covering up your face. Go out and act as crazy as you want, but most importantly have fun.

10) **Take Care of Your Costume**—If your costume stinks and looks bad, nobody will want to be around you. When you have finished using it, hang it up to dry or wash it if you can. Keeping the costume looking good is an important part of a mascot's job.

Becoming a good mascot is not hard. All it takes is a little pride and dedication. With effort, some experience in front of the crowd, and a whole lot of fun experimenting on new ideas, you can become the best crowd motivator around without ever having to yell. In no time at all, being a mascot will become second nature to you.

Remember that in life you control your attitude and your effort. Choose to live with a positive attitude. Give your 100% best effort at whatever you set your mind to do, and great things will happen. God bless you on your adventure!

Acknowledgements

I am a very blessed man. God has surrounded me with an amazing family and many wonderful friends. I have a long list of people to thank for helping me on my journey and my long road to recovery. Without their love and encouragement I would not be where I am today, and this book would never have become a reality. At the very top of the list is my wife.

Cam: Tarzan had Jane, Mickey had Minnie and I'm thankful I have you. I can never thank you enough for your love, sacrifice and support throughout our married life and during my recovery. You are the most beautiful woman I know both inside and out. Thanks for being my friend, lover and soul mate. I'm grateful I get to live out this adventure called life with you. I will love you forever and always.

Mycah, Aaron and Mallory: I've wiped your tears, noses and bottoms, and even though I loved your childhood years, I'm thankful you now handle most of those wiping responsibilities yourself. You have each been a huge blessing in my life. Nothing I've ever done compares to the joy I find in being your dad. Even if you weren't mine, I would still think you were great kids. I love you, and I'm very proud of each of you.

Mom and Dad: Thanks for being my biggest cheerleaders and modeling for me that true success is found in service, not status. You are the two most giving people I know. Thanks for all the blood, sweat, tears and prayers you have invested in my life. I love you!

Jim and Nancy Cochran: I'm not sure if I would give a mascot permission to marry one of my daughters, but I'm very grateful you did. Thanks for your love and support and for letting me be a part of the Cochran Clan.

Honey, Dave and Stacey, Tom and Kerry, Jim and Kristen, nieces, nephews, in-laws, out-laws and everyone else who is somehow related to me: Our family truly is like fudge and whether you're sweet or one of the nuts, I love you all.

The Hunt family: Thank you for the privilege of serving as KC Wolf for over 25 years. It is truly an honor to work for a sports franchise that is committed to excellence, both on the field and in the community. Go Chiefs!

My Kansas City Chiefs coworkers: I not only have the best job in the world, but I also work with the greatest people in the world. Thanks for your friendship and for putting up with the Director of Shenanigans, even when I arrive at work smelling "less than fresh."

Chiefs Kingdom: Thank you for making my job fun. You truly are the greatest fans in the NFL. Thanks to you, work has never felt like work.

Tony Dungy: Thanks for taking the time in the midst of your busy schedule to write a foreword for my book. I appreciate your friendship and for all you have taught me about living a life of significance.

Dr. Steven Wilkinson: Thanks for the two titanium rods and the cool new scar. My mom wouldn't let me get a tattoo, but a scar is even better because it comes with a cool story. Plus my wife tells me "Chicks Dig Scars."

The doctors and nurses at Centerpoint Medical Center: It wasn't exactly a bed and breakfast, but thanks for making my nine day stay as enjoyable as possible. Even though I felt like a human pin cushion, at least you smiled while you were sticking me. Thanks for your compassionate care.

Rod Handley, Mike DeBacker, William Hanna, Fred Olson, Bruce Rehmer and Travis Bourbon: Thank you for holding me accountable and for challenging me to be the man God intended for me to be. Life is a team sport, and I'm glad you guys are on my team. I love you guys.

Ed Knapp and my friends at Summit Strength Physical Therapy: Thanks for helping this Old Wolf get his dance moves back. I'll see you again when my hips need to be replaced.

Gordon Thiessen: Thank you for taking on this book project with me. Writing a book is like eating an elephant. I'm glad I got to share the meal with you.

LeAnn Adams, Matt Bartle, Don Hilkemeier, Patty McWilliams, Michelle Montgomery and Dan Smith: Thanks for your assistance with the proofreading and pictures. Your feedback and advice was extremely helpful.

ACKNOWLEDGEMENTS 221

Laura Maxwell: Sorry I didn't pay closer attention in English class. Thanks for editing this book and cleaning up my grammar.

My KC Wolf backups—Jon Kindler, Andrew Johnson, Shawn Emerson, Ky Turner, Brady Testorff and Wade Shapp: Thanks for being Characters with Character. I couldn't ask for a better group of guys with whom to share an identity.

My NFL Furternity Brothers: We may be two peas short of a casserole, but what we lack in smarts, we make up for in fun. Thanks for all the great memories.

My friends and everyone who prayed for me: Thank you. God answers prayers (James 5:16).

My Lord and Savior Jesus Christ: Thank You that my identity isn't found in being a mascot, but my true identity is found in You. Thank You for adopting me into Your family and allowing this wolf to become one of Your sheep. You never promised me a life free from pain, but You did promise to walk with me along the journey. Thank You for Your faithfulness and for always keeping Your promises.

About the Author

Dan Meers goes to work each day like many other men, dressed in a suit. The only difference is that instead of wearing a tie with his suit, Dan wears a tail. You see, Dan is a professional mascot.

Dan began his career in 1986 at the University of Missouri—Columbia. Dressed as the school mascot, Truman Tiger, it didn't take long for Dan to establish himself as one of the top college mascots in the nation. After finishing second in 1988, Dan was selected the nation's #1 college mascot at the 1989 National Collegiate Mascot Championships. As graduation approached, Dan began to receive offers to use his talents at the professional level. After graduating with honors, Dan decided to trade in his tiger stripes for bird feathers and began his professional career as Fredbird, the mascot for the St. Louis Cardinals baseball team. Although many thought Dan's "bird legs" were a perfect match for his costume in St. Louis, Dan stayed only a short time. He was offered a job in professional football and decided to exchange his bird suit to become a wolf.

Today Dan is widely known as KC Wolf, the official mascot of the Kansas City Chiefs. He travels throughout the United States and the world, entertaining thousands of people both in and out of costume. Dan is in high demand not only as a mascot but also as a humorous and motivational speaker to audiences of all ages. His enthusiasm, optimism and love for life are contagious and make Dan an inspiration to all those he meets.

After listening to Dan, you realize what makes him so truly special is his genuine desire to motivate others to enjoy life as much as he does. The constant smile he wears comes from within. The humorous message he shares has encouraged thousands to strive for the best in life and enjoy it each and every step along the way.

If you are interested in having Dan Meers speak to your organization, church, school or ministry please contact him at: **dmeers@chiefs.nfl.com** or **www.characterthatcounts.org**

Follow KC Wolf on Facebook at KC Wolf
on Twitter@KCWOLF
or at: www.kcchiefs.com/cheerleaders/kc-wolf.html or at
www.DanMeers.org

NOTE ON BOOK PROCEEDS

All net proceeds and royalties from the sale of this book will be used to fund missions and ministries aiding orphans and the poor around the world through the 501(c)(3) ministry of Character That Counts. See www.characterthatcounts.org for more information.

"Religion that God our Father accepts as pure and faultless is this: to look after orphans and widows in their distress and to keep oneself from being polluted by the world" (James 1:27).